A CHRISTIAN CHRONOLOGY OF HISTORY

A TIME LINE OF HUMAN HISTORY
FROM A CHRISTIAN PROSPECTIVE

"God's Friend"

Order this book online at www.trafford.com
or email orders@trafford.com

Most Trafford titles are also available at major online book retailers.

Printed in the United States of America.

ISBN: 978-1-4907-3981-6 (sc)
ISBN: 978-1-4907-3983-0 (hc)
ISBN: 978-1-4907-3982-3 (e)

Library of Congress Control Number: 2014911267

Trafford rev. 06/19/2014

Trafford
PUBLISHING   www.trafford.com
North America & international
toll-free: 1 888 232 4444 (USA & Canada)
fax: 812 355 4082

IF YOU WOULD LIKE TO HELP
THE CAMBODIAN MISSION EFFORT
MENTIONED IN THESE PAGES FOLLOWING
2000A.D.
PLEASE CONTACT:
Cambodian Missions
Melrose Church of Christ
221 Main Street
(Mail: 1462 Curry Rd AN)
Melrose, N.M. 88124

Before we get into the time chronology, I would like to describe some principles and basic understandings that have lead me to challenge some dates I confidently consider inaccurate though politically correct. If you believe that the Bible, as originally delivered, is the infallible Word of God, and I do, then you expect the Bible to accurately describe historic events. If some human has decided to disagree with the Bible, I may pity his error, but will not knowingly join his folly. Some of the secular scholars' misunderstandings come from a failure to understand the religious Jewish calendar used in the Bible, and to incompletely read ancient historians and the Bible. Often ancient historians do not know what they think they know and they always know incompletely. The same is true of modern historians and me. To help us in the discovery of an accurate though grossly incomplete chronology from a Christian prospective, I am first introducing you to some notes on the Jewish religious calendar and the ending of Herod the Great's life. Herod's death has a lot to do with the proper dating of Jesus' birth, life and death, an important series of Christian events that have been misdated by many.

NOTES ON THE JEWISH RELIGIOUS CHALENDAR

The Bible calendar is not understood, or is misunderstood in the literature. Secular scholars worry too much about tying things to the things in the second heaven and ignore plain statements and commands against the worship of such things. This limits the accuracy of the available information. Much of what we read belongs in file thirteen and can best be described as mounds of misinformation with small amounts of imbedded truth. Most refer to the Jewish month as a lunar month and designate them as being 29 and 30 days. There are no 29 day months in the Bible. Although a moon phase cycle is about 29 and ½ days long, the moon cycle is 27.321661 days long. All Bible months are 30 days long. Bible years normally consist of twelve thirty day months that are 360 days long. There are some Bible years that are 390 days long and consist of 13 30 day months. These years are rare.

Some "authorities" have said that an extra month was added to the year about every three years to adjust the normal Jewish year to the solar year. I believe these "authorities" never did the math involved in the adjustment they are claiming. A solar year is about 365.25636 days long. If you add 30 days every three years to the Bible's normal 360 day year, you are long over 237 days in a fifty year period, and that is accumulative. That did not happen.

The Bible calendar does function on a fifty year Jubilee cycle with years 7, 14, 21, 28, 35, 42, and 49 being special Sabbath years. The fiftieth year is a very special year of Jubilee (Lev. 25). If the Sabbath years and the year of Jubilee are given extra 30 day months, the fifty year cycle is less than 23 days off from the natural solar calendar. I feel certain that is what happened. The year before Jesus' death was a Sabbath year with 390 days. Daniel prophesied Jesus' ministry would be 3 ½ years long and have 1290 days in it. Jesus was crucified during the thirtieth year of Jubilee.

Luke and Daniel indicate the ministry of Jesus began on about the 30th birthday of Jesus on the 15th of Ethanim (Tishri). This corresponds to the time Jews were instructed by the Torah to start the service of those who served the tabernacle and stood before the Lord to minister to Him and to bless in His name (Deut. 10:8,9; Num. 4; Luke 1; Gen. 3:15; Luke 2:1-19). Because of Joseph, Jesus was of the tribe of Judah and lineage of David. The Bible calls Him a "priest for ever after the order of Melchisedec" (Hebrews 7). Matthew 1 and Luke 3 both trace Jesus' lineage through Joseph (Ecclesiastic History Book 1, Ch. 7).

Some "authorities" suggest that at some unknown times 7 or 8 days were also added to the three annual festivals. If you add an eight day period to two of the annual festivals on the year of Jubilee and a seven day period to the third annual festival of that year, the Bible calendar would be off from the solar calendar by less than 4 ½ hours over a fifty year period. That is more accurate than our modern day solar calendar. I believe that is what was done.

Some pretend the three annual festivals were always the same number of days apart. That is not so. The Passover and the Feast of Tabernacles were always on the same date on the Jewish Ceremonial Calendar. Because of the calendar adjustments described above, those dates moved about by as much as seventy-three days on our calendar. Most "authorities" accept the movement as about two months. The Pentecostal Festival was tied to the barley harvest and moved less on our calendar due to its dating being largely controlled by the natural solar year. That means it shifted in its relationship to the Passover by over two months during the fifty year cycle. Daniel prophesied it would fall on the 45th day after Passover day on the year of Jesus' death (the cross of the Messiah-the abomination that makes desolate). Since Pentecost always fell on Sunday, Jesus died on Thursday, the Day of Preparation for the Feast of Unleavened Bread. A usually non-Saturday Sabbath Day (the 15th of Nisan or Abib) followed that day. The Bible Religious Calendar counted the evening and then the following morning to make-up a twenty-four hour day. Jesus ate the Passover feast with his apostles and was arrested during the evening of the Passover (the 14th of Nisan). He was then taken before Pilot and crucified during the morning of the 14th of Nisan. It was on this Day of

Preparation that all leaven was to be removed from the homes so the Jews could properly participate in the Feast of Unleavened Bread.

The Sadducee tradition of the dark ages agrees with this, but the Pharisee tradition does not. Pharisees do not link Pentecost to the barley harvest as the Bible (Torah) does, but link it to the giving of the law on Mount Sinai. They count fifty days from the Passover and use Siv 6ᵗʰ as Pentecost, saying that is the date on which God first gave the Law to Israel. The Torah dates Israel's arrival at Sinai as Siv 14ᵗʰ (Ex. 19:1; 12:30-51), and then records the giving of some laws a few days later. The erroneous Pharisee tradition causes Pentecost to always be on the same day on the religious calendar, but not always on Sunday as the Torah instructions require and as a prophesy of Daniel indicates. The Modern Pharisee calendar is credited to Rabbi Hillel II, a Jewish authority between 330 and 365 A.D. Although Rabbi Hillel is credited with the modern Pharisee Hebrew Calendar, most agree that it evolved over about 500 years and was not accepted until after 800 A.D. It produces years that are 353, 354, 355, 383, 384, and 385 days long. The Bible does not support any of these year lengths. During Jesus' life on earth, Jesus rebuked the Pharisees for doing many things according to their traditions, setting aside the commandments of God. Jesus taught this made their worship vain (Mark 7:1-13).

NOTE ON HEROD THE GREAT

Another area of misinformation in the literature is about the death of Herod the Great. According to Josephus, there was an eclipse the night Herod removed Matthias from the High Priesthood and burnt alive another Matthias, a teacher of the Law. This eclipse can be dated as March the 13th in 4 B.C. Many give that as the date of Herod's death, but it is merely a date from which Josephus says his sickness became worse.

Herod remained active after March 13th, 4 B.C., seeking medical attention. He traveled beyond the Jordan to bath in the warm healing waters at Calirrhoe. He then returned to Jericho to summon and arrest many Jewish leaders. Herod acknowledged he was dying and wanted the community leaders killed at his death so there would be massive mourning when he died. He later received communications, Caesar announcing the execution of Acme and giving Herod permission to execute Antipater. Herod executed Antipater five days before his own death. Herod died about two weeks before the Passover of 3 B.C. (late March/ early April, 3 B.C. on our calendar).

The Passover of 3 B.C. was very close to Herod's death. It was before Archelaus, Herod's heir apparent, sailed for Rome to have his inheritance validated by Caesar, something I believe he would do as soon as possible. Official mourning for Herod lasted the customary two weeks. As the mourning ended, the people of Jerusalem were granted an audience with Archelaus. This audience became riotous and Archelaus responded with force. The riotous clash between the people of Jerusalem and the soldiers of Archelaus was at the beginning of the Passover and the Feast of Unleavened Bread in 3 B.C.

Table of Contents

CHAPTER ONE
A CHRISTIAN CHRONOLOGY OF HISTORY
(CREATION – 2231 B.C.)
A TIME LINE OF HUMAN HISTORY
FROM A CHRISTIAN PROSPECTIVE
Compiled by "God's Friend"

4179 B.C.	CREATION: EVE'S SEED PROPHESIED TO CRUSH SATAN'S HEAD (SEE 7B.C. – 30 A.D.) (Genesis 3:15; 5:1-3)
4174 B.C.	CAIN'S BIRTH
4173 B.C.	ABEL'S BIRTH
4049 B.C.	SETH'S BIRTH (Genesis 5:3,6)
3944 B.C.	ENOS'S BIRTH (Genesis 5:6,9)
3854 B.C.	CAINAN'S BIRTH (Genesis 5:9, 12)
3784 B.C.	MAHALALEEL'S BIRTH (Genesis 5:12, 15)
3719 B.C.	JARED'S BIRTH (Genesis 5:15, 18)
3557 B.C.	ENOCH'S BIRTH (Genesis 5:18, 21)
3492 B.C.	METHUSELAH'S BIRTH (Genesis 5:21, 25)
3305 B.C.	LAMECH'S BIRTH (Genesis 5:25, 28-29)
3249 B.C.	ADAM'S DEATH (Genesis 5:3,4)
3137 B.C.	SETH'S DEATH (Genesis 5:6,7)
3123 B.C.	NOAH'S BIRTH (Genesis 5:28-32)
2623 B.C.	JAPHETH'S BIRTH (Genesis 5:32)
2621 B.C.	SHEM'S BIRTH (Genesis 7:6; 11:10)

THE STORM THAT RESULTED IN NOAH'S FLOOD WAS TRULY AWESOME

2523-22 B.C.

NOAH'S FLOOD: IN ABOUT MAY (THE MONTH OF THE FLOWERS), THE EARTH IS STRUCK BY A COMET (AN ICE STORM FROM OUTER SPACE). THE CRUST IS MOVED ABOUT FIVE THOUSAND MILES TO THE EAST IN RELATIONSHIP TO THE EARTH'S CORE. THE PACIFIC OCEAN IS SPLASHED OUT OF ITS BASIN AND WASHES OVER CANADA. SHOCK WAVES ENCOUNTER MAJOR RESISTANCE IN THE MIDDLE OF THE ATLANTIC AND CRACKS THE CRUST FROM THE ARCTIC TO THE ANTARTIC. THE CRUST FOLDS LIKE AN ACCORDION LEAVING MAGNETIC STRIPES THE SAME WIDTH AS THE THICKNESS OF THE OCEAN BOTTOM CRUST. THE CRUST CRACKS INTO ABOUT TWENTY LARGE PIECES (CRUSTAL PLATES).

ICE FROM THE COMET CREATES GLACIERS ON THE SLOPES OF TROPICAL ISLANDS AND DEPOSITS OUR POLAR ICE CAPS ATOP TROPICAL JUNGLES. HERDS OF GIANT ELEPHANTS (MAMMOTHS) ARE QUICK FROZEN AS THEY MUNCH ON BLOOMING BUTTERCUPS.

THE EARTH IS TILTED ON ITS AXIS BY THE FORCE OF THE IMPACTS. MAGMA IS DRIVEN UP FROM THE MANTEL AND BOILS THE GROUND WATER DRIVING IT INTO THE ATMOSPHERE. THE INCOMING, SUPER COLD ICE,

PRECIPITATES ALL MOISTURE OUT OF THE ATMOSPHERE. HEAVY METALS ARE SPLASHED UP FROM THE MANTEL INTO THE CRUST SURROUNDING THE NORTH PACIFIC IMPACT ZONE. HEAVY METALS ARE ALSO DRIVEN UP INTO THE CRUST ON THE OPPOSITE SIDE OF THE PLANET (IN AFRICA).

THE CLIMATE IS CHANGED SO THAT WHAT USE TO BLOOM IN APRIL OR MAY IS NOW BLOOMING IN JULY. THE ENVIRONMENT IS SO CONTAMINATED THAT MAN'S LIFE EXPECTANCY IS REDUCED TO A TENTH OF THAT BEFORE THE FLOOD. THE PACIFIC OCEAN FLOOR IS DRIVEN UNDER SURROUNDING CONTINENTS. MOST FOSSILS, COAL DEPOSITS AND OIL DEPOSITS ARE FORMED.

2522 B.C. THE DESCENDANTS OF CANAAN, A SON OF HAM, A SON OF NOAH, IS PROPHESIED TO BECOME THE SLAVE OF SLAVES (SEE 1471 B.C.). HAM'S DESCENDANTS SETTLE AFRICA AND THE FERTILE CRESENT.

THE DESCENDANTS OF SHEM (ISRAELITES, ARABS, AND SOUTHERN-CENTRAL ASIANS) ARE TO BE BLESSED WITH A SPECIAL RELATIONSHIP WITH GOD. (THEY ARE USED BY GOD TO WRITE THE BIBLE AND PROVIDE THE LINEAGE OF JESUS. ALL BIBLE PROPHETS WHO ARE USED BY THE SPIRIT OF GOD TO WRITE THE BIBLE AND THE APOSTLES COME FROM THIS LINE.)

THE DESCENDANTS OF JAPHETH
(EUROPEANS, NORTH ASIANS, AND
AMERICAN INDIANS) ARE TO HAVE
THEIR TERRITORIES EXTENDED AND
COME TO LIVE IN SHEM'S HOUSE.
(THE TERRITORIES CONTROLED
BY THIS GROUP TODAY INCLUDES
ALL OF EUROPE, MOST OF ASIA,
A LARGE PART OF AFRICA, ALL OF
NORTH AND SOUTH AMERICA,
AUSTRALIA, ICELAND, GREENLAND,
AND NUMEROUS ISLANDS. MOST
OF THOSE WHO CALL THEMSELVES
CHRISTIANS OR CATHOLICS ARE
FROM THIS GROUP. ACCORDING
TO NEW TESTAMENT DOCTRINE,
THE CHRISTIANS TODAY HAVE THE
SPECIAL RELATIONSHIP THAT USE
TO BE HELD BY THE JEWS. THIS
RELATIONSHIP IS OPEN TO ALL WHO
OBEY THE GOSPEL TAUGHT BY JESUS
AND HIS APOSTLES. THEY ARE THE
"NEW ISRAEL, AND SONS OF GOD,"
THE PRINCES OF GOD.
(Galatians 4:21-31; 5:4, 18; 6:15, 16;
Ephesians 2:11-14, 18-22; Romans 8:14-17;
9:6-8; 24-27; 11:7-23; NOTE: Some Jews have
chosen to become Christians, and therefore
still have their privileged relationship.
Matthew 21:33-46; 22:1-14; Mark 12:1-12;
Luke 14: 7-11; 15-24; 20:9-19)

Noah's Ark

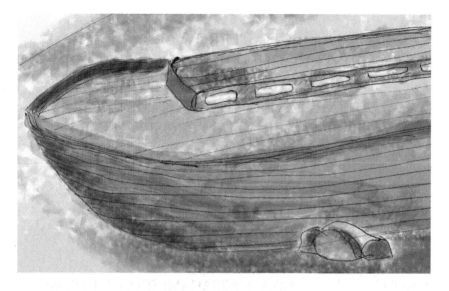

Noah's Ark as described by George Herropean. He, as a youth, was taken by his uncle to the ark on Mt. Ararat and helped to climb on to its top.

2521 B.C.	ARPHAXAD'S BIRTH TWO YEARS AFTER THE FLOOD. (Genesis 11:10, 12)
2486 B.C.	SALAH'S BIRTH (Genesis 11: 12, 14)
2456 B.C.	EBER'S BIRTH (Genesis 11:14, 16)
2422 B.C.	PEGLEG'S BIRTH (Genesis 11:16, 18)
2392 B.C.	REU'S BIRTH (Genesis 11:19, 20)
2360 B.C.	SEGAR'S BIRTH (Genesis 11:20, 22)
2350 B.C.	PEPI I DEFEATS REBELS AT THE GAZELLE'S HEAD IN THE VALLEY OF JEZREEL NEAR MEGIDDO.
2330 B.C.	NAHOR'S BIRTH (Genesis 11: 22, 24)
2301 B.C.	TERAH'S BIRTH (Genesis 11:24, 26)
2282 B.C.	NAHOR, FATHER OF TERAH, DIES (Genesis 11: 25)
2231 B.C.	BIRTH OF ABRAHAM SHORTLY FOLLOWED OR ACCOMPANIED BY THE BIRTHS OF NAHOR AND HARAN (Genesis 11:26; 11:10; 5:32).

CHAPTER TWO
A CHRISTIAN CHRONOLOGY OF HISTORY
(ABRAHAM'S BIRTH – 1117 B.C.)
A TIME LINE OF HUMAN HISTORY
FROM A CHRISTIAN PROSPECTIVE
Compiled by "God's Friend"

2231 B.C.	ABRAHAM'S BIRTH (Genesis 11:26, 21:5)
2183 B.C.	PEGLEG'S DEATH (Genesis 11:19)
2173 B.C.	NOAH'S DEATH (Genesis 9:28)
2156 B.C.	ABRAM (ABRAHAM) SETS OUT FROM HARAN (Genesis 12:4).
2154 B.C.	ABRAM AND LOT COME TO CANAAN FROM EGYPT AND LOT SEPARATES TO SODOM AND GOMORRAH.
2153 B.C.	REU'S DEATH (Genesis 11:21)
2147 B.C.	MELCHISEDEK BUILDS SALEM (JERUSALEM) VIA JOSEPHUS.
2146 B.C.	KEDORLAOMER, KING OF ELAM, CONQUERS THE SODOM AREA AND TAKES LOT PRISONER. ABRAM RESCUES.
2145 B.C.	ISHMAEL IS BORN.
2145-30 B.C.	ISHMAEL AND HIS DESCENDANTS (ARABS) RECEIVE A BLESSING FROM GOD AT ABRAHAM'S REQUEST. HE IS TO PRODUCE 12 RULERS (KINGDOMS) AND BE GREATLY MULTIPLIED. HIS HAND WILL BE AGAINST EVERYONE, AND EVERYONE'S HAND WILL BE AGAINST HIM. HE WILL BE A WILD DONKEY OF A MAN. (SEE THE MODERN ARAB NATIONS AND THEIR RECENT HISTORIES). GOD

	ALSO PROMISED TO ESTABLISH HIS COVENANT OF BLESSINGS THROUGH ISAAC. (JESUS COMES THROUGH ISAAC). (Genesis 16:6-16; 17:15-21)
2132 B.C.	HOMOSEXUAL SODOM AND GOMORRAH ARE DESTROYED. (Genesis 17:1)
2131 B.C.	ISAAC'S BIRTH (Genesis 21:5)
2130 B.C	SERUG'S DEATH (Genesis 11:23)
2129 B.C.	GOD HAS ABRAHAM SEND HAGAR AND ISHMAEL AWAY, AND ISAAC BECOMES ABRAHAM'S ONLY SON. ISHMAEL IS COMPLETELY BLOCKED FROM SHARING IN ABRAHAM'S INHERITANCE. THIS IS REPRESENTED AS A FIGURATIVE ASSURANCE THAT GOD HAS LIMITED SALVATION AND WILL NOT RETURN TO THE LAW OF MOSES. THOSE THAT DO NOT APPROACH GOD THROUGH CHRIST WILL NOT SHARE IN GOD'S INHERITANCE. (Gal. 4:21-31; Deut. 18:18-19; Acts 3:22-23; John 14:6; Acts 4:10-12)
c2120 B.C.	ABRAHAM OBEYS GOD IN HIS WILLINGNESS TO OFFER HIS ONLY SON ISAAC AS A SACRIFICE, AND IS PROMISED BY GOD THAT GOD WILL BLESS ALL NATIONS THROUGH HIS SEED BECAUSE OF THIS (Genesis 22: 1-19)
2091 B.C.	ISAAC MARRIES REBEKAH (Genesis 25:20)
2096 B.C.	DEATH OF TERAH (Genesis 11: 32)
2083 B.C.	DEATH OF ARPHAXAD (Genesis 11:13)
2071 B.C.	ESAU AND JACOB'S BIRTH (Genesis 25:6)
2056 B.C.	ABRAHAM'S DEATH (Genesis 25:7, 8)
2053 B.C.	DEATH OF SALAH (Genesis 11:13)
2021 B.C.	SHEM'S DEATH (Genesis 11:11)
1994 B.C.	JACOB LEAVES ISAAC AND REBEKAH FOR HARAN AND LABAN'S HOUSEHOLD.
1992 B.C.	DEATH OF EBER (Genesis 11:17)

1980 B.C.	BIRTH OF JOSEPH NEAR HARAN
1974 B.C.	JACOB LEAVES HARAN AND LABAN'S HOUSEHOLD.
1963 B.C.	JOSEPH IS SOLD INTO EGYPT. (Genesis 37:2)
1951 B.C.	ISAAC'S DEATH (Genesis 35:28, 29)
1950 B.C.	JOSEPH BEGINS TO ADMINISTER EGYPT (POSSIBLY UNDER SENUSRET I). (Genesis 41:46)
1941 B.C.	JACOB GOES TO EGYPT, (Genesis 47:9)
1941-1511 B.C.	JOB WRITTEN IN SAUDI ARABIA BY UNKOWN AUTHOR.
1780-1591 B.C.	THE ISRAELITES ESTABLISH THEMSELVES AS A NATION IN THE LAND OF GOSHEN (THE EASTERN NILE DELTA). THEY ARE KNOWN TO THE EGYPTIANS AS HYKSOS.
1605-1595 B.C.	A NEW DYNASTY THAT IS OPPRESSIVE TOWARD THE ISRAELITES ESTABLISHES ITSELF IN EGYPT.
1591 B.C.	THE BIRTH OF MOSES (Under Intef VI or VII?).
1511 B.C.	MOSES LEADS THE ISRAELITES OUT OF EGYPT AFTER A 430 YEAR SOJOURN IN EGYPT (probably under Thutmoses I) (Exodus 12:40). THEY TRAVEL TO MOUNT SINAI, RECEIVE THE LAW AND BUILD ON THE TABERNACLE.
1510 B.C.	THE TABERNACLE IS COMPLETED AND ISRAEL MOVES TO PARAN. THEY THEN CONTINUE TO KADESH-BARNEA AND SPY OUT THE PROMISED LAND.
1510-1471 B.C.	ISRAEL IS CURSED WITH FORTY YEARS WANDERINGS IN THE WILDERNESS FOR UNBELIEF. DURING THESE YEARS ALL OVER 20, BUT JOSHUA AND CALEB, DIE. THESE YEARS ARE USED BY GOD AS AN EXAMPLE FOR CHRISTIANS TO

SHOW THEM HOW TO LIVE AND NOT
LIVE THEIR CHRISTIAN LIVES. THE
CROSSING OF THE RED SEA IS USED TO
REPRESENT THE BEGINNING OF THE
CHRISTIAN LIFE AT BAPTISM. DURING
THEIR CHRISTIAN LIFE THEY ARE
TRAINED BY CHRIST WHO IS THEIR
SPIRITUAL ROCK. MOST DIE BECAUSE
OF UNBELIEF AND THEIR FAILURES
IN FAITHFULLY FOLLOWING GOD.
THEIR CROSSING JORDAN INTO THE
PROMISED LAND IS REPRESENTATIVE
OF PASSING INTO HEAVEN.
(1 Cor. 10:1-13)

MOSES WRITES GENESIS, EXODUS,
LEVITICUS, NUMBERS AND
DEUTERONOMY. HE PROPHESIES THAT
THE MESSIAH WILL COME FROM THE
LINEAGE OF EVE, SHEM, ABRAHAM,
ISAAC, JACOB, AND JUDAH (Genesis 3:15;
12:3; 22:18; 26:4; 28:14; 49:10.) HE WILL
BE A PROPHET LEADER LIKE MOSES.
WHOEVER DOESN'T LISTEN TO HIM
WILL HAVE TO ANSWER DIRECTLY TO
GOD FOR THE INSULT. HE WILL BLESS
ALL NATIONS. (SEE 7-1 B.C.; 26-30 A.D.;
70 A.D.) JUDAH WILL HAVE A KING
AND LAWGIVER ON THE THRONE
FOREVER (UNTIL SHILOH("rest") COME
– the great rest of God...Genesis 49:8-12;
Hebrews 3:11-4:11). IF ISRAEL OBEYS
GOD'S COMMANDS THEY WILL HAVE
UNBELIEVABLE SUCCESS. IF ISRAEL
DOES NOT OBEY GOD'S COMMANDS
THEY WILL HAVE UNBELIEVABLE
HORRORS (Duet. 28:1-68).

GOD COMMANDS THREE ANNUAL
FEASTS DURING WHICH THE PEOPLE
WILL RETURN TO JERUSALEM. THE
FEASTS ARE ARRANGED TO COINCIDE
WITH THE BIRTH OF JESUS IN THE
EARLY FALL, THE DEATH OF JESUS
IN THE EARLY SPRING, AND THE
PREACHING OF THE FIRST GOSPEL
SERMON ON SUNDAY IN THE EARLY
SUMMER. GOD SETS UP THE JEWISH
CALENDER ON A 50 YEAR CYCLE. EVERY
SEVENTH YEAR THE LAND IS TO REST.
CROPS ARE NOT TO BE SOWN, PRUNED
OR HARVESTED, BUT THE CROPS MAY
BE EATEN BY ALL. THE FIFTIETH YEAR
IS A YEAR OF JUBILEE. ON THAT YEAR
THEY ARE TO PROCLAIM LIBERTY
THROUGH OUT THE LAND. AGAIN
THE CROPS MAY BE EATEN BY ALL,
BUT NEITHER SOWN NOR REAPED. ON
THAT YEAR ALL ARE TO RETURN TO
THEIR ORIGINAL LAND GRANTS, AND
DEBTS ARE FORGIVEN. ALL ISRAELITE
SLAVES (SLAVES WHO ARE SONS OF
GOD – HAVE A SPECIAL RELATIONSHIP
WITH GOD) ARE TO GO FREE AND ALL
DEBTS FORGIVEN (SEE Lev. 25). THOSE
WHO DO NOT HAVE THE SPECIAL
RELATIONSHIP WITH GOD DO NOT GO
FREE. THE COUNTING OF THE FIFTY
YEAR CYCLES IS TO BEGIN WHEN THE
ISRAELITES ENTER THE PROMISED
LAND. THIS FIFTY YEAR CYCLE CAUSES
THE YEAR OF JUBILEE TO COINCIDE
WITH THE DEATH OF JESUS WHEN THE
OBEDIENT ARE SET FREE FROM THEIR
SINS. (SEE 30 A.D.)

1471 B.C.	MOSES DIES, THE ISRAELITES ENTER THE PROMISED LAND, AND JOSHUA BEGINS THE CONQUEST OF CANAAN. THE CANAANITES ARE NEVER COMPLETELY DRIVEN OUT, BUT ARE USED FOR FORCED LABOR (Judges 1:27-33; Genesis 9:24-27)
1471-70 B.C.	THE LAND IS DIVIDED BETWEEN THE TRIBES. CITIES OF REFUGE AND A GOVERNMENT SYSTEM OF LOCAL RULE AND AUTONOMY UNDER GOD ARE ESTABLISHED AT GOD'S DIRECTION.
1471-30 B.C.	THE WRITING OF JOSHUA: DESCRIBES THE CONQUEST AND DIVIDING OF THE PROMISED LAND AMONG THE CHILDREN OF ISRAEL.
1457-56 B.C.	THUTMOSE III, OF EGYPT, BARELY DEFEATS MESOPOTAMIAN HITITES AT MEGIDDO.
c.1440-33 B.C.	CHUSHRANISHATHAIM, (Subbiliuliuma: to his own, "the Great King, the Noble King of Hatti", but to Israel, "he of the two fold crimes of Chush"), ENSLAVES THE ISRAELITES.
c1433-1394 B.C.	OTHNIEL DELIVERS ISRAEL FROM CHUSHRANISHATHAIM AND ISRAEL HAS 40 YEARS PEACE AS HE JUDGES.
1421 B.C.	FIRST YEAR OF JUBILEE (Lev. 25)
c.1394-1377B.C.	EGLON OF MOAB ENSLAVES ISRAEL.
c. 1377-1298 B.C.	EHUD KILLS EGLON AND ISRAEL HAS REST.
1371,1321 B.C.	THE SECOND AND THIRD YEARS OF JUBILEE
c.1298-79 B.C.	JABIN OF CANAAN OPPRESSES ISRAEL.
c.1279-1240B.C.	DEBORAH AND BARAK DEFEAT SISERA AT TAANACH AND MOUNT TABOR NEAR MEGIDDO. ISRAEL HAS REST FOR 40 YEARS.
1271 B.C.	THE 4TH YEAR OF JUBILEE.

c.1240- 1234B.C.	MIDIA TORMENTS ISRAEL.
c. 1234 -1195 B.C.	GIDEON DEFEATS THE MIDIANITES AND AMALEKITES AT ENDOR AND MOREH. ISRAEL HAS 40 YEARS OF REST.
1221 B.C.	THE FIFTH YEAR OF JUBILEE
c. 1200 B.C.	TROY FALLS AND REFUGEES HELP ESTABLISH ROME. SAMUEL IS BORN.
c. 1195-1193 B.C.	ABIMELECH IS A TYRANT IN ISRAEL. HE MURDERS SEVENTY OF HIS BROTHERS WITH THE SUPPORT OF SHECHEM. THEN HE AND THE PEOPLE OF SHECHEM FUED AND MANY OF THEM DIE BEFORE HE IS KILLED.
c. 1193-1171 B.C.	TOLA JUDGES ISRAEL. RUTH AND NAOMI RETURN TO BETHLEHEM
c. 1182 –1143 B.C.	THE PHILISTINES TORMENT ISRAEL. MOST OF THIS TIME THEY ARE IN CONFLICT WITH SAMSON.
1171-1150B.C.	JAIR JUDGES ISRAEL
1171 B.C.	THE SIXTH YEAR OF JUBILEE
1160-1143 B.C.	AMMON OPPRESSES ISRAEL.
c.1143-1138 B.C.	JEPHTHAH DEFEATS AMORITES AND JUDGES ISRAEL.
c.1143 B.C.	ELI DIES AT 98 YEARS OLD AND HIS TWO SONS ARE KILLED. THE PHILISTINES TAKE THE ARK OF GOD AND THEN RETURN IT.
c.1138-1132 B.C.	IBZAN JUDGES ISRAEL.
c.1132-1123 B.C.	ELON JUDGES ISRAEL.
c.1123-1117 B.C.	ABDON JUDGES ISRAEL.
c.1123-1070 B.C.	THE PHILISTINES RENEW THEIR CONFLICT WITH ISRAEL.
1121 B.C.	THE SEVENTH YEAR OF JUBILEE.

CHAPTER THREE
CHRISTIAN CHRONOLOGY OF HISTORY
(REIGN OF SAUL – 738 B.C.)
A TIME LINE OF HUMAN HISTORY
FROM A CHRISTIAN PROSPECTIVE
Compiled by "God's Friend"

1117-1075 B.C.	REIGN OF KING SAUL, DURING WHICH DAVID, SON OF JESSE, BECOMES A CHAMPION OF ISRAEL.
c.1100 B.C.	THE WRITING OF JUDGES.
1110-1091 B.C.	SAMUAL PROBABLY WRITES RUTH AND THE FIRST 24 CHAPTERS OF 1 SAMUEL. SAMUEL REORGANIZES GOD'S PEOPLE FROM A SYSTEM BUILT AROUND LOCAL RULE AND AUTONOMY UNDER GOD, TO A HIGHLY CENTRALIZED KINGDOM SYSTEM. HE DID THIS AT THE INSISTENCE OF THE PEOPLE. THEY SAID THEY WANTED TO BE LIKE OTHERS AROUND THEM. GOD SAID THIS WAS A REJECTION OF GOD. GOD WARNED THEM OF THE MISERY THEY WERE CREATING, BUT PERMITTED IT AND CONTINUED TO WORK WITH THEM. (SEE 66-67; 380; 1776; 1787, AND 1992 A.D.).
1075 B.C.	THE PHILISTINES DEFEAT SAUL AND JONATHAN AT MOUNT GILBOA NEAR MEGIDDO.
1071 B.C.	EIGHTH YEAR OF JUBILEE

1069 B.C.	KING DAVID CAPTURES JERUSALEM AND UNITES ISRAEL.
1069-1020 B.C.	NATHAN AND GAD WRITE THE REST OF 1 SAMUEL AND 2 SAMUEL. NATHAN PROPHESIES TO DAVID ABOUT THE ACCOMPLISHMENTS OF HIS LINEAGE AFTER HIM. HE TELLS HIM HIS DESCENDANT WILL BUILD A HOUSE FOR GOD AFTER HIM. SOLOMON FULFILLS THIS IN A PHYSICAL SENSE IN 1031 B.C. AND JESUS FULFILLS THIS IN A SPIRITUAL SENSE IN 30 A.D. A DESCENDANT OF DAVID IS TO RULE GOD'S PEOPLE FOREVER (30A.D. – THE END OF THE WORLD IS THE RULE OF JESUS THROUGH HIS CHURCH. THERE ARE PASSAGES THAT ESTABLISH HIS RULE BEFORE THEN) (SEE 2 Samuel 7:12-17; 1 Chronicles 17:11-15).
1069-1041 B.C.	DAVID WRITES PSALMS, PROPHESYING THE MESSIAH WILL HAVE HIS HANDS AND FEET PIERCED AND SOLDIERS WILL DIVIDE HIS GARMENTS, CASTING LOTS FOR HIS VESTURE. HIS BODY WILL NOT BE LEFT IN THE GRAVE, BUT HE WILL BE RESURRECTED AND SEATED AT THE RIGHT HAND OF GOD. HE WILL BECOME A PRIEST LIKE MELCHIZEDEK. (SEE Matthew 27: 35-36; 26-30 A.D.)
1043 B.C.	THE APPROXIMATE TIME THE CHILDREN OF ISRAEL QUIT HONORING JUBILEE AND SABBATH YEARS. (RENT ON LAND OWED TO GOD).
1034 B.C.	SOLOMON BEGINS TO REIGN.
1031 B.C.	CONSTRUCTION ON SOLOMON'S TEMPLE BEGINS. (1Kings 6:1)
1021 B.C.	NINETH YEAR OF JUBILEE

1020-1006 B.C.	SOLOMON WRITES PROVERBS, SONG OF SOLOMON AND ECCLESIASTES.
994 B.C.	DIVIDED KINDDOM (JUDAH/ISRAEL) BEGINS (1 Kings 11:42).
994-978 B.C.	REHOBOAM, SON OF SOLOMON, RULES JUDAH (1 Kings 14:21).
994-973 B.C.	JEROBOAM 1ST RULES ISRAEL (1Kings 14:20).
986 B.C.	SHOSHENQ I (SHISHAK) DEFEATS MEGIDDO.
977-975 B.C.	ABIJAM RULES JUDAH (1 Kings 15:1, 2).
975-935 B.C.	ASA RULES JUDAH (1 Kings 15: 9-10).
974-973 B.C.	NADAB RULES ISRAEL (1 Kings 15:25).
973-950 B.C.	BAASHA RULES ISRAEL (1Kings 15:33).
971 B.C.	10TH YEAR OF JUBILEE
950-949 B.C.	ELAH RULES ISRAEL (1Kings 16:8).
949 B.C.	ZIMRI KILLS ELAH AND RULES ISRAEL FOR 7 DAYS. THEN OMRI BESIEGES ZIMRI, AND ZIMRI DIES (1Kings 16:15).
948-945 B.C.	CIVIL WAR IN ISRAEL BETWEEN OMRI AND TIBNI.
945-934 B.C.	OMRI RULES ISRAEL AND BUILDS SAMARIA (1Kings 16:23-24).
938-917 B.C.	AHAB RULES ISRAEL (1 Kings 16:29).
935-911B.C.	JEHOSHAPHAT RULES JUDAH (1Kings 22:42).
921 B.C.	ELEVENTH YEAR OF JUBILEE
919-918 B.C.	AHAZIAH RULES ISRAEL (1 Kings 22:51).
919-914 B.C.	JEHORAM OF JEHOSHAPHAT HAS A CO-REGENCY IN JUDAH (2 Kings 8:16, 17; 2 Kings 1:17).
918 B.C.	ELISHA WATCHES ELIJAH CARRIED TO HEAVEN BY A CHARIOT OF FIRE (2 Kings 2:11, 12).
918-907 B.C.	JEHORAM OF AHAB RULES ISRAEL (2Kings 3:1).
914-907 B.C.	JEHORAM'S FULL REGENCY IN JUDAH (2 Kings 8:16).

910 B.C.	EDOM REBELLS FROM UNDER JUDAH (2 Kings 8:20; Genesis 27:38-40).
907 B.C.	AHAZIAH, JEHOSHAPHAT'S GRANDSON, RULES JUDAH (2 Kings 8:25, 26).
907 B.C.	ELISHA HAS JEHU ANOINTED KING OVER ISRAEL. JEHU THEN KILLS JEHORAM OF AHAB AND AHAZIAH, AFTER JEHORAM IS WOUNDED BY THE SYRIANS AT JEZREEL, NEAR MEGIDDO. HE SLAYS OR HAS SLAIN JEZEBEL AND ALL THE HOUSE OF AHAB, ALONG WITH AHAZIAH AS PROPHESIED BY ELIJAH. HE ALSO SLAYS THE PRIESTS AND PROPHETS OF BAAL. (2 Kings Chapter 9,10) HOWEVER, HE KEPT THE GOLDEN CALVES AT BETHEL AND DAN.
906-879 B.C.	JEHU RULES ISRAEL (2 Kings 10:36).
906-901 B.C.	ATHALIAH RULES JUDAH (2 Kings 11) SHE ATTEMPTS TO DESTROY THE LINEAGE OF DAVID. JOASH, THE SON OF AHAZIAH, SURVIVED, PROTECTED BY JEHOIADA THE PRIEST.
900-861 B.C.	JEHOASH (JOASH) RULES JUDAH (2 Kings 12:1).
878-862 B.C.	JEHOAHAZ RULES ISRAEL (2 Kings 13:1).
871 B.C.	THE TWELFTH YEAR OF JUBILEE.
864-849 B.C.	JEHOASH, SON OF JEHOAHAZ, RULES ISRAEL (2 Kings 13:10-25).
863-835 B.C.	AMAZIAH RULES JUDAH (2 Kings 14:1, 2).
860 B.C.	AN UPRISING IN TYRE RESULTS IN THE KING'S DAUGHTER, ELISSA (DIDO), AND NOBLEMEN FROM TYRE, FLEEING AND ESTABLISHING CARTHAGE IN NORTH AFRICA.
850 B.C.	HOMER WRITES THE ILIAD AND THE ODYSSEY.

849-809 B.C.	JEROBOAM II RULES ISRAEL (2 Kings 14:23).
840 B.C.	JONAH WRITES "JONAH" (2 Kings 14:25). THE THREE DAYS JONAH SPENDS IN THE BELLY OF THE FISH BECOMES SYMBOLIC OF THE MESSIAH'S STAY IN THE TOMB (SEE Matthew 12:39-41; 30 A.D.).
823-772 B.C.	AZARIAH (UZZIAH) RULES JUDAH (2 Kings 15:1-2).
821 B.C.	THE THIRTEENTH YEAR OF JUBILEE.
825 B.C.	JOEL WRITES "JOEL". HE PROPHESIES THERE WILL COME A TIME WHEN GOD POURS HIS SPIRIT OUT ON ALL NATIONS. MANY MIRACLES WILL BE DONE. WONDERS WILL BE SHOWN IN THE HEAVENS AND WHOEVER CALLS ON THE NAME OF THE LORD WILL BE SAVED. (SEE Acts 2:16-43; 30 A.D.)
820-725 B.C.	ISAIAH WRITES ISAIAH. HE PROPHESIES THE MESSIAH WILL NOT BE HANDSOME. HE WILL BE CALLED WONDERFUL COUNSELOR, MIGHTY GOD, EVERLASTING FATHER, AND PRINCE OF PEACE. HE WILL RULE ON DAVID'S THRONE FOREVER. THERE WILL BE NO END TO THE INCREASE OF HIS GOVERNMENT AND PEACE. THE SPIRIT OF THE LORD WILL REST ON HIM (SEE John 3:31-36). HE WILL STRIKE WITH THE ROD OF HIS MOUTH. PEACE WILL BE IN UNNATURAL PLACES AND THE EARTH WILL BE FULL OF THE KNOWLEDGE OF GOD. HE WILL BE FROM THE ROOT OF JESSE, A COVENANT FOR GOD'S PEOPLE AND A LIGHT FOR THE GENTILES. HIS STRENGTH IS TO BE IN HIS MOUTH

AND THE WORDS HE SPEAKS
(SEE John 12: 44-50).

HE WILL BE DESPISED, FORSAKEN, AND
A MAN OF SORROW. HE WILL BRING
GOOD TIDINGS. HIS TEACHINGS
ARE TO BE GIVEN IN ZEBULIN AND
NAPHTALI, BY THE SEA, GALILEE OF
THE NATIONS. HE WILL DO MANY
MIRACLES. DESPITE ALL THESE SIGNS,
THE PEOPLE WILL REJECT HIM. (SEE
John 18:36- 19:16)

HE IS TO BE LED LIKE A LAMB TO THE
SLAUGHTER. THROUGH INJUSTICE HE
IS TO DIE BEING ASSOCIATED WITH
THE WICKED AND A RICH MAN IN HIS
DEATH (SEE Matthew 27:38, 57-60). HE
WILL BE SLAIN FOR OUR INIQUITIES.

A BOOK IS TO BE GIVEN TO LEAD
PEOPLE OUT OF DARKNESS. ALL
NATIONS ARE TO FLOW INTO HIS
KINGDOM (SEE Revelation 22: 18, 19;
2 Thessalonians 1:8, 9; 2:15- 17; A.D. 26-30).

THE ISRAELITE PEOPLE, BECAUSE OF
THEIR SIN, WILL BE CARRIED OFF INTO
SLAVERY, BUT WILL BE RETURNED
TO START THE NATION AGAIN. A
PAGAN NAMED "CYRUS" WILL HELP
ACCOMPLISH THE RETURN
(SEE 2 Kings 20:16-19; 25:1-30; 2
CHRONICLES 36:22, 23; Ezra 1:1-4).

815 B.C.   AMOS WRITES AMOS. HE PROPHESIES
THAT DAMASCUS WILL BE CONQUERED
AND CARRIED INTO SLAVERY TO KIR.

	THE PHILISTINES SHALL PERISH. ISRAEL IS TO BE DESTOYED BY ASSYRIA (SEE 753-736, 608 B.C.).
800-740 B.C.	HOSEA WRITES HOSEA. HE PROPHESIES ISRAEL WILL BE SCATTERED AMONG THE NATIONS BECAUSE SHE HAS NOT BEEN FAITHFUL TO GOD. BECAUSE OF THEIR IGNORANCE ABOUT GOD THEY WILL COME TO RUIN (SEE 737 AND 608 B.C.). THOSE THAT WERE NOT GOD'S PEOPLE WILL BE CALLED HIS PEOPLE (SEE 30 A.D. and Romans chapters 9-11).
786 B.C.	ZACHARIAH RULES ISRAEL SIX MONTHS. HE IS KILLED BY SHALLUM WHO RULES ONE MONTH. SHALLUM IS KILLED BY MENAHEM.
785-776 B.C.	MENAHEM RULES ISRAEL (2 Kings 15:14-18).
774-773 B.C.	PEKAHIAH RULES ISRAEL (2 Kings 15:23-26).
772-753 B.C.	PEKAH RULES ISRAEL (2 Kings 15:27-31).
771 B.C.	THE FOURTEENTH YEAR OF JUBILEE.
771-715 B.C.	MICAH WRITES MICAH. HE PROPHESIES THE MESSIAH WILL BE BORN IN BETHLEHAM (SEE 5 B.C.; Matthew 2:1-6).
771-756 B.C.	JOTHAM RULES JUDAH (SEE 2 Kings 15:32, 33).
757-741 B.C.	AHAZ RULES JUDAH (2Kings 16:1, 2).
756-730 B.C.	REZIN OF SYRIA AND PEKAH OF ISRAEL ATTACK AHAZ OF JUDAH. AHAZ CONTRACTS WITH ASSYRIA FOR HELP. ASSYRIA CONQUERS DAMASCUS AND CARRIES THE INHABITANTS INTO SLAVERY AT KIR. LATER ASSYRIA ATTEMPTS TO CONQUER THE WHOLE REGION, CARRYING SAMARIA INTO SLAVERY AND DESTROYING ALL THE CITIES OF JUDAH, BUT JERUSALEM.

DIVINE INTERVENTION, IN WHICH
A HUNDRED AND EIGHTY-FIVE
THOUSAND ASSYRIANS DIE IN
ONE NIGHT, SAVES JERUSALEM.
FOUR DIFFERENT ASSYRIAN KINGS
PARTICIPATE IN THESE CAMPAIGNS,
TIGLATH-PILESER (PUL), SHALMANESER,
SARGON, AND SENNACHERIB.

746-738 B.C.	HOSEA RULES ISRAEL (2 Kings 17:1).
744-716 B.C.	HEZEKIAH RULES IN JUDAH (2 Kings 18:1, 2).
738 B.C.	THE FALL OF SAMARIA TO SARGON DURING HOSEA'S REIGN IN ISRAEL. SARGON CARRIES OFF THE NORTHERN TRIBES.

CHAPTER FOUR
CHRISTIAN CHRONOLOGY OF HISTORY
(THE FALL OF SAMARIA –604 B.C.)
A TIME LINE OF HUMAN HISTORY
FROM A CHRISTIAN PROSPECTIVE
Compiled by "God's Friend"

738 B.C.	FALL OF SAMARIA
730 B.C.	THE DIVINE DEFEAT OF SENNACHERIB'S ARMY AT JERUSALEM DURING HEZEKIAH'S REIGN IN JUDAH. 185,000 DIE IN ONE NIGHT.
721 B.C.	FIFTEENTH YEAR OF JUBILEE
715-661 B.C.	MANASSEH RULES JUDAH (2 Kings 21:1).
671 B.C.	SIXTEENTH YEAR OF JUBILEE.
661-660 B.C.	AMON RULES JUDAH (2 Kings 21:19).
660-630 B.C.	JOSIAH RULES JUDAH (2 Kings 22:1).
650-630 B.C.	NAHUM WRITES NAHUM. HE PROPHESIES THAT LIKE THE FALL OF THEBES, THE FALL OF ASSYRIA WILL BE AMAZING, TERRIBLE, AND UNMOURNED, BUT APPLAUDED BY MANY (SEE 630 B.C.).
648-607 B.C.	JEREMIAH WRITES LAMENTATIONS, 1 KINGS, AND MOST OF JEREMIAH AND 2 KINGS. DANIEL HAD ACCESS TO AT LEAST SOME OF JEREMIAH'S WRITINGS (Daniel 9), AND I BELIEVE, MADE A SMALL ADDITION TO THE ENDS OF JEREMIAH AND 2 KINGS. JEREMIAH PROPHESIED THAT GOD WOULD GIVE A NEW COVENANT

OR TESTAMENT, NOT LIKE THE ONE
DELIVERED BY MOSES (SEE 30-96
A.D.). GOD WILL PROVIDE A GOOD
SHEPHERD FOR HIS PEOPLE. THIS
SHEPHERD WILL LOOK AFTER GOD'S
PEOPLE AS A SHEPHERD LOOKS AFTER
HIS SHEEP. GOD WILL RAISE UP A
RIGHTEOUS BRANCH FROM KING
DAVID THAT WILL SAVE THE PEOPLE
(SEE 5-30 A.D.).

GOD WILL RETURN THE CAPTIVES
FROM THE NORTH COUNTRY (SEE
536-444 B.C.). JERUSALEM AND ALL
NEIGHBORING NATIONS WILL BE
DESTROYED BY BABYLON (SEE 619-608
B.C.). RESISTING BABYLON'S RULE WILL
ONLY MAKE MATTERS WORSE. MOAB,
AMMON, ELAM, AND JUDAH WILL BE
RESTORED. BABYLON WILL BE MADE
DESOLATE SEVENTY YEARS AFTER THE
DESOLATION OF JUDAH. THEN THE
CAPTIVES WILL BE SENT HOME (SEE
608 B.C., 538 B.C., AND 536 B.C.).

647-626 B.C. NEBOPOLLASSAR RULES BABYLON
(NEBUCHADNEZZAR'S FATHER). NOTE
AS REGUARDS THE BABYLONIAN
DYNASTY: THE BIBLE DATES
NEBUCHADNEZZAR AND EVIL-
MURDOCK. IT ALSO ENDORSES THE
REIGN OF BELSHAZZAR, BUT HELPS
DATE ONLY THE END OF THAT REIGN,
INDICATING HE REIGNED AT LEAST
THREE YEARS. JOSEPHUS LISTS THE
KINGS IN THIS DYNASTY IN ORDER
GIVING LENGTHS OF REIGN. THOSE
LENGTHS ARE IMPOSSIBLE. HE ALSO
FAILS TO MENTION NABONIDUS,

BUT ATTRIBUTES A SIMILAR NAME
TO BELSHAZZAR. A SIGNIFICANT
COLLECTION OF CUNEIFORM
TABLETS DOCUMENT THE CO-
REGENCY OF BELSHAZZAR AND HIS
FATHER, NABONIDUS. I'VE MERGED
INFORMATION ABOUT THE KINGS
FROM JOSEPHUS AND DR. E.J. YOUNG'S,
THE PROPHECY OF DANIEL. I THEN
USED WHAT SEEMED REASONABLE
TO ME. I MUST ADMIT THAT THERE
IS ARBITRARINESS IN SOME OF THE
LENGTH'S AND THEREFORE DATES.
HOWEVER, THE OVER ALL PERIOD OF
BABYLONIAN CAPTIVITY IS RELIABLE
AND VERIFIED BY JEREMIAH AND
DANIEL.

645 B.C.   ZEPHANIAH WRITES ZEPHANIAH.
HE PROPHESIES THE DESTRUCTION
OF THE CITIES OF THE PHILISTINES,
MOAB, AMMON, ETHIOPIA AND
ASSYRIA. NINEVEH IS TO BECOME
COMPLETELY DESOLATE. A PURIFIED
REMNANT OF ISRAEL AND JERUSALEM
WILL BE PROTECTED (SEE 630-536 B.C.).

645 B.C.   EZEKIEL IS BORN.

630 B.C.   PHARAOH- NECHO IS REFUSED
PASSAGE BY JOSIAH. JOSIAH IS SLAIN
AT MEGIDDO. NECHO GOES TO FIGHT
THE ASSYRIANS AT CHARCHEMISH
ALLIED WITH THE BABYLONIANS.
ASSYRIA IS DEFEATED, AND LATER
NINEVEH DESTROYED.

630 B.C.   JEHOAHAZ RULES JUDAH 3 MONTHS
(2 Kings 23:30-31).

630-619 B.C.   HABAKKUK WRITES HABAKKUK. HE
PROPHESIES THAT THE CALDEANS
HAVE BEEN BROUGHT TO PUNISH THE

NATION, BUT THEY TOO SHALL BE
PUNISHED FOR THEIR VIOLENCE (SEE
538 B.C.).

629-619 B.C.   ELIAKIM (JEHOIAKIM) RULES JUDAH
(2 Kings 23: 34-37).

629-627 B.C   BABYLON INVADES JUDAH AND TAKES
EVERYTHING FROM THE NILE TO THE
EUPHRATES FROM EGYPT. DANIEL
AND OTHERS ARE CARRIED INTO
BABYLONIAN SLAVERY.

627-583 B.C.   NEBUCHADNEZZAR RULES BABYLON.

627 B.C.   NEBUCHADNEZZAR ASSUMES
COMMAND OF BABYLON'S ARMY
AND SUBJUGATES JEHOIAHKIM AND
OTHERS, TAKING DANIEL AND HIS
FRIENDS CAPTIVE. DANIEL DATES HIS
RULE FROM THIS DATE.

627-625 B.C.   JEHOIAKIM SERVES BABYLON AND
THEN WITHOLDS TRIBUTE.

626 B.C.   NEBUCHADNEZZAR'S FATHER DIES IN
BABYLON AND NEBUCHADNEZZAR
RETURNS TO BABYLON TO BE
RECOMFIRMED AS KING. HE THEN
GOES TO BATTLE AT CARCHEMISH
WHERE HE DEFEATS THE EGYPTIANS.
JEREMIAH DATES HIS RULE FROM HIS
RECONFIRMATION AFTER HIS FATHER'S
DEATH.

626 B.C.   DANIEL REVEALS AND INTERPRETS
NEBUCHADNEZZAR'S DREAM OF THE
GREAT IMAGE. IN THIS HE PROPHESIES
BABYLON'S FALL TO ANOTHER
KINGDOM, (THE MEDES AND PERSIANS)
WHICH WOULD FALL TO A THIRD
KINGDOM, (THE GREEKS) WHICH
WOULD FALL TO A FOURTH KINGDOM
(THE ROMANS). DURING THE FOURTH
KINGDOM GOD WOULD SET UP HIS

	OWN KINGDOM, REPRESENTED BY A GREAT ROCK, AND THAT KINGDOM WOULD NEVER BE DESTROYED, BUT WOULD BREAK ALL OTHER KINGDOMS AND GROW AND FILL THE EARTH. IT WOULD LAST FOREVER (SEE 1069, 538,336-323, 133-27 B.C.; 30-the present A.D.).
623-534 B.C.	DANIEL WRITES DANIEL. (NEBUCHADNEZZAR WRITES CHAPTER FOUR OF DANIEL). DANIEL PROPHESIES PERSIA WILL CONQUER BABYLON (SEE 538 B.C.). GREECE WILL CONQUER PERSIA (SEE 336 B.C.). THE GREEK EMPIRE WILL BE DIVIDED INTO FOUR KINGDOMS (SEE 323 B.C.), AND THE ROMANS WILL CONQUER THE GREEK EMPIRE (SEE 168-27 B.C.). DURING THE ROMAN RULE GOD WILL SET UP A KINGDOM (SEE 30 A.D.) THAT WILL GROW AND FILL THE EARTH. HE ALSO PROPHESIED THAT FROM A DECREE TO RESTORE JERUSALEM TO THE MESSIAH'S (THE ETERNAL, WORLD KING) COMING WILL BE 483 YEARS (SEE 458B.C. AND 26 A.D.). THE MESSIAH WILL STAY FOR THREE AND A HALF YEARS, AND THEN LEAVE (SEE 30 A.D.) THE THREE AND A HALF YEARS WILL HAVE 1290 DAYS. 45 DAYS AFTER HIS DEPARTURE THERE WILL BE SOMETHING VERY SPECIAL THAT WILL HAPPEN (SEE PENTECOST IN 30 A.D.). THEN JERUSALEM WILL BE DESTROYED. (SEE 70 A.D., 1 CHRONICLES 17: 11-15; DANIEL ALSO PROPHESIES A DETAILED STRING OF EVENTS OCCURING BETWEEN 323 B.C. TO 30 A.D.)

621 B.C.	THE SEVENTEENTH YEAR OF JUBILEE
619 B.C.	JEHOIACHIN AND 10,000 JERUSALEM CAPTIVES ARE REMOVED BY THE BABYLONIANS (NEBOCHADNEZZAR). EZEKIEL IS INCLUDED IN THE CAPTIVES.
618-608 B.C.	ZEDEKIAH RULES JUDAH (2 Kings 24: 17, 18).
618-608 B.C.	EZEKIEL WRITES EZEKIEL. HE PROPHESIES THAT THE CAPTIVES SHOULD WORK TO MAKE LIVES IN THE LAND THEY HAVE BEEN CARRIED TO, BECAUSE JERUSALEM WILL NOT RISE UP AND FREE THEM. HE TELLS OF A MESSIAH THAT WILL BE A TEACHER, SHEPHERD OF GOD'S PEOPLE.

HE ALSO PROPHESIES THAT IN A DISTANT TIME, IN THE LAST DAYS, THAT NATIONS (SOMALIANS OR SUDANIANS, IRANIANS, LIBYANS, GERMANIC PEOPLES, MONGOLIANS (POSSIBLY CHINA (SEE 1279 A.D.), AND A PEOPLE THAT LIVED NORTH OF THE GERMANS, LEAD BY RUSSIA) WILL INVADE A LAND FULL OF PEOPLE WHO HAVE POWER WITH GOD (OR PRINCES OF GOD, SONS OF GOD-ISRAEL TRANSLATED). THEY WILL BE IN A VERY PROSPEROUS LAND THAT USE TO BE EMPTY, BUT IS NOW FULL OF PEOPLE. THEIR VILLAGES WILL NOT BE FORTIFIED.

GOD'S PEOPLE WILL HAVE COME FROM MANY DIFFERENT NATIONS (SEE 1620 A.D.). THE SPANISH AND ARABS WILL BE BYSTANDERS. THE EVIL NATIONS WILL ATTACK SEEKING

PLUNDER. GOD WILL DEFEND AND
THE ATTACKING NATIONS WILL DIE IN
A LARGE VALLEY EAST OF THE OCEAN
WHERE TRAVELERS GO. THE INVADING
NATIONS WILL BE DESTROYED
BY FAMINE, DISEASE, INTERNAL
FIGHTING, AND FIRE, HAIL, AND RAIN
FROM THE SKY (SEE 57 A.D., 96 A.D., 2000
A.D. AND AFTERWARDS).

610-604 B.C.   NEBUCHADNEZZAR BESIEGES
JERUSALEM, DESTROYS IT AND CARRIES
OFF CAPTIVES AGAIN. THE REMAINING
JUDEANS KILL THE LEADER APPOINTED
BY THE BABYLONIANS AND RUN OFF
TO EGYPT. JEREMIAH IS FORCED TO GO
WITH THEM.

608 B.C.   ZEDEKIAH IS CAPTURED, HIS SONS ARE
SLAIN BEFORE HIM AND HIS EYES ARE
PUT OUT.
JERUSALEM AND ALL THE HOMES
THERE ARE BURNT TO THE GROUND.
THE FIRST TEMPLE, BUILT BY KING
SOLOMON, IS DESTROYED BY
NEBUCHADNEZZAR (SEE Jeremiah 3:12;
2 Kings 25:8, 9).

606 B.C.   OBADIAH WRITES OBADIAH. HE
PROPHESIES THE DESOLATION OF
EDOM BECAUSE OF ITS REJOICING IN
THE DESTRUCTION OF JUDAH. AT THIS
TIME EDOM IS A SIGNIFICANT PEOPLE
TO THE SOUTHEAST OF JUDAH. BY
THE TIME OF CHRIST THEIR LAND IS
DESOLATE.

CHAPTER FIVE
CHRISTIAN CHRONOLOGY OF HISTORY
(THE FALL OF JERUSALEM - 27 B.C.)
A TIME LINE OF HUMAN HISTORY
FROM A CHRISTIAN PROSPECTIVE
Compiled by "God's Friend"

608 B.C.	JERUSALEM IS DESTROYED BY NEBUCHADNEZZAR (Jeremiah 3:12; 2 Kings 25:8, 9).
591-585 B.C.	THE PROBABLE YEARS OF NEBUCHADNEZZAR'S INSANITY (Daniel chapter 4).
582-565 B.C.	EVILMERODACH RULES BABYLON. HE TAKES JEHOICHIN FROM PRISON, GIVING HIM AN ALLOWANCE FOR THE REST OF HIS LIFE (Jeremiah 52:31-34; 2 Kings 25:27-30).
571 B.C.	EIGHTEENTH YEAR OF JUBILEE.
565-561 B.C.	NEGLISSAR (NERIGLISAR) RULES BABYLON.
563 B.C.	BIRTH OF SIDDHARTHA GAUTAMA, FOUNDER OF THE BUDDHIST SECTS. HE IS BORN IN INDIA NEAR A REGION UNDER PERSIAN CONTROL.
560 B.C.	LABOSORADACUS RULES BABYLON FOR NINE MONTHS.
560-538 B.C.	NABONIDAS (NABOANDELUS) RULES BABYLON.
554-538 B.C.	BELSHAZZAR (BALTASAR) RULES BABYLON. HE IS SECOND IN COMMAND

SHARING RULE WITH HIS FATHER, NABONIDAS.

554 B.C. DANIEL HAS A VISION OF FOUR BEASTS. FOUR BEASTS CAME UP FROM THE SEA. THE FIRST WAS LIKE A LION WITH WINGS (BABYLON). ITS WINGS WERE PLUCKED FROM IT. THE SECOND BEAST WAS LIKE A BEAR WITH THREE RIBS BETWEEN ITS TEETH (THE MEDOPERSIAN EMPIRE). THE THIRD BEAST WAS LIKE A LEOPARD WITH FOUR WINGS AND FOUR HEADS (THE GREEK EMPIRE). THE FOURTH BEAST WAS TERRIBLE WITH TEN HORNS (THE ROMAN EMPIRE). ANOTHER HORN CAME UP THAT PLUCKED UP THREE OF THE FIRST HORNS.

THEN THE ANCIENT OF DAYS SITTING ON A THRONE CAME. THE BEAST WAS SLAIN AND THE REST OF THE BEASTS HAD THEIR DOMINION TAKEN AWAY. THE SON OF MAN (JESUS) CAME TO THE ANCIENT OF DAYS AND WAS GIVEN AN ETERNAL KINGDOM. THE HORN REPRESENTED TEN KINGS OR DYNASTIES. THE SMALL HORN WAS A KING OR DYNASTY THAT MADE WAR AGAINST GOD'S PEOPLE FOR 1260 YEARS (TIME, TIMES AND A DIVIDED TIME 360 X 3 ½). THEN DOMINION WAS GIVEN TO GOD'S PEOPLE. (POSIBLE MEANING: Constantine replaced three ruling families to take the rule of the Roman empire. His grand son tried to declare the church under his rule and set-up rule of the secular kings over the religion allowed the masses. He laid the ground work for the Catholic Church. This power was reversed 1260 years later when

Parliament declared freedom of religion and
reversed the rule of the kings in religious matters.
Then people were freed to follow the apostolic
pattern in the Bible, The pattern commanded to
be followed in 2 Thessalonians 2:15.
(SEE: 380 A.D. and 1640 A.D.; Daniel 7).

552 B.C.

DANIEL HAS A VISION OF A TWO
HORNED RAM AND A ONE HORNED
GOAT (Daniel 8). THIS DREAM
PROPHESIED THE FALL OF MEDOPERSIA
TO GREECE (SEE 336-323 A.D.). THEN IT
PROPHESIED ALEXANDER THE GREAT
BEING REPLACED BY FOUR OF HIS
GENERALS (SEE 323 B.C.). FROM ONE OF
THE GENERALS CAME A RULER THAT
CAUSED THE DAILY SACRIFICE IN THE
JEWISH TEMPLE TO CEASE FOR 2300
SACRIFICES, OR 1115 DAYS AT TWO A
DAY. (SEE: 168 B.C.-165 B.C.)

538 B.C.

BELSHAZZAR SEES THE HAND WRITING
ON THE WALL AND PROMISES A THIRD
OF HIS KINGDOM OR THE THIRD RANK
IN THE KINGDOM TO ITS INTERPRETER.
DANIEL TRANSLATES REVEALING GOD
HAD NUMBERED THE BABYLONIAN
KINGDOM AND FINISHED IT. IT WAS
GIVEN TO THE MEDES AND PERSIANS.

538-536 B.C.

AFTER JERUSALEM HAS BEEN DESOLATE
FOR SEVENTY YEARS, BABYLON IS
DESTROYED AS WAS PROPHESIED
(2 Chronicles 36:16-23; Jeremiah 25:8-14;
29:10; 52:12-34; Daniel 9:1-19). THE FALL
OF BABYLON TO THE MEDO-PERSIANS
(DARIUS THE MEDE RULES). DANIEL
IS THROWN IN THE LIONS' DEN.
WHEN HE SURVIVES, DARIUS ORDERS,
"THAT IN ALL THE DOMINION OF

HIS KINGDOM MEN ARE TO TREMBLE AND FEAR BEFORE THE GOD OF DANIEL..." DANIEL BECOMES CHIEF ADMINISTRATOR OF THE ENTIRE EMPIRE. DANIEL PROPHESYS THE COMING OF THE GREAT MESSIAH 483 YEARS AFTER THE ORDER THAT RESTORES JERUSALEM. DATING FROM EZRA'S ORDER TO GO TO JERUSALEM AND TEACH THE WORD OF GOD, IT IS 483 YEARS TO THE BAPTISM OF JESUS AND THE BEGINNING OF JESUS' PERSONAL MINISTRY. DANIEL SAYS THE MESSIAH WILL THEN LEAVE IN THREE AND A HALF YEARS. THREE AND A HALF YEARS AFTER THE BEGINNING OF JESUS' MINISTRY, JESUS IS CRUCIFIED, RESURRECTED, AND ASCENDS INTO HEAVEN. DANIEL THEN SAYS A PRINCE WILL COME AND DESTROY JERUSALEM. TITUS, SON OF THE EMPEROR OF ROME, DESTROYS JERUSALEM (SEE: 70 A.D.). DANIEL MAKES A WRITTEN RECORD OF THE PROPHECY. DANIEL PREDICTS THE COMING OF THE MESSIAH IN ABOUT 500 YEARS. HE ALSO INDICATES THE THREE AND ½ YEARS WILL HAVE 1290 DAYS IN IT AND PENTICOST WILL BE 45 DAYS FROM THE DEATH OF JESUS (SEE Daniel 12 AND 30 A.D.).

536 B.C.   CYRUS BEGINS TO RULE (SEE 521 B.C.). CYRUS DECREES THAT JEWS MAY RETURN FROM CAPTIVITY TO REPOPULATE JERUSALEM AND REBUILD THE TEMPLE (A fulfillment of Isaiah 44:24-45... SEE 820-725 B.C.).

535 B.C.   FOUNDATION OF THE SECOND TEMPLE IS LAID.

SI-A-MEETREY

JESUS CHRIST

Bassano, Jacopo

Si-A-Meetrey (meaning: the highest God, the creator of every thing, the Lord of mercies) is known by the Buddhists for being the Lord of Lords and King of Kings. He knows more than all men and all angels. He is the only one that will ever be able to forgive sins. In Cambodia this mural from a king's palace shows him on his throne (and of course he is Asian). They don't know about the cross, but they do know about the bloody hands and feet, the pierced side, and the scared forehead. They will often mark the specialness of these areas with spirals, triangles, or flowers. Similarly, you will note that Europeans always make Jesus a European.

534 B.C.

BUDDHA BEGINS TRAINING TO BE A
RELIGIOUS LEADER, HAVING BEEN
ORDERED BY THE PERSIAN EMPEROR
(Darius the Mede- SEE 538-536 B.C.) TO
HONOR DANIEL'S GOD ABOVE ALL
OTHERS. BUDDHA IS ON THE FAR EDGE
OF THE PERSIAN EMPIRE (about 1400 miles
in a straight line). BUDDHA TEACHES HIS
FOLLOWERS THAT THE HIGHEST GOD,
CREATOR OF EVERYTHING, THE LORD
OF MERCIES, (SI-A-MEETREY), WILL BE
KNOWN AS LORD OF LORDS AND THE
KING OF KINGS. HE WILL COME IN
THE FUTURE. HE WILL BE THE ONLY
ONE TO EVER BE ABLE TO FORGIVE
SINS. HE WILL HAVE BLOODY HANDS,
BLOODY FEET, A HOLE IN HIS SIDE,
AND SCARES ON HIS FOREHEAD. HIS
ARMY WILL CONQUER THROUGH LOVE
AND COMPASSION. BUDDHA TELLS
THE BUDDHIST FOLLOWERS TO LEAVE
THEIR OLD WAYS AND JOIN HIS ARMY
WHEN IT COMES TO THEIR LANDS. IN
A DISCUSSION ON WOMEN PRIESTS HE
SAYS THE BUDDHIST FAITH WILL ONLY
LAST ABOUT FIVE HUNDRED YEARS
(SEE: 1069-1041 B.C.; 538-536 B.C.;
Psalms 22:16-18; Daniel 9).
BUDDHA LIVES IN A PAGAN WORLD
AND INCORPORATES MANY PAGAN
BELIEFS INTO HIS TEACHING. WHEN
BUDDHA WAS YOUNG HE WAS
PROTECTED FROM AGING, SUFFERING
AND SICKNESS. WHEN HE LEARNS OF
THESE THINGS HE OBSESSES ON THESE
THINGS. THE FOCUS OF MUCH OF HIS
STUDY IS TO ELIMINATE THEM. SINCE
HE BELIEVES IN REINCARNATION, HIS

	SOLUTION IS TO BE GOOD ENOUGH TO NOT HAVE TO BE REBORN. HIS HEAVEN BECOMES TO CEASE TO EXIST.
529 B.C.	DEATH OF CYRUS.
529-521 B.C.	CAMBYSES RULES PERSIA
522 B.C.	WORK ON THE SECOND TEMPLE STOPPED.
521 B.C.	NINETEENTH YEAR OF JUBILEE.
521 B.C.	SMERDIS (PSEUDO) RULES PERSIA. THIS APPEARS TO BE AN ATTEMPT BY THE MAGI (A SECT OF THE MEDES) TO REGAIN CONTROL OF THE EMPIRE. WHILE REASSERTING HIS AUTHORITY CAMBYSES DIES. I BELIEVE EITHER CAMBYSES OR DARIUS HYSTAPSIS PURGED THE HISTORIC RECORDS TO REMOVE THE EARLY RECORD OF MEDE (HILL PEOPLE) LEADERSHIP, ATTRIBUTING MUCH OF WHAT DARIUS THE MEDE ACCOMPLISHED TO CYRUS (PERSIAN -VALLEY PEOPLE).
521-486 B.C.	DARIUS HYSTAPSIS (DARIUS I) REIGNS IN PERSIA (FROM THIS POINT ON THE VALLEY PEOPLE DOMINATE LEADERSHIP IN PERSIA).
520 B.C.	HAGGAI WRITES HAGGAI. WORK ON THE SECOND TEMPLE BEGINS AGAIN.
520-518 B.C.	FOUR MONTHS AFTER HAGGAI BEGINS PROPHESYING, ZECHARIAH BEGINS PROPHESYING AND WRITES ZECHARIAH. HE PROPHESIES THE SECOND DESTRUCTION OF JERUSALEM SHORTLY AFTER THE DEATH OF THE MESSIAH (SEE 70 A.D.). GOD'S PEOPLE WILL BEGIN DENYING THE GIFT OF PROPHESY TO LIMIT DECEIT. THE MESSIAH WILL HAVE A TRIUMPHANT ENTRY INTO JERUSALEM RIDING ON A

COLT, THE FOAL OF AN ASS (SEE 30 A.D.;
96 A.D.; Matthew 21:1-16; Zechariah 9:9;
John 12:12-16).

515 B.C.	THE SECOND JERUSALEM TEMPLE IS COMPLETED.
485-465 B.C.	XERXES RULES PERSIA. THIS IS THE EMPEROR OF PERSIA THAT ATTEMPTS THE CONQUEST OF GREECE AND MACEDONIA.
485 B.C.	XERXES SETS OUT TO INVADE GREECE FROM SARDIS.
483 B.C.	BUDDHA DIES. HE HAS TOLD HIS FOLLOWERS OF A COMING MESSIAH, "SIRA-ADIA-MEETREY," WHO HAS A SCARED FOREHEAD, BLOODY HANDS, FEET AND SIDE. HE IS THE PRINCE OF MERCY, KING OF KINGS, AND LORD OF LORDS, WHO CAN FORGIVE SINS. HIS ARMY IS TO COME FROM THE WEST WITH WEAPONS OF LOVE, COMPASSION AND MERCY. BUDDHA TELLS HIS FOLLOWERS THAT WHEN THE ARMY COMES, THEY SHOULD LEAVE THEIR OLD WAYS AND JOIN IT. SIRA-ADIA-MEETREY IS TO COME IN ABOUT 500 YEARS. BUDDHA DOES NOT WRITE HIS TEACHINGS DOWN, BUT THEY ARE PASSED ON BY WORD OF MOUTH.
471 B.C.	TWENTIETH YEAR OF JUBILEE.
464-422 B.C.	ARTAXERXES LONGIMANUS RULES PERSIA. JOSEPHUS SAYS THAT HE IS THE HUSBAND OF ESTHER, AS DOES THE SEPTUAGINT.
462 B.C.	ESTHER IS CHOSEN AS SUCCESSOR FOR VASHTI, QUEEN OF PERSIA.
458 B.C.	DECREE IS ISSUED SENDING EZRA TO JERUSALEM EARLY THE NEXT YEAR TO TEACH THE BIBLE TO THE

	PEOPLE. SPIRITUAL RESTORATION OF JERUSALEM BEGINS. (SEE 538-536 B.C. and 26 A.D.-This activates the prophecy of Daniel 9 that dates the coming of the messiah).
456-445 B.C.	EZRA WRITES 1 AND 2 CHRONICLES AND EZRA. EZRA REPEATS THE PROPHECY OF NATHAN THAT PROMISES THE LINAGE OF DAVID WILL PRODUCE AN ETERNAL KING THAT WILL HAVE AN ETERNAL KINGDOM (SEE 1 Chronicles 17:11-14).
453 B.C.	HAMAN PLOTS AGAINST THE JEWS. ESTHER INTERVENES AND MORDECAI BECOMES SECOND IN COMMAND IN THE PERSIAN EMPIRE. THE CELEBRATION OF PURIM BEGINS DURING THE 12TH MONTH, ADAR.
452-450 B.C.	UNKNOWN AUTHOR WRITES ESTHER.
445-444 B.C.	NEHEMIAH SENT TO JERUSALEM TO REBUILD THE WALLS OF JERUSALEM.
440 B.C.	NEHEMIAH WRITES NEHEMIAH.
440 B.C.	MALACHI WRITES MALACHI. HE PROPHESIES THAT A PROPHET WILL PREPARE THE WAY BEFORE THE MESSIAH (SEE 26 A.D.). GOD SHALL SEND ELIJAH BEFORE THE GREAT AND DREADFUL DAY OF THE LORD.
422-404 B.C.	DARIUS II RULES PERSIA.
421 B.C.	TWENTY-FIRST YEAR OF JUBILEE.
404-358 B.C.	ARTAXERXES II RULES PERSIA.
371 B.C.	TWENTY-SECOND YEAR OF JUBILEE.
358-338 B.C.	ARTAXERXES III RULES PERSIA.
356 B.C.	ALEXANDER THE GREAT IS BORN.
338-336 B.C.	ARSES RULES PERSIA.
336-323 B.C.	ALEXANDER THE GREAT CONQUERS THE KNOWN WORLD. HE ORDERS JERUSALEM TO SEND HIM SUPPLIES. THEY REPLIED THAT THEY COULD NOT

COMPLY BECAUSE OF THEIR OATH TO THE PERSIAN EMPEROR. THEY REFUSE TO FIGHT AGAINST HIM. AFTER ALEXANDER HAD TAKEN TYRE AND GAZA THROUGH SIEGE, HE MARCHED ON JERUSALEM. THE JEWS OPENED THEIR GATES AND THE PRIESTS MET ALEXANDER IN THEIR OFFICIAL ATTIRE. ALEXANDER SAID HE HAD HAD A VISION OF THE HIGH PRIEST AND GAVE SPECIAL RIGHTS TO THE JEWS, INCLUDING FREEDOM FROM TRIBUTE REQUIREMENTS ON THE SABBATH YEARS. (SEE Josephus Book 11, Chapter 8). THE BOOK OF DANIEL WAS SHOWN ALEXANDER AND ALEXANDER WAS REASSURED BY DANIEL'S PROPHESIES THAT THE PERSIAN EMPIRE WOULD BE DESTROYED BY GREEKS.

336-331 B.C.	DARIUS III CODOMANNUS RULES PERSIA. HE IS DEFEATED BY ALEXANDER THE GREAT AT THE BATTLE OF GAUGMELA (OR ARBELA).
334 B.C.	ALEXANDER INVADES ASIA MINOR
323 B.C.	DEATH OF ALEXANDER THE GREAT ON MAY 21ST. HE DIVIDES HIS EMPIRE AMONG GREEK GENERALS PTOLEMY, CASSANDER, LYSMACHUS, AND SELEUCUS. PTOLEMY'S EMPIRE CENTERS IN EGYPT AND SELEUCUS' IN SYRIA. THEY ARE THE ONES WHO IMPACT PALESTINE (Daniel 7:6; 8:8, 22).
323-30 B.C.	THE PTOLEMY DYNASTY RULES EGYPT.
323-285 B.C.	PTOLEMY I (SOTER) RULES EGYPT (Daniel 11:5).
321 B.C.	TWENTY-THIRD YEAR OF JUBILEE.
320-204 B.C.	THE PTOLEMY DYNASTY RULES EGYPT AND PALESTINE.

312-65 B.C.	THE SELEUCID DYNASTY RULES SYRIA.
312-280 B.C.	SELEUCUS I (NICATOR) RULES SYRIA.
300 B.C.	THE BEGINNING OF THE MAYA EMPIRE IN MEXICO.
285-246 B.C.	PTOLEMY II (PHILADELPHUS) RULES EGYPT (Daniel 11:6).
285 B.C.	PTOLEMY PHILADELPHUS ORDERS THE SEPTUAGINT TRANSLATED. (This translation of the Old Testament documents that the whole Old Testament pre-dates the New Testament fulfillment of the Old Testament prophesies about the Messiah. Numerous Messianic prophesies were fulfilled in the life of Jesus.)
274-232 B.C.	RAJA ASHOKA BECOMES A SUPPORTING MEMBER OF THE BUDDHIST FAITH AND COMMISSIONS AN EVANGELISTIC OUT REACH TO TIBET, CHINA AND SOUTHEAST ASIA. THE TEACHINGS OF BUDDHA ARE PUT INTO WRITTEN FORM FOR THE FIRST TIME. THEY ARE THEN LOST AT SEA, RESCUED AND RESTORED. AFTER RESTORATION THE MANUSCRIPTS READ THAT THE GREAT SAVIOR (Si-A-MEETREY) WILL COME IN 5,000 YEARS INSTEAD OF 500 YEARS. HOWEVER, IN A SECTION DISCUSSING WOMEN PRIESTS, THEY STILL TEACH THAT THE BUDDIST FAITH IS TO LAST ONLY 500 YEARS.
271 B.C.	TWENTY FOURTH YEAR OF JUBILEE.
261-246 B.C.	ANTIOCHUS II (THEOS) RULES SYRIA.
246- 226 B.C.	SELEUCUS II (CALLINICUS) RULES SYRIA (Daniel 11:9).
246-221 B.C.	PTOLEMY III (EUERGETES I) RULES EGYPT (Daniel 11:7, 8).
242 B.C.	THE ROMANS DEFEAT THE CARTHAGINIANS AT SEA ENDING THE 1ST PUNIC WAR.

226-223 B.C.	SELEUCUS III (CERAUNUS) RULES SYRIA (Daniel 11:9).
223-187 B.C.	ANTIOCHUS III (The Great) RULES SYRIA (Daniel 11:10-18).
221 B.C.	TWENTY-FIFTH YEAR OF JUBILEE.
221-204 B.C.	PTOLEMY IV (PHILOPATER) RULES EGYPT (Daniel 11:11, 12, 14).
218 B.C.	ANTIOCHUS III DEFEATS PTOLEMY AT MOUNT TABOR NEAR MEGIDDO.
204-165 B.C.	THE SELEUCIDS RULE SYRIA AND PALESTINE.
201 B.C.	HANNIBAL IS DEFEATED BY THE ROMANS, ENDING THE SECOND PUNIC WAR.
187-175 B.C.	SELEUCUS IV (PHILOPATOR) RULES SYRIA (Daniel 11: 20).
181-145 B.C.	PTOLEMY VI (PHILOMETOR) RULES EGYPT.
175-164 B.C.	ANTIOCHUS IV (EPIPHANES) RULES SYRIA (Daniel11:21-35).
171 B.C.	TWENTY-SIXTH YEAR OF JUBILEE.
171 B.C.	ANTIOCHUS EPIPHANES SENDS ORDERS TO JERUSALEM AND THE CITIES OF JUDAH THAT THEY SHOULD NOT FOLLOW THE LAW OF MOSES. HE FORBIDS WHOLE BURNT OFFERINGS, SACRIFICES, AND DRINK OFFERINGS IN THE SANCTUARY. THE SABBATHS AND FEASTS ARE TO BE IGNORED AND THE SANCTUARY AND PRIESTS ARE TO DO THINGS THAT WOULD CAUSE THEM TO BE CONSIDERED POLLUTED (I Maccabees 1).
168 B.C.	MACCABEAN (Hasmonean) REVOLT AGAINST ANTIOCHUS, A SELEUCID KING, BEGINS. MACEDONIA IS CONQUERED BY ROME. IT IS DIVIDED

	INTO FOUR SELF-GOVERNING REGIONS PAYING TRIBUTE TO ROME.
165 B.C.	THE JERUSALEM TEMPLE IS CLEANSED AND REDEDICATED.
165-163 B.C.	HASMONEAN KINGS RULE JUDAH. THREE MACCABEAN BROTHERS (JOHNATHAN, JUDAS, AND SIMON), LEAD THE FIGHT FOR JUDEAN INDEPENDENCE. JOHNATHAN SERVES AS HIGH PRIEST, JUDAH LEADS THE ARMY. JUDAH DIES AND SIMON TAKES OVER HIS ROLE. JOHNATHAN DIES AND SIMON TAKES OVER HIS ROLE, BECOMING A HIGH PRIEST-KING. SOME CHALLENGE THE CONCEPT OF MACCABEAN HIGH PRIESTS OF THE WRONG LINEAGE FOR HIGH PRIESTS.
164-162 B.C.	ANTIOCHUS V (EUPATOR) RULES SYRIA.
162-150 B.C.	DEMETRIUS I (SOTER) RULES SYRIA.
150-145B.C.	ALEXANDER BALAS RULES SYRIA.
149-146 B.C.	THIRD PUNIC WAR ENDS WITH THE DESTRUCTION OF CARTHAGE.
148-146 B.C.	A MACEDONIAN REVOLT IS PUT DOWN AND IT BECOMES A ROMAN PROVINCE.
142-135 B.C.	SIMON RULES PALESTINE AS A HIGH PRIEST-KING.
135 B.C.	MATHIAS CURTIS, THE GREAT GRAND FATHER OF JOSEPHUS, IS BORN TO THE DAUGHTER OF JOHNATHAN, THE ORIGINAL MACCABEAN HIGH PRIEST.
135-104 B.C.	JOHN HYRCANUS, SIMON'S SON, BECOMES A HIGH PRIEST- KING OF PALESTINE. THE QUMRAN COMMUNITY DOES ITS FIRST BUILDING.
133 B.C.	SPAIN AND PERGAMUS COME UNDER ROMAN RULE.
121 B.C.	TWENTY-SEVENTH YEAR OF JUBILEE.

109 B.C.	ARMENIA MAJOR BECOMES A ROMAN PROVINCE.
104-103 B.C.	ARISTOBULUS, SON OF JOHN HYRCANUS, BECOMES HIGH PRIEST-KING OF PALESTINE. QUMRAN BECOMES OCCUPIED.
103-76 B.C.	ALEXANDER JANNACUS, SON OF ARISTOBULUS, BECOMES HIGH PRIEST-KING OF PALESTINE. HE PLUNDERS SECTS OF JEWS WHO OBJECT TO HIS DUAL ROLE (THIS INCLUDES THOSE OF QUMRAN). JULIUS CAESAR IS BORN (7/12 OR 13/100 B.C.). SOME OF THE DEAD SEA SCROLLS ARE WRITTEN.
76-67 B.C.	SALOME ALEXANDRA, WIFE OF ALEXANDER JANNAEUS, RULES PALESTINE. SHE FAVORS FUNDAMENTALISTS. PHARISEES SHARE HER POWER. HYRCANUS II IS HIGH PRIEST.
75 B.C.	BITHYNIA COMES UNDER ROMAN RULE.
71 B.C.	TWENTY-EIGHTH YEAR OF JUBILEE.
67 B.C.	JOSEPH, THE GRAND FATHER OF JOSEPHUS, IS BORN.
67-63 B.C.	CIVIL WAR IN PALESTINE BETWEEN JOHN HYRCANUS II AND ARISTOBULUS II, BOTH SONS OF SALOME. BOTH APPEAL TO POMPEY THE GREAT (ROME) FOR HELP. ROME SUPPORTS JOHN. ARISTOBULUS DECLARES HIMSELF HIGH PRIEST-KING, AND DEFEATS JOHN IN BATTLE.
63 B.C.	POMPEY THE GREAT TAKES JERUSALEM, REINSTATES JOHN AS HIGH PRIEST, BUT MAKE AN IDUMEAN (EDOMITE), ANTIPATHER (HEROD THE GREAT'S FATHER) KING.

57 B.C.	GAUL BECOMES A ROMAN PROVINCE.
55 B.C.	GABINIUS DEFEATS ALEXANDER AT MOUNT TABOR NEAR MEGGIDO.
50-48 B.C.	CIVIL WAR BETWEEN JULIUS CAESAR AND POMPEY ENDS IN THE DEATH OF POMPEY THE GREAT.
44 B.C.	JULIUS CAESAR IS KILLED IN THE ROMAN SENATE ON MARCH 15TH BY BRUTUS, CASSIUS, AND MARK ANTONY.
43 B.C.	CONSULS HIRTIUS AND PANSA JOIN WITH OCTAVIAN TO DEFEAT ANTONY AT MODENA. THE CONSULS ARE SLAIN IN THE CONFLICT, BUT ANTONY IS BEATEN AND RETREATS ACROSS THE ALPS WHERE HE JOINED LEPIDUS. OCTAVIUS THEN JOINED ANTONY AND LEPIDUS TO FORCE ROME TO RECOGNIZE THEM AS A RULING TRIUMVIRATE.
42 B.C.	OCTAVIUS CEASAR AND ANTONY DEFEAT BRUTUS AND CASSIUS AT PHILIPPI.
40-37 B.C.	PARTHIA INVADES PALESTINE. ANTIGONUS, SON OF ARISTOBULUS, BECOMES HIGH PRIEST-KING IN JERUSALEM AS A PARTHIAN PUPPET.
37 B.C.	HEROD THE GREAT IS PLACED ON THE JEWISH THRONE AFTER HE RETAKES JERUSALEM FOR ROME. HE FAVORS THE ESSENES (QUMRAN SECT) BECAUSE THEY PREDICTED HIS VICTORY.
35 B.C.	SEXTUS POMPEY, SON OF POMPEY THE GREAT, IS SLAIN.
31 B.C.	THE ROMAN EMPIRE IS DIVIDED BETWEEN OCTAVIUS (WEST), AND ANTONY (EAST).
30 B.C.	OCTAVIUS DEFEATS MARK ANTONY IN A NAVAL BATTLE AT ACTIUM. AN

EARTH QUAKE IN THE JERUSALEM
AREA KILLS 30,000. QUMRAN BECOMES
UNOCCUPIED.

27 B.C.   MARK ANTONY AND CLEOPATRA (THE
LAST OF THE PTOLEMIES) DIE. EGYPT
BECOMES A ROMAN PROVINCE.
OCTAVIUS IS GIVEN THE TITLE,
"AUGUSTUS".

CHAPTER SIX
CHRISTIAN CHRONOLOGY OF HISTORY
(THE FIRST ROMAN EMPEROR - 96 A.D.)
A TIME LINE OF HUMAN HISTORY
FROM A CHRISTIAN PROSPECTIVE
Compiled by "God's Friend"

27 B.C.-14 A.D.	OCTAVIUS IS GIVEN THE TITLE, "AUGUSTUS". HE RULES AS THE FIRST ROMAN EMPEROR.
21 B.C.	TWENTY-NINTH YEAR OF JUBILEE.
20 B.C.	BIRTH OF PHILO, ALEXANDRIAN JEWISH PHILOSOPHER.
5-3 B.C.	BIRTH OF JOHN THE BAPTIST AND JESUS, DEATH OF THE BABIES AROUND BETHLEHEM. JOHN WAS BORN AROUND THE FEAST OF UNLEAVENED BREAD IN 5 B.C. JESUS WAS BORN NEAR OR ON THE START OF THE FEAST OF TABERNACLES IN 5 B.C. IT WAS AT THAT TIME (ABOUT THE END OF OCTOBER) THAT THE ANGEL AND HEAVENLY HOST APPEARED TO THE SHEPHERD IN THE FIELDS NEAR BETHLEHEM. THE BABIES AROUND BETHLEHEM WERE KILLED BETWEEN THE FEAST OF TABERNACLES IN 4 B.C. AND THE FIRST OF NISAN IN 3 B.C., WHICH WAS ABOUT WHEN HEROD DIED. JESUS WAS BORN OF A VIRGIN IN BETHLEHEM. HE WAS OF THE LINEAGE OF SHEM, ABRAHAM, ISAAC, JACOB, JUDAH, JESSE,

AND DAVID. JOSEPH TAKES JESUS TO EGYPT AFTER BEING WARNED BY AN ANGEL OF HEROD'S COMING ATTEMPT TO KILL JESUS. AFTER HEROD'S DEATH THE CHILD IS BROUGHT OUT OF EGYPT AND RAISED IN NAZARETH (FROM A ROOT WORD (NAZAR) THAT MEANS "BRANCH"). IT WAS AROUND THE FEAST OF TABERNACLES IN 4 B.C. THAT THE MAGI (PRIEST/WARRIORS OF THE MEDES FROM THE FOOTHILLS OF INDIA) CAME TO JERUSALEM LOOKING FOR THE PROMISED KING OF THE JEWS (AN ETERNAL KING WITH AN ETERNAL KINGDOM). THEY WERE SENT TO BETHLEHEM WHERE THEY FOUND JESUS AND BESTOWED GIFTS ON HIM.

5 B.C.   BIRTH OF JESUS (Luke 3:23; Daniel 9:24-27; 12:1-13) (Birth probably on 15th of Ethanim 5 B.C.-1st day of the Feast of Tabernacles; about Oct. 29th, 5 B.C. He was probably circumcised on the last day of the Feast of Tabernacles. SEE Luke 2:21-38; 29 A.D. was a Sabbath year with an extra thirty day month, 390 days long).

LATE 4 B.C.   MAGI (MEDES FROM THE MOUNTAINS OF INDIA, NORTH OF NEPAL) VISIT HEROD LOOKING FOR THE NEWLY BORN MESSIAH. HEROD KILLS THE BABY BOYS TWO YEARS OLD AND UNDER LIVING AROUND BETHLEHEM (MATTHEW 2:1-18).

3 B.C.-39 A.D.   HEROD THE GREAT DIES AND HEROD ANTIPAS RULES AS TETRARCH OF GALILEE AND PERAEA.

3 B.C.-6 A.D.   HEROD ARCHELAUS RULES JUDEA. AN ANGEL APPEARS TO JOSEPH AND CALLS HIS FAMILY OUT OF EGYPT, WHERE THEY WERE SENT TO PROTECT JESUS.

	FROM HEROD THE GREAT (Matthew 2:13-23).
3 B.C.	JOSEPH AND MARY TAKE JESUS TO BE RAISED IN NAZARETH (the city of the branch- SEE Matthew 2:23; Luke 2:39; Zechariah 3:8; 6:12; Jeremiah 23:5; 33:15; Isaiah 11:1).
1 B.C.	QUMRAN REPAIRED AND REOCCUPIED.
3-9 A.D.	BIRTH OF MATTHIAS, FATHER OF JOSEPHUS.
12 A.D.	TIBERIUS CAESAR BEGINS RULING AS CO-REGENT WITH AUGUSTUS. HE BECOMES SOLE ROMAN EMPEROR ON AUGUST 19, 14 A.D., WHEN AUGUSTUS DIES. TIBERIUS DIES ON 3/16/37 A.D.
14 A.D.-37A.D.	TIBERIUS RULES AS SOLE ROMAN EMPEROR.
23 A.D.	BIRTH OF PLINY THE ELDER, UNCLE OF AND ADOPTIVE FATHER TO PLINY THE YOUNGER.
26 A.D.-29 A.D.	JOHN THE BAPTIST BEGINS PREACHING THE BAPTISM OF REPENTENCE FOR THE REMISSION OF SINS. HE SAYS THE ONE THAT COMES AFTER HIM IS SO HIGH THAT JOHN IS NOT EVEN WORTHY TO CARRY OR FASTEN HIS SHOES, THAT HE WILL BAPTIZE WITH FIRE AND THE HOLY SPIRIT (SEE 30 A.D.). JOHN IS THEN ARRESTED AND BEHEADED BY HEROD ANTIPAS.
26 A.D.-30 A.D.	JESUS IS BAPTIZED AND BEGINS HIS MINISTRY AS THE FEAST OF TABERNACLES BEGINS AND AS HE TURNS 30 YEARS OLD, THE AGE FOR PRIEST TO BEGIN DIVINE SERVICE (Numbers 4; Luke 3:1, 21-23; PSALMS 110:4; Hebrews 5:5, 6). (In respect to the genealogies of Matthew and Luke note <u>Ecclesiastic History</u>:

Book 1, Chapter 7; Deuteronomy 25:5-6).
(Early Christian tradition says both genealogies
are Joseph's that were complicated by re-
marriages, half siblings, and the Law of Moses.
One writer followed the blood line and the other
followed the Law of Moses inheritance line.)
Jesus' ministry began on the 15th of Ethanim in
26 A.D. as Jesus turned 30 years old (as counted
by Daniel and Luke, under inspiration of the
Holy Spirit – Daniel 9:25-27; 12:1-12; Luke
3:1, 23; SEE 458 B.C., 12 A.D. and 30 A.D.).

JESUS TAUGHT THAT HE WAS A KING,
BUT HIS KINGDOM WAS NOT OF THIS
WORLD (John 12:12-16; 18:36-37; Luke
17:20-21). HIS KINGDOM WOULD LAST
FOREVER (Matthew 16:13-18; 28: 18-20).

JESUS WENT ON TO TEACH THAT HE
CAME NOT TO JUDGE THE WORLD,
BUT TO SAVE IT, BUT THE WORDS HE
SPOKE WOULD JUDGE THE ONE WHO
REJECTS HIM AT THE LAST DAY
(John 12: 44-50; Deuteronomy 18: 18, 19).

JESUS DID MUCH OF HIS TEACHING IN
ZEBULUN AND NAPHTALI BY THE SEA
IN THE LAND BEYOND THE JORDAN,
GALILEE OF THE NATIONS. HE HEALED
THE SICK DOING MANY MIRACLES. A
WEEK BEFORE HIS DEATH HE RODE
INTO JERUSALEM ON A COLT, THE FOAL
OF AN ASS, AND THE MULTITUDES
RAN BEFORE HIM SPREADING THEIR
GARMENTS AND TREE BRANCHES IN
HIS PATH. AS THEY DID THAT THEY
CRIED OUT, "HOSANNA TO THE SON OF
DAVID, BLESSED IS HE THAT COMES IN

THE NAME OF THE LORD, HOSANNA IN
THE HIGHEST" (SEE: Isaiah 9:1-7;
Chapter 53; Malachi 4:1-6; Matthew 4:23;
Zechariah 9:9-11; Luke 19: 28-44;
John 12:12-16).

JESUS TAUGHT THAT THE JEWS WOULD
KILL HIM, BUT THAT HE WOULD
RETURN FROM THE GRAVE IN THREE
DAYS. JESUS FURTHER WARNED THAT
AFTER HIS DEATH, DURING THE LIVES
OF SOME HEARING HIM, JERUSALEM
AND HEROD'S TEMPLE WOULD BE
DESTROYED. HE TOLD HIS FOLLOWERS,
WHEN THE EAGLES GATHER OUTSIDE
OF THE CITY, THAT THEY SHOULD RUN
FOR THEIR LIVES (SEE 70 A.D.; 30 A.D.
Isaiah Chapter 53; Luke 21: 20-24; Matthew
12:40; 24:1-35; 26:1, 2, 31-34; Mark 8:31-33;
John 2:18-22).

JESUS WAS THEN ARRESTED AND TRIED
IN A WAY THAT BROKE MANY OF THE
LAWS OF MOSES. HE WAS LED LIKE
A LAMB TO THE SLAUGHTER. PILOT
DECLARED HIM INNOCENT SEVERAL
TIMES, BUT THE PEOPLE CRIED FOR
HIS BLOOD AND ASKED FOR ANY
BLOOD GUILT TO BE PLACED ON
THEM AND THEIR CHILDREN. HE WAS
TAKEN, BEATEN, AND HIS FOREHEAD
BECAME SCARED. HIS APPEARANCE
WAS DISFIGURED BEYOND THAT OF
ANY MAN, AND HIS FORM WAS MARRED
BEYOND HUMAN LIKENESS. HE WAS
THEN CRUCIFIED. NAILS WERE DRIVEN
THROUGH HIS HANDS AND FEET
AND THE GUARDS AT THE FOOT OF

THE CROSS DIVIDED HIS GARMENTS,
CASTING LOTS FOR HIS VESTURE.
TWO THIEVES WERE CRUCIFIED WITH
HIM. BEFORE HE WAS TAKEN DOWN
FROM THE CROSS A ROMAN SOLDIER
RAN A SPEAR THROUGH HIS SIDE TO
MAKE SURE HE WAS DEAD. AFTER HIS
DEATH, A RICH MAN PETITIONED FOR
HIS BODY, AND HE WAS LAID IN A NEW
TOMB (Isaiah Chapter 53; Zechariah 13:7-9;
12:10-14; Psalms 22:1-18; Matthew 27:11-66;
Mark 15:1-39; Luke 23:1-55;
John 18:28-19:42).

BECAUSE OF JESUS' PROPHESY THAT
HE WOULD LEAVE THE GRAVE WITHIN
THREE DAYS, THE TOMB WAS SEALED
AND A GUARD WAS POSTED TO
SECURE HIS BODY. ON THE THIRD DAY
THE SEAL WAS BROKEN, THE STONE
ROLLED BACK AND HE WALKED OUT
OF THE TOMB. THE GUARDS COULD
DO NOTHING. NO ONE WAS INJURED,
BUT HIS BODY WAS GONE. HE THEN
APPEARED TO OVER 500 PEOPLE WHO
KNEW HIM. HE GAVE HIS DISCIPLES,
THOSE WHO KNEW HIM BEST,
OPPORTUNITY TO ASSURE THEMSELVES
THAT HE HAD REALLY RISEN FROM THE
DEAD. THEY ASSURED THEMSELVES TO
THE POINT THAT EVERY ONE OF THEM
WAS WILLING TO DIE AND HAVE THEIR
FAMILIES TORTURED RATHER THAN
DENY THE RESURRECTION
(Matthew 27:62- 28:20; Mark 16:1-16;
Luke 24:1-53; John 20:1-21:24; Acts 1:1-11;
1 Corinthians 15:3-8).

30 A.D.	THE YEAR THAT JESUS WAS CRUCIFIED WAS THE THIRTIETH YEAR OF JUBILEE, A YEAR OF RELEASE FROM DEBT. IT FOLLOWS A SABBATH YEAR THAT HAS 390 DAYS INSTEAD OF THE NORMAL 360 DAYS.
30 A.D.	THIRTIETH YEAR OF JUBILEE. (Jesus' ministry lasts 3 ½ years, or 1290 days (29 A.D. is a Sabbath year with an added month.)). He begins his ministry on the first day of the Feast of Tabernacles in 26 A.D. as he turns 30 years old (15th of Ethanim (Tishri)). He dies on the 14th of Abib (Nisan) in 30 A.D. It is a Thursday (the Day of Preparation for the Feast of Unleavened Bread and the Passover Day, the day all leaven is removed from the Jewish homes). The 15th of Nisan is a special Sabbath day that normally does not fall on Saturday. It is the first day of the Feast of Unleavened Bread (John 19:14, 31; Exodus 12: 14-20; 13:3-10; Leviticus 23: 4-8). 45 days after the 14th of Nisan is a Sunday that is Pentecost, the day of the first gospel sermon (Leviticus 23:9-21; Daniel 12:10-12).
30 A.D.	ON PENTECOST, FORTY-FIVE DAYS AFTER JESUS' DEATH, THE CHURCH BEGINS IN JERUSALEM. JESUS BAPTIZES THE APOSTLES WITH THE HOLY SPIRIT FROM HEAVEN AND THEY BEGIN SPEAKING IN TONGUES (FOREIGN LANGUAGES). PEOPLE FROM DIFFERENT REGIONS HEAR THEM TEACHING IN THEIR NATIVE LANGUAGES (Daniel 12: 1, 2, 7, 10-12; Matthew 27:50-54; Mark 15:38; Luke 23:44-47; Acts 2:1-12).
32-33 A.D.	MARTYRDOM OF STEVEN, CONVERSION OF PAUL, SPREAD OF THE

	CHURCH THROUGH OUT PALESTINE, SYRIA, AND SAMARIA.
36-70 A.D.	THOMAS PREACHES TO THE PARTHIANS, MEDES, PERSIANS, CARMANIANS, HYRCANIANS, BACTRIANS, MAGIANS, AND IS KILLED FOR THE GOSPEL IN CALAMINA, INDIA. SIMON ZELOTES PREACHES THE GOSPEL IN MAURITANIA, AFRICA, AND BRITAIN BEFORE BEING CRUCIFIED FOR THE GOSPEL. BARTHOLOMEW CARRIES THE GOSPEL TO INDIA AND TRANSLATES THE GOSPEL OF MATTHEW INTO THEIR LANGUAGE. HE THEN PREACHES IN ARMENIA WHERE HE IS CRUCIFIED.
37 A.D.	BIRTH OF JOSEPHUS.
37-41 A.D.	CALIGULA (CAIUS CAESAR GERMANICUS) RULES IN ROME.
37 A.D.	HEROD AGRIPPA I BECOMES KING OF GAULONITIS, TRACHONITIS, AND PANEAS.
37-60 A.D.	MATTHEW WRITES HIS GOSPEL. HE SAID JESUS TAUGHT THAT THE REAL GOD IS NOT GOD OF THE DEAD, BUT OF THE LIVING. HE RECORDS THAT JESUS TOLD HIS FOLLOWERS TO CORRECT ERRANT BROTHERS THROUGH VERBAL AND SOCIAL PERSUASION, AND NOT THROUGH PHYSICAL OR SECULAR COERCION. VENGEANCE IS RESERVED FOR GOD. JESUS TAUGHT THAT THE RELIGIOUS TITLE OF "FATHER" WAS TO BE RESERVED FOR GOD ONLY.
39 A.D.	HEROD AGRIPPA I RECEIVES THE ADDITIONAL TERRITORIES OF GALILEE AND PERAEA.

40 A.D.	HEROD AGRIPPA I RECEIVES TERRITORIES OF JUDEA AND SAMARIA.
41-54 A.D.	CLAUDIUS CAESAR RULES IN ROME AFTER KILLING CAIUS.
43 A.D.	JAMES, THE BROTHER OF JOHN IS KILLED BY HEROD AGRIPPA I.
44 A.D.	HEROD AGRIPPA I IS KILLED BY GOD.
47 A.D.	PAUL BEGINS HIS FIRST MISSIONARY JOURNEY.
49 A.D.	THE JERUSALEM COUNCIL DISCUSSES WHAT SHOULD BE BOUND ON THE CHRISTIAN FROM THE LAW OF MOSES. THE HOLY SPIRIT SAYS THAT THE ONLY THINGS TO BE BOUND ON THE CHRISTIAN FROM THE LAW OF MOSES IS TO ABSTAIN FROM MEAT OFFERED TO IDOLS, FROM BLOOD, FROM THINGS STRANGLED, AND FROM SEXUAL IMMORALITY.
50 A.D.	PAUL BEGINS HIS SECOND MISSIONARY JOURNEY. JEWS ARE EXPELLED FROM ROME. PHILO DIES.
50-63 A.D.	JAMES THE BROTHER OF JESUS WRITES JAMES. HERE WE ARE TOLD THAT WE ARE JUSTIFIED BY WORKS AND NOT FAITH ONLY. FAITH WITHOUT WORKS IS DEAD. THE DEVILS ALSO BELIEVE AND TREMBLE.
52-53 A.D.	PAUL WRITES 1 AND 2 THESSALONIANS. HE STATES THAT JESUS WILL TAKE VENGEANCE ON THEM THAT KNOW NOT GOD AND THAT OBEY NOT THE GOSPEL. THE CHURCH IS WARNED OF A COMING APOSTASY IN WHICH LEADERS OF THE CHURCH WILL USURP THE AUTHORITY OF GOD (SEE 380, 395, 408, 1022, 1099,1150, 1209, 1215, 1572,1598,1608, 1610,1628, AND 1640 A.D.).

TO KEEP YOUR SALVATION YOU MUST
HOLD TO THE APOSTLES' TEACHINGS.
THE APOSTASY IS TO LAST UNTIL;
JESUS RETURNS. SOME ONE (PROBABLY
THE HOLY SPIRIT) IS RESTRAINING
THE APOSTASY THROUGH "IT"
(PROBABLY THE GIFT OF MIRACULOUS
KNOWLEDGE), BUT WILL GET OUT OF
THE MIDDLE OF THINGS BEFORE THE
APOSTASY BEGINS. DAMNATION COMES
THROUGH A LACK OF LOVE FOR THE
TRUTH.

52-60 A.D.   ANTONIUS FELIX IS ROMAN PREFECT
IN JUDEA.

53 A.D.   PAUL BEGINS HIS THIRD MISSIONARY
JOURNEY.

53-56 A.D.   JOSEPHUS, IN JERUSALEM, STUDIES THE
ESSENES, PHARISEES, AND SADDUCEES
TO DETERMINE WHICH GROUP HE
WANTS TO JOIN. HE CHOOSES THE
PHARISEES.

54 A.D.   JEWS RETURN TO ROME AFTER
CLAUDIUS' DEATH.

54-68 A.D.   NERO RULES IN ROME.

57 A.D. –58 A.D.   PAUL WRITES GALATIANS, 1 AND
2 CORINTHIANS, ROMANS. HE
PROPHESIES THAT THE HOLY
SPIRIT WILL QUIT GIVING THE
GIFT OF TONGUES, PROPHESY AND
MIRACULOUS KNOWLEDGE WHEN THE
MATURE BODY OF CHRIST OR PERFECT
THING COMES, BUT WILL CONTINUE
TO GIVE THE GIFTS OF FAITH, HOPE
AND LOVE (SEE 96 A.D.). HE FURTHER
TEACHES THAT THE CHRISTIANS
ARE NOW THE ISRAEL OF GOD, SONS
OF GOD, AND THE CHILDREN OF
PROMISE. ALL JEWS AND NON-JEWS

HAVE ACCESS TO THIS RELATIONSHIP
THROUGH OBEDIENT FAITH IN
JESUS. WHOREMONGERS, IDOLATERS,
HOMOSEXUALS, DRUNKARDS AND
THIEVES SHALL NOT INHERIT THE
KINGDOM OF GOD. SUCH <u>WERE</u> SOME
OF YOU, BUT YOU ARE WASHED, ARE
SANCTIFIED, AND ARE JUSTIFIED IN
THE NAME OF JESUS.

60-62 B.C. PORCIUS FESTUS IS ROMAN PREFECT IN
JUDEA.

60-65? A.D. PAUL DICTATES HEBREWS (HIS BEST
SCRIBAL HELPERS ARE ABSENT AND
HE HAS POOR VISION). HE DECLARES
THE NEW COVENANT IS SUPERIOR
TO THE OLD COVENANT IN EVERY
WAY. CHRIST IS MORE WORTHY THAN
MOSES. CHRIST'S HIGH PRIESTHOOD
IS BETTER THAN AARON'S. BY THE
ETERNAL PRIESTHOOD OF CHRIST THE
LEVITICAL PRIESTHOOD OF AARON IS
ABOLISHED. CHRIST'S SELF SACRIFICE
IS BETTER THAN THE ANIMAL
SACRIFICES OF THE LAW OF MOSES. WE
HAVE A GREAT HERITAGE OF FAITH.
BEWARE OF STRANGE DOCTRINES.
FORSAKE NOT THE ASSEMBLING
TOGETHER. OFFER THE SACRIFICE OF
PRAISE TO GOD CONTINUALLY.

62 A.D. MARK WRITES PETER'S GOSPEL.
PLINY THE YOUNGER IS BORN. MARK,
LUKE, AND MATTHEW ALL SAID JESUS
PROPHESIED THE DESTRUCTION OF
JERUSALEM IN THEIR GENERATION.
THE CHRISTIANS WERE TOLD TO RUN
FROM JERUSALEM WHEN THEY SEE THE
EAGLES GATHER OUTSIDE THE WALLS
OF JERUSALEM (SEE 68 A.D.). MARK

WARNS JESUS TAUGHT THAT WE ARE SAVED WHEN WE BELIEVE AND ARE BAPTIZED, BUT IF WE DO NOT BELIEVE WE WILL NOT BE SAVED. (Mark 16:16).

62-63 A.D. PAUL WRITES EPHESIANS, PHILIPPIANS, COLOSSIANS, AND PHILEMON WHILE HE IS A PRISONER IN ROME. LUKE WRITES PAUL'S GOSPEL AND THE BOOK OF ACTS. PAUL TEACHES THAT THE GENTILES USE TO BE ALIENATED FROM THE COMMON WEALTH OF ISRAEL, BUT NOW JESUS RECONCILES BOTH INTO ONE BODY AND THEY ARE CITIZENS WITH THE SAINTS AND MEMBERS OF THE HOUSEHOLD OF GOD. WE ARE TOLD THAT WE ARE SAVED BY GRACE THROUGH FAITH, NOT BY OUR WORKS. WE ARE CREATED IN CHRIST TO DO GOOD WORKS WHICH GOD ORDAINED THAT WE SHOULD WALK IN. BE NOT DECEIVED; WHATEVER A MAN SOWS, THAT SHALL HE ALSO REAP. BE NOT WEARY IN WELL DOING. FORGIVENESS OF SINS COMES THROUGH REPENTANCE AND BAPTISM. THERE IS NO GOSPEL EXCEPT THAT THAT WAS DELIVERED BY THE APOSTLES. ANY MAN PREACHING A DIFFERENT GOSPEL IS ACCURSED. THERE IS ONE BODY (CHURCH), ONE SPIRIT, ONE HOPE, ONE LORD, ONE FAITH, ONE BAPTISM. BE KIND TO ONE ANOTHER, TENDER HEARTED, FORGIVING ONE ANOTHER. THINK ON THINGS THAT ARE TRUE, HONEST, JUST, PURE, LOVELY, OF GOOD REPORT, FULL OF VIRTUE, AND PRAISE. WHATSOEVER

	YOU DO IN WORD OR DEED, DO ALL IN THE NAME OF JESUS.
63 A.D.	PAUL IS RELEASED FROM PRISON AND GOES TO PREACH IN SPAIN.
63-64 A.D.	JOSEPHUS IN ROME PLEADED WITH NERO'S WIFE FOR URGENT RELEASE OF JEWISH PRIESTS BROUGHT TO ROME IN BONDS.
63-68 A.D.	PETER WRITES 1 AND 2 PETER. HE PROPHESIES THAT IN THE LAST DAYS EVIL SCOFFERS WILL MAKE JEST OF CHRISTIANS, ASKING, "WHEN IS JESUS COMING AGAIN?" THEY WILL SAY, "ALL THINGS HAVE ALWAYS PROCEDED THE SAME," FORGETTING ABOUT NOAH'S FLOOD. GOD IS PRESERVING OUR WORLD FOR DESTRUCTION BY FIRE, IS PATIENT, GIVING THEM TIME TO REPENT, NOT WANTING THEM TO PERISH (SEE 1795,1830,1837,1858, AND 1881 A.D.).
66-67 A.D.	PAUL WRITES 1 TIMOTHY AND TITUS. CHURCHES WERE ORGANIZED WITH JESUS AS KING IN HEAVEN, AND EACH CONGREGATION UNDER THE LEADERSHIP OF MORAL, LOCAL, FAMILY MEN KNOWN AS BISHOPS. HE PROPHESIED THAT IN LATER TIMES SOME WILL LEAVE THE FAITH, ORDERING OTHERS TO NOT MARRY AND TO ABSTAIN FROM MEATS.
66-67 A.D.	JOSEPHUS LED A TRANS-JORDAN ARMY OF OVER 150,000.
67 A.D.	VESPASIAN DEFEATED JEWISH FORCES AT MOUNT TABOR, NEAR MEGGIDO.
68 A.D.	PAUL WRITES 2 TIMOTHY. HE ASSERTS THAT THE INSPIRED SCRIPTURES CAN MAKE A MAN OF GOD COMPLETE,

THOROUGHLY FURNISHED UNTO
ALL GOOD WORKS. PAUL AND
PETER WERE EXECUTED IN ROME.
JOSEPHUS WAS CAPTURED BY THE
ROMANS. THE QUMRAN COMMUNITY
IS ANNIHILATED BY THE ROMAN
GARRISON AT JERICHO. NERO DIED.

68-86 A.D.   THE ROMANS, WHO HAD COME TO
BESIEGE JERUSALEM, BRIEFLY LIFTED
THE SIEGE TO ESCORT VESPASIAN
TO THE SEA SO HE COULD GO TO
ROME WHERE HE HOPED TO BECOME
EMPEROR. BECAUSE OF PROPHECY, THE
CHRISTIANS FLED JERUSALEM
(SEE 62 A.D.). ESSENES CEASED TO EXIST.
ROMANS OCCUPIED THE RUINS OF
QUMRAN.

69 A.D.   GALBA, OTHO, VITELLIUS, AND
VESPASIAN CONTEST THE THRONE
OF ROME.

69-79 A.D.   VESPASIAN RULES IN ROME.

70-74 A.D.   DESTRUCTION OF JERUSALEM WITH
HORRID CONSEQUENCES FOR ANY
INHABITANTS AFTER 68 A.D. ROMANS
CONDUCT MOP-UP OPERATIONS
THROUGHOUT JUDEA. TITUS, SON OF
VESPASIAN, LEADS THE ASSAULT ON
JERUSALEM. 1,100,000 JEWS DIE, NOT
COUNTING THOSE IN GALILEE. 17,000
ARE SOLD INTO THE PROVINCES AS
SLAVES. TWO THOUSAND ARE TAKEN
TO ROME FOR TITUS' TRIUMPH AND
THEN ARE SLAIN OR DEVOURED IN
THE GAMES.

70-79 A.D.   THE EPISTLE OF BARNABAS IS
WRITTEN, BUT NOT ACCEPTED AS
INSPIRED OF GOD. IT PREDICTS THE
END OF THE WORLD ABOUT SIX

	THOUSAND YEARS AFTER CREATION; 2,000 YRS. INTO THE CHRISTIAN AGE (ABOUT 2030 A.D.).
74 A.D.	MASADA, THE LAST JEWISH STRONGHOLD, FALLS.
79 A.D.–81 A.D.	TITUS RULES AS ROMAN EMPEROR.
79 A.D.	DEATH OF PLINY THE ELDER AT THE ERUPTION OF MT. VESUVIUS THAT DESTROYED POMPEII. PLINY WAS A PROLIFIC NATURALIST AUTHOR, AND ADMIRAL OF THE ROMAN NAVY. DRUSILLA AND HER SON, AGRIPPA III, ALSO DIED IN THIS ERUPTION. DRUSILLA WAS WIFE OF FELIX, DAUGHTER OF HEROD AGRIPPA I, SISTER OF HEROD AGRIPPA II.
80 A.D.	ANDREW, AFTER PREACHING TO THE SCYTHIANS AND ETHIOPIANS, IS CRUCIFIED IN ACHAIA.
80 A.D.	THIRTY FIRST YEAR OF JUBILEE
81-96 A.D.	DOMITIAN RULES IN ROME.
90 A.D.	JOHN WRITES 1, 2, 3, JOHN. HE TEACHES THAT ANYONE WHO DENIES THE FATHER AND JESUS, OR SAYS THAT JESUS IS NOT THE CHRIST (ANOINTED ONE-MESSIAH) IS AN ANTICHRIST.
90-96 A.D.	PERSECUTION OF THE CHRISTIANS UNDER DOMITAIN.
95 A.D.	CLEMENT OF ROME WRITES TO THE CORINTHIAN CHURCH. HIS WRITING IS NOT ACCEPTED AS INSPIRED OF GOD.
96 A.D.-97 A.D.	JOHN WRITES REVELATION AND THE GOSPEL OF JOHN. HE PROPHESIES OF A ROMAN RELIGIOUS MOTHER OF HARLOTS THAT WILL KILL THE SAINTS AND FORBID THEM THE RIGHT OF COMMERCE. HER POWER IS TO LAST 1260 YEARS (SEE 380, 1640 A.D.).

(NOTE: I MAY BE SUGGESTING SOME
HISTORICAL DATES THAT MAY HELP
EXPLAIN SOME OF THE PROPHESIES,
BUT YOU SHOULD STUDY THE BOOK
CAREFULLY BEFORE REACHING ANY
CONCLUSIONS. I AM NOT GIVING
ENOUGH FOR THE FORMATION OF
DOGMATIC CONCLUSIONS).

MOVING FROM JOHN'S TIME,
HE PREDICTS CONQUEST AND
PROSPERITY (SEE 98 A.D.) FOLLOWED
BY WAR AND SLAUGHTER (SEE 180
A.D.), FOLLOWED BY FAMINE WITH
PROTECTION OF GRAPES AND OLIVES
(SEE 293 A.D.), FOLLOWED BY MUCH
DYING. THEN THERE WOULD BE A
FALSE EXPECTATION OF RELIEF FROM
PERSECUTION FOR THE CHRISTIAN
(SEE 315 A.D.), THEN A COLLAPSE IN
LEADERSHIP (SEE 325 A.D., 360 A.D., AND
380 A.D.).

DESTRUCTION WOULD FIRST COME BY
LAND (SEE 378, 403, 408, AND 410 A.D.),
THEN BY THE SEA (SEE 429, 439, AND 455
A.D.), THEN DOWN THE RIVER VALLEYS
(SEE 450, 452, AND 453 A.D.). THIS
WOULD BE FOLLOWED BY ANOTHER
COLLAPSE IN LEADERSHIP
(SEE 476 A.D.).

THERE WOULD THEN COME TORMENT
FROM THOSE LEAD BY THE KING OF
THE DEAD FOR ONE HUNDRED AND
FIFTY YEARS (SEE 612 A.D. AND 762 A.D.
AND Matthew 22:32). DURING THIS TIME
PLANT LIFE WOULD BE PROTECTED

(SEE 632 A.D.). THEN THERE WOULD BE
A SECOND WAVE OF TORMENT FROM
THOSE LEAD BY THE KING OF THE
DEAD FROM ACROSS THE EUPHRATES
RIVER. THIS WOULD LAST FOR 391
YEARS (SEE 1062 AND 1453 A.D. AND
Matthew 22:32). THEIR NUMBER WOULD
BE EXTREMELY LARGE. THEY WOULD
USE FIRE AND BRIMSTONE IN THEIR
WEAPONS.

THEN A BOOK, SWEET AT FIRST, BUT
WITH SOME BITTER AFTER EFFECTS,
WILL BE USED AND THE TEACHINGS
WILL GO BEFORE MANY NATIONS. THE
TEMPLE OF GOD WILL BE MEASURED.
TWO WITNESSES WILL PROPHESY FOR
1260 YEARS IN SACK CLOTH (WITH
MUCH SORROW) (SEE 380 AND 1640;
1455, 1530, 1615, 1804-1830 A.D.).

THE TEACHING WILL BE STOPPED FOR
A SHORT TIME (31/2 DAYS OR YEARS-
PROBABLY YEARS) (SEE 1861-1865 A.D).
THE WITNESSES WILL BE REVIVED
AND 7000 SLAIN BY GOD. KINGDOMS
WILL SUBMIT TO GOD. THIS WILL
MAKE THE NATIONS ANGRY. GOD WILL
JUDGE THE DEAD AND REWARD HIS
SERVANTS. GOD WILL DESTROY THEM
THAT DESTROY THE EARTH (Ezekiel 38,
39; Revelation 20: 7-10).

THERE APPEARS TO BE A SECOND
CYCLING THROUGH HISTORY. THE
FIRST CYCLE IS IN CHAPTERS 6-11. THE
SECOND CYCLE IS IN CHAPTERS 12-20.

GOD'S PEOPLE BRING FORTH JESUS
WHO DOOMS SATAN. SATAN IS CAST
DOWN TO EARTH WHERE HE MAKES
WAR ON THOSE WHO OBEY GOD. GOD
PROVIDES HIS PEOPLE A HIDDING
PLACE FOR 1260 YEARS. GOD'S PEOPLE
OVERCOME THROUGH THE BLOOD OF
JESUS, THEIR TESTIMONY AND THEIR
WILLINGNESS TO GIVE THEIR LIFE FOR
THE CAUSE.

A BEAST RISES OUT OF THE SEA THAT
IS A COMPOSITE OF ROME, GREECE,
PERSIA, AND BABYLON (Daniel 7). THE
COMPOSITE BEAST RECEIVES POWER
FROM SATAN. THIS BEAST FAUGHT
AGAINST THE SAINTS AND PREVAILED.
A SECOND BEAST COMES UP FROM THE
EARTH THAT APPEARS LIKE THE LAMB
OF GOD BUT RECEIVES POWER FROM
THE COMPOSITE BEAST THAT SATAN
ENPOWERED. HE DECEIVED THOSE
ON THE EARTH BY GREAT WONDERS.
THE LAST BEAST'S NUMBER IS 666. HE
CONTROLED COMMERCE AND SPOKE
AS SATAN.

JESUS STANDS ON MOUNT SION WITH
A COMPLETE COMPANY OF GOD'S
PEOPLE. THEY ARE GIVEN VICTORY
OVER THE BEAST AND THE EARTH IS
HARVESTED. SEVEN VIALS FULL OF
GOD'S WRATH ARE POURED OUT.
THE FIRST IS POURED OUT ON THE
EARTH AND SICKNESS AND SORES
WERE ON THEM THAT WORSHIPED
THE BEAST. THE SECOND WAS
POURED ON THE SEA AND EVERY

LIVING SOUL IN THE SEA DIED. THE
THIRD VIAL WAS POURED ON THE
RIVERS AND FOUNTAINS OF WATER
AND THEY BECAME BLOOD. THE
FOURTH WAS POURED ON THE SUN
AND IT SCORCHED MEN (LEADERSHIP
BECOMES UNBARABLY HARSH).

THE FITH POURED ON THE THRONE
AND LEADERSHIP BECAME DARK
(LACKED UNDERSTANDING AND
WISDOM). THE SIXTH DRIED UP THE
EUPHRATES AND THE KINGS OF THE
EAST WERE PREPARED.

SATAN ISSUES THREE FROGS (GREAT
LIES) (POSSIBLY: EVOLUTION,
COMMUNISM, ISLAM)

FALL OF BABYLON, THE MOTHER OF
HARLOTS.

SATAN IS BOUND FOR A
COMPLETENESS OF TIME AND THEN IS
LOOSED TO GO DECEIVE THE NATIONS
AND GATHER THEM FOR BATTLE
(THOSE ALLIED WITH RUSSIA AND
MONGOLIA). THEY WILL SURROUND
THE CAMPS OF THE SAINTS AND TRY
TO DESTROY GOD'S PEOPLE
(SEE 608 B.C. AND 1279, 1917, 1932,
1947, 1959, 1974, 1984, 1986, AND
1996-PRESENT A.D.). GOD WILL
DESTROY THEM (SEE 619-608 B.C. EZE.
38, 39). THEN THE FINAL JUDGMENT
AND HEAVEN WILL COME. JOHN
WARNS THAT ANYONE ADDING TO THE

BOOK OF PROPHESIES WILL RECEIVE
THE PLAGUES OF THE BOOK.

96-98 A.D.	NERVA RULES THE ROMAN EMPIRE.
98-100 A.D.	THE DEATH OF JOHN, THE LAST LIVING APOSTLE.

CHAPTER SEVEN
A CHRISTIAN CHRONOLOGY OF HISTORY
(COMPLETION OF THE BIBLE–476 A.D.)
A TIME LINE OF HUMAN HISTORY
FROM A CHRISTIAN PROSPECTIVE
Compiled by "God's Friend"

96-97 A.D.	JOHN WRITES REVELATION AND THE GOSPEL OF JOHN.
96-98 A.D.	NERVA RULES THE ROMAN EMPIRE.
98-117 A.D.	TRAJAN RULES IN ROME. HE IS FROM CRETE, AN AREA RENOWNED FOR ARCHERS. HE EXPANDS THE EMPIRE OVER THE NATIONS OF THE EAST FROM THE MOUNTAINS OF ARMENIA TO THE PERSIAN GULF.
98-180 A.D.	EMPERORS ARE SELECTED FOR MERIT, NOT LINEAGE.
100 A.D.	THIS IS A TIME OF EXPANSION, PROSPERITY, AND UNITY.
110-115 A.D.	JOHN AND JOSEPHUS DIE. (JOHN IS THE LAST OF THE APOSTLES).
113 A.D.	LETTERS OF IGNATIUS. PLINY THE YOUNGER, GOVERNOR OF BYTHYNIA DIES.
115 A.D.	IGNATIUS OF ANTIOCH MARTYRED AND THROWN TO THE LIONS AT ROME.
130 A.D.	THIRTY SECOND YEAR OF JUBILEE.
132 A.D.	HADRIAN BUILDS A TEMPLE TO JUPITER IN JERUSALEM.
132-135 A.D.	THE SECOND JEWISH REVOLT IN JERUSALEM. JEWISH REBELS OCCUPY

	QUMRAN. QUMRAN LEFT DESERTED FROM 135 A.D. TO THE PRESENT.
136 A.D.	HADRIAN ESTABLISHES A HEATHEN TEMPLE AND REBUILDS JERUSALEM AS A PAGAN CITY WHICH IS RENAMED "AELIA CAPITOLINA" AND WHICH THE JEWS ARE FORBIDDEN TO ENTER.
138-161 A.D.	ANTONINUS PIUS RULES AS ROMAN EMPEROR.
155-156 A.D.	POLYCARP, A STUDENT OF THE APOSTLE JOHN, AN ELDER TO THE CHURCH AT SMYRNA IS MARTYRED.
161-180 A.D.	MARCUS AURELIUS RULES AS ROMAN EMPEROR.
180 A.D.	THIRTY-THIRD YEAR OF JUBILEE
180-285 A.D.	OVER FIFTY EMPERORS AND TWENTY PRETENDERS ASCEND THE THRONE OF ROME. FEW DIE A NATURAL DEATH. THIS IS A PERIOD OF CONSTANT CIVIL STRIFE FROM JEALOUSY, PERSONAL AMBITION, AND GREED.
180-192 A.D.	COMMODUS RULES AS ROMAN EMPEROR.
192-193 A.D.	PERTINAX RULES AS ROMAN EMPEROR.
193 A.D.	DIDIUS JULIANUS RULES AS ROMAN EMPEROR.
193-211 A.D.	SEPTIMUS SEVERUS RULES AS ROMAN EMPEROR.
193-194 A.D.	PESCENNIUS NIGER RULES AS ROMAN EMPEROR.
193-197 A.D.	CLODIUS ALBINUS RULES AS ROMAN EMPEROR.
211-217 A.D.	ANTONINUS (CARACALLA) RULES AS ROMAN EMPEROR.
211 A.D.	GETA RULES AS ROMAN EMPEROR.
217-218 A.D.	MARCIAN RULES AS EASTERN EMPEROR.
218 A.D.	DIADUMENIANUS RULES AS ROMAN EMPEROR.

218-222 A.D.	ELAGABALUS, SELEUCUS, URANIUS, GELLIUS MAXIMUS AND VERUS RULE AS ROMAN EMPERORS.
222-225 A.D.	SEVERUS ALEXANDER AND TAURINUS RULE AS ROMAN EMPERORS.
225-227 A.D.	L. SEIUS SALLUSTIUS RULES AS ROMAN EMPEROR.
230 A.D.	THIRTY-FOURTH YEAR OF JUBILEE.
235-238 A.D.	MAXIMINUS THRAX, MAGNUS, AND QUARTINUS RULES AS ROMAN EMPERORS.
238 A.D.	GORIAN I, GORIAN II, PUPIENUS (MAXIMUS), AND BALBINUS RULE AS ROMAN EMPERORS.
238-244 A.D.	GORDIAN III RULES AS ROMAN EMPEROR.
240 A.D.	SABINIANUS RULES AS ROMAN EMPEROR.
244-249 A.D.	PHILIP THE ARAB, SILBANNACUS, AND SPONSIANUS RULE AS ROMAN EMPERORS.
248 A.D.	PACATIANUS AND IOTAPIANUS RULE AS ROMAN EMPERORS.
247-249 A.D.	PHILIP IUNIOR RULES AS ROMAN EMPEROR.
250 A.D.	L. PRISCUS AND IULIUS VALENS LICINIANUS RULE AS ROMAN EMPERORS.
251-253 A.D.	TREBONIUS GALLUS AND VOLUSIANUS RULE AS ROMAN EMPERORS.
253 A.D.	URANIUS ANTONINUS AND AEMILIUS EMILIANUS RULE AS ROMAN EMPERORS.
253-260 A.D.	VALERIAN AND MAREADES RULE AS ROMAN EMPERORS.
253-268 A.D.	GALLIENUS, CELSUS, AND SATUENINUS RULE AS ROMAN EMPERORS.

260 A.D.	INGENUUS AND REGALIANUS RULE AS ROMAN EMPERORS.
260-261 A.D.	MACRIANUS SENIOR, MACRIANUS IUNIOR, AND QUIETUS RULE AS ROMAN EMPERORS.
260-269 A.D.	POSTUMUS, A GALLIC EMPEROR, RULES.
261 A.D.	PISO, VALENS, BALLISTA, AND MUSSIUS AEMILIANUS RULE AS ROMAN EMPERORS.
262 A.D.	MEMOR RULES AS ROMAN EMPEROR.
262-268 A.D.	AUREOLUS RULES AS ROMAN EMPEROR.
268-270 A.D.	CLAUDIUS II, GOTHICUS, AND CENSORINUS RULE AS ROMAN EMPERORS.
269 A.D.	LAELIANUS AND MARIUS, GALLIC EMPERORS, RULE.
269-270 A.D.	VICTORINUS, A GALLIC EMPEROR, RULES.
270 A.D.	QUINTILLUS RULES AS ROMAN EMPEROR.
270-275 A.D.	AURELIAN RULES AS ROMAN EMPEROR.
270-271 A.D.	FELICISSIMUS RULES AS ROMAN EMPEROR.
271-272 A.D.	DOMITIANUS, URBANUS, AND SEPTIMIUS RULE AS ROMAN EMPERORS.
271-274 A.D.	TETRICUS I, A GALLIC EMPEROR, RULES.
272 A.D.	VABALLATHUS RULES AS ROMAN EMPEROR.
273 A.D.	FIRMUS RULES AS ROMAN EMPEROR.
273 A.D.	FAUSTINUS, A GALLIC EMPEROR, RULES.
273-274 A.D.	TETRICUS II, A GALLIC EMPEROR, RULES.
275-276 A.D.	TACITUS RULES AS ROMAN EMPEROR.
276 A.D.	FLORIANUS RULES AS ROMAN EMPEROR.
276-282 A.D.	PROBUS RULES AS ROMAN EMPEROR.
280 A.D.	THIRTY-FIFTH YEAR OF JUBILEE.
280 A.D.	BONOSUS RULES AS ROMAN EMPEROR.

280-281 A.D.	PROCULUS RULES AS ROMAN EMPEROR.
281 A.D.	SATURNINUS RULES AS ROMAN EMPEROR.
282-283 A.D.	CARUS RULES AS ROMAN EMPEROR.
283-284 A.D.	NUMERIANUS RULES AS ROMAN EMPEROR.
283-285 A.D.	CARINUS RULES AS ROMAN EMPEROR.
284-305 A.D.	DIOCLETIAN RULES AS ROMAN EMPEROR.
285-310? A.D.	MAXIMIANUS HERCULIUS AND IULIANUS RULE AS ROMAN EMPERORS.
285-286 A.D.	AMANDUS AND AELIANUS RULE AS ROMAN EMPERORS.
286-293 A.D.	CARAUSIUS, A BRITISH EMPEROR, RULES.
293-296 A.D.	CONSTANTIUS I CHLORUS RULES AS ROMAN EMPEROR.
293-297 A.D.	ALLECTUS, A BRITISH EMPEROR, RULES.
293-311 A.D.	GALERIUS RULES AS ROMAN EMPEROR. A VERY STRICT, RIGOROUS INQUISITION INTO THE OWNERSHIP OF PROPERTY IS UNDERTAKEN FOR TAXATION PURPOSES. TORTURE IS FREELY EMPLOYED TO OBTAIN CONFESSION OF ADDITIONAL WEALTH. A LAW IS ENACTED THAT SAYS, "IF ANYONE SHALL RELIGIOUSLY CUT A VINE, OR STINT THE FRUIT OF PROLIFIC BOUGHS, AND CRAFTILY FEIGN POVERTY IN ORDER TO AVOID A FAIR ASSESSMENT, HE SHALL, IMMEDIATELY, ON DETECTION, SUFFER DEATH, AND HIS HIS PROPERTY BE CONFISCATED."
297 A.D.	L. DOMITIUS DOMITIANUS RULES AS ROMAN EMPEROR.
297-298 A.D.	AURELIUS ACHILLEUS RULES AS ROMAN EMPEROR.
303 A.D.	EUGENIUS RULES AS ROMAN EMPEROR.

305-307 A.D.	II SEVERUS RULES AS ROMAN EMPEROR.
305-313 A.D.	MAXIMINUS DAIA RULES AS ROMAN EMPEROR
306-312 A.D.	MAXENTIUS RULES AS ROMAN EMPEROR.
306-337 A.D.	CONSTANTINE I IS EMPEROR OF ROME.
308-309 A.D.	L. DOMITIUS ALEXANDER RULES AS ROMAN EMPEROR.
311 A.D.	WITH THE BACKING OF A ROMAN BISHOP, A BISHOP IS CHOSEN IN CARTHAGE THAT HAD LEFT THE CHURCH DURING THE DIOCLETIAN PERSECUTIONS. THERE WAS A SPLIT IN WHICH MANY CARTHAGIANS OPPOSED ANY ROMAN INTERFERENCE IN THEIR CHURCH. THE ANTI-ROME MOVEMENT SPREAD THROUGHOUT NORTH AFRICA AND REMAINED UNTIL THE ARAB CONQUEST (SEE 670-732 A.D.). AT ITS HEIGHT THIS MOVEMENT HAD OVER 270 BISHOPS.
312 A.D.	CONSTANTINE BECOMES A CHRISTIAN.
314 A.D.	VALENS RULES AS ROMAN EMPEROR.
315 A.D.	CONSTANTINE ORDERS A STOP TO THE PERSECUTION OF CHRISTIANS, AND COMMISSIONS A CHRISTIAN HISTORY BY EUSEBIUS.
324 A.D.	MARTINIANUS RULES AS ROMAN EMPEROR.
325 A.D.	CONSTANTINE LAYS THE GROUND WORK FOR A CHRISTIAN STATE CULT THAT EVOLVES INTO THE MODERN CATHOLIC CHURCH.
330 A.D.	THIRTY-SIXTH YEAR OF JUBILEE.
333-334 A.D.	CALOCAERUS RULES AS ROMAN EMPEROR.
337-340 A.D.	CONSTANTINE II RULES AS ROMAN EMPEROR.

337-350 A.D.	CONSTANTS I RULES AS ROMAN EMPEROR.
337-361 A.D.	CONSTANTIUS II RULES AS ROMAN EMPEROR.
350 A.D.	NEPOTIAN AND VETRANIO RULE AS ROMAN EMPERORS.
350-353 A.D.	MAGNENTIUS RULES AS ROMAN EMPEROR.
355 A.D.	SILVANUS RULES AS ROMAN EMPEROR.
360-363 A.D.	JULIAN RULES AS ROMAN EMPEROR. HE TRIES TO RETURN THE EMPIRE TO PAGANISM. ONLY PAGANS ARE ELEVATED TO HIGH RANK.
363-364 A.D.	JOVIAN RULES AS ROMAN EMPEROR.
364-375 A.D.	VALENTINAN RULES AS ROMAN EMPEROR.
364-378 A.D.	VALENS RULES AS ROMAN EMPEROR.
365-366 A.D.	PROCOPIUS RULES AS ROMAN EMPEROR.
366 A.D.	MARCELLUS RULES AS ROMAN EMPEROR.
367-383 A.D.	GRATIAN RULES AS ROMAN EMPEROR.
370-376 A.D.	THE HUNS OVERRUN OSTROGOTHIC AND VISIGOTHIC TERRITORIES, DRIVING THEM INTO THE ROMAN EMPIRE.
375 A.D.	FIRMUS RULES AS ROMAN EMPEROR.
375-392 A.D.	VALENTINIAN II RULES AS ROMAN EMPEROR.
376 A.D.	THE GOTHS (VISIGOTHS) IMPLORE THE PROTECTION OF ROME AGAINST THE HORDES OF HUNS POURING OUT OF MONGOLIA INTO NORTHEASTERN EUROPE. THEY WERE PLACED IN THRACE AND MOESIA AFTER HAVING THEIR WEAPONS AND CHILDREN TAKEN FROM THEM.
376-435 A.D.	THE HUNS PILLAGE THE UPPER RIVER REGIONS OF EUROPE.

378 A.D.	THE GOTHS RAVAGE THRACE, CONQUERING BY LAND.
378-395 A.D.	THEODOSIUS I RULES AS ROMAN EMPEROR. HE RECRUITS AND TRAINS THE GOTHS AS SOLDIERS. AMONG THEM IS ALARIC.
380 A.D.	THE THIRTY-SEVENTH YEAR OF JUBILEE.
380 A.D.	THEODOSIUS I ORDERS THE ROMAN ARMIES TO DO WHATEVER THEY CAN AGAINST ANY WHO DISAGREE RELIGIOUSLY WITH BISHOP DAMASCUS OF ROME. HE ALSO MADE PAGAN WORSHIP A CRIME OF HIGH TREASON. THIS IS THE BEGINNING OF STATE DICTATED AND CONTROLLED CHRISTIAN RELIGION. IT USHERS IN 1260 YEARS OF A MANDATED FORM OF CORRUPT "CHRISTIAN" STYLE RELIGIOUS PRACTICE.
383-388 A.D.	MAGNUS MAXIMUS RULES AS ROMAN EMPEROR.
384-388 A.D.	FLAVIUS VICTOR RULES AS ROMAN EMPEROR.
392-394 A.D.	EUGENIUS RULES AS ROMAN EMPEROR.
393-423 A.D.	HONORIUS RULES AS EMPEROR, AND THEN AS WESTERN EMPEROR. THE GOTHS REVOLT AND PILLAGE GREECE AND ITALY.
395 A.D.	THE ROMAN EMPIRE IS PARTITIONED INTO THE EASTERN AND WESTERN EMPIRE. THE STATE SPONSORED CHURCH IN THE WEST CONTINUES TO EVOLVE INTO THE CATHOLIC CHURCH. THE STATE SPONSORED CHURCH IN THE EAST EVOLVES INTO THE GREEK ORTHODOX CHURCH.
395-408 A.D.	ARCADIUS RULES AS EASTERN EMPEROR.

403 A.D.	THE GOTHS ARE PAID TO QUIT PILLAGING ITALY.
407 A.D.	IT IS DECLARED THAT CHRISTIANS WHO DISAGREE WITH ROMAN RELIGIOUS AUTHORITY ARE TO BE TREATED AS TRAITORS WHO REBEL AGAINST THE SECULAR AUTHORITY OF THE EMPEROR.
407-411 A.D.	CONSTANTINE III RULES AS WESTERN EMPEROR.
408 A.D.	ALERIC, LEADER OF THE GOTHS, RETURNS WITH ARMY TO ITALY AND BESIEGES ROME. AGAIN HE IS PAID OFF.
408-450 A.D.	THEODOSIUS II RULES AS EASTERN EMPEROR.
408-456 A.D.	68 LAWS DECLARING PUNISHMENT FOR CHRISTIANS WHO RESIST THE RELIGIOUS AUTHORITY OF ROME ARE ENACTED. FORCE IS USED IN FAVOR OF THE STATE CHURCH.
409 A.D.	ALARIC RETURNS AND AGAIN BESIEGES ROME. THIS TIME HE PICKS ATTALUS, A FRIEND, TO BE EMPEROR AND MAKES HIMSELF MASTER GENERAL OF ALL THE WESTERN ARMIES.
409-410 A.D.	PRISCUS ATTALUS RULES AS WESTERN EMPEROR.
409-411 A.D.	CONSTANS II AND MAXIMUS RULE AS WESTERN ROMAN EMPERORS.
410 A.D.	ALARIC BECOMES UPSET WITH ATTALUS, BESIEGES ROME, AND REMOVES HIM FROM THE THROWN. THE GOTHS TAKE ROME AND KILL AND PLUNDER FOR SIX DAYS. THEY THEN SETTLE IN SOUTHERN FRANCE.
410 A.D.	AN ALLIANCE IS MADE BETWEEN ROME AND THE HUNS. ATILLA IS SENT AS A ROMAN HOSTAGE TO INSURE THE

	TREATY. AISHIUS IS SENT AS A HUN HOSTAGE TO INSURE THE TREATY. EACH LEARNS THE WAYS OF THE OTHER'S CULTURE.

411-413 A.D. JOVINUS RULES AS WESTERN EMPEROR.

412-413 A.D. SEBASTIANUS RULES AS WESTERN EMPEROR.

421 A.D. CONSTANTIUS III RULES AS WESTERN EMPEROR.

425-455 A.D. VALENTINIAN III RULES AS WESTERN EMPEROR. HE ISSUES AN EDICT COMMANDING ALL TO OBEY THE BISHOP OF ROME ON THE GROUND THAT THE LATTER HELD THE PRIMACY OF ST. PETER.

429 A.D. THE VANDALS (OSTROGOTHS), RUNNING BEFORE THE HUNS, CROSS THE PILLARS OF HERCULES (STRAITS OF GIBRALTAR) AND INVADE NORTH AFRICA (PART OF THE ROMAN EMPIRE).

430 A.D. THE THIRTY-EIGHTH YEAR OF JUBILEE.

435 A.D. ATILLA BECOMES KING OF THE HUNS.

439-490 A.D. VANDALS CONQUER CARTHAGE. THEY THEN BUILD A NAVY AND RAID THE ROMAN COASTS OF THE MEDITERRANEAN. THEY CONQUER SICILY, SACK PALERMO, AND FREQUENTLY RAID THE COAST OF LUCANIA. THEY ARE A PLAGUE BY SEA.

440-461 A.D. LEO I AS BISHOP IN ROME DEVELOPED THE CLAIM THAT ROME, AS THE SEE OF PETER, SHOULD BE SUPREME OVER THE UNIVERSAL (CATHOLIC) CHURCH.

450 A.D. ATILLA MASSES HIS ARMY ALONG THE RHINE AND PREPARES TO CONQUER THE ROMAN EMPIRE.

450-457 A.D. MARCIAN RULES AS EASTERN EMPEROR.

451 A.D.	ATTILA THE HUN HAS HIS FIRST SIGNIFICNT DEFEAT AT CHALONS IN GAUL. THE OPPOSING GENERAL IS AISHIUS. THE SLAUGHTER IS MASSIVE ON BOTH SIDES (THE DEAD ARE ESTIMATED TO NUMBER 162,000 TO 300,000-ALL DYING IN A SINGLE DAY).
452 A.D.	THE CITIES OF VENETIA ARE SACKED BY THE GREATLY REDUCED HUN ARMY.
453 A.D.	ATILLA, THE MAIN HUN CHIEFTAIN, DIES. HE PLAGUED THE UPPER RIVER VALLEYS OF EUROPE. HIS MONGOLIAN HORDES RETREAT AND SETTLE IN THE PLAINS OF HUNGARY.
455 A.D.	PETRONIUS MAXIMUS RULES AS WESTERN EMPEROR. A VANDAL ARMY LED BY GENSERIC SACKS ROME. THEY PILLAGE ROME FOR FOURTEEN DAYS AND NIGHTS AND THEN CARRY OFF SUCH CITIZENS AS THEY DESIRE AS SLAVES.
455-456 A.D.	AVITUS RULES AS WESTERN EMPEROR.
457-461 A.D.	MAJORIAN RULES AS WESTERN EMPEROR.
457-474 A.D.	LEO I RULES AS EASTERN EMPEROR.
461-465 A.D.	LIBIUS SEVERUS RULES AS WESTERN EMPEROR.
467-472 A.D.	ANTHEMIUS RULES AS WESTERN EMPEROR.
472 A.D.	OLYBRIUS RULES AS WESTERN EMPEROR.
473-474 A.D.	GLYCERIUS RULES AS WESTERN EMPEROR.
474 A.D.	LEO II RULES AS EASTERN EMPEROR.
474-475 A.D.	JULIUS NEPOS RULES AS WESTERN EMPEROR.
474-491 A.D.	ZENO RULES AS EASTERN EMPEROR.

475-476 A.D.	ROMULUS AUGUSTULUS RULES AS WESTERN EMPEROR.
476 A.D.	THE WESTERN ROMAN EMPEROR, ROMULUS, IS DEPOSED BY ODOACER, A GERMAN CHIEF, AND THE WESTERN ROMAN EMPIRE ENDS. NO ONE WANTS TO BE THE WESTERN EMPEROR. IT IS TOO DANGEROUS A JOB.

CHAPTER EIGHT
A CHRISTIAN CHRONOLOGY OF HISTORY
(FALL OF THE WESTERN EMPIRE–1453 A.D.)
A TIME LINE OF HUMAN HISTORY
FROM A CHRISTIAN PROSPECTIVE
Compiled by "God's Friend"

476 A.D.	FALL OF THE WESTERN ROMAN EMPIRE.
480 A.D.	THE THIRTY-NINTH YEAR OF JUBILEE.
485 A.D.	GERMANICUS WRITES THE ROMAN BISHOP (POPE) COMPLAINING THAT THE CHRISTIANS OF BRITAIN DENY ROME'S RELIGIOUS AUTHORITY AND DON'T RECOGNIZE INFANT BAPTISM BECAUSE INFANTS CAN NEITHER BELIEVE NOR REPENT (ADDITIONAL BIBLE REQUIREMENTS FOR SALVATION).
491-518 A.D.	ANASTASIUS RULES AS EASTERN EMPEROR.
518-527 A.D.	JUSTIN (JUSTINIAN DYNASTY) RULES AS EASTERN EMPEROR.
527-565 A.D.	JUSTINIAN RULES AS EASTERN EMPEROR.
530 A.D.	THE FORTIETH YEAR OF JUBILEE
565-578 A.D.	JUSTIN II RULES AS EASTERN EMPEROR.
570 A.D.	BIRTH OF MOHAMMED.
578-585 A.D.	TIBERIUS I CONSTANTINE RULES AS EASTERN EMPEROR.
582-602 A.D.	MAURICE RULES AS EASTERN EMPEROR.
596 A.D.	GREGORY, BISHOP OF ROME, ORDERED AUGUSTINE (NOT OF HIPPO) TO

	EVANGELIZE ENGLAND FOR THE CATHOLIC CHURCH. MUCH OF ENGLAND WAS CHRISTIAN, BUT NOT CATHOLIC. HE ARRIVED THERE THE NEXT YEAR WITH FORTY MONKS. CATHOLIC CENTERS OF INFLUENCE WERE ESTABLISHED AT CANTERBURY AND YORK, BUT THE CHRISTIANS ON THE WESTERN PART OF THE ISLAND BECOME ANTAGONIZED.
602-610 A.D.	PHOCAS RULES AS EASTERN EMPEROR.
601-641 A.D.	HERACLIUS RULES AS EASTERN EMPEROR.
c612 A.D.	MOHAMMED BEGINS THE RELIGION OF ISLAM.
622 A.D.	MOHAMMED IS EXILE FROM MECCA.
633 A.D.	MOHAMMED RETURNS TO MECCA.
632 A.D.	MOHAMMED DIES AND ABUBEKER LEADS THE MOSLEMS IN THE CONQUEST OF PERSIA AND SYRIA. HE ORDERS HIS SOLDIERS TO, "DESTROY NO PALM TREE, NOR BURN ANY FIELDS OF CORN. CUT DOWN NO FRUIT TREES, NOR DO ANY MISCHIEF TO CATTLE, ONLY SUCH AS YOU KILL TO EAT."
641 A.D.	HERACLONAS AND CONSTANTINE III RULE AS EASTERN EMPERORS.
641-668 A.D.	CONSTANS II RULES AS EASTERN EMPEROR.
646-647 A.D.	GREGORY RULES AS EASTERN EMPERPOR.
649-653 A.D.	OLYMPIUS RULES AS EASTERN EMPEROR.
668-685 A.D.	CONSTANTINE IV RULES AS EASTERN EMPEROR.
669 A.D.	MEZEZIUS RULES AS EASTERN EMPEROR.

670 A.D.	ARABIAN MOSLEMS INVADE THE BYZANTINE (EASTERN) EMPIRE.
670-732 A.D.	ARABS SWEEP ACROSS NORTH AFRICA AND CONQUER SPAIN.
685-695 A.D.	JUSTINIAN II RULES AS EASTERN EMPEROR (BANISHED).
c690 A.D.	CHRISTIAN CELTS ATTEMPT, WITH SOME SUCCESS, TO UNDO THE CATHOLIC INFLUENCE AROUND CANTERBURY AND YORK.
695-698A.D.	LEONTIUS RULES AS EASTERN EMPEROR.
698-705 A.D.	TIBERIUS II RULES AS EASTERN EMPEROR.
705-711 A.D.	JUSTINIAN II RULES AS EASTERN EMPEROR (RESTORED).
711-713 A.D.	BARDANES RULES AS EASTERN EMPEROR.
713-716 A.D.	ANASTASIUS II RULES AS EASTERN EMPEROR.
716-717 A.D.	THEODOSIUS III RULES AS EASTERN EMPEROR.
717-741 A.D.	LEO III (ISAURIAN DYNASTY) RULES AS EASTERN EMPEROR.
741 A.D.	THE MOSLEM ARMIES ARE FINALLY TURNED BACK BY CHARLES MARTEL AT POITIERS IN FRANCE.
741-775 A.D.	CONSTANINE V COPRONYMUS RULES AS EASTERN EMPEROR.
742-743 A.D.	ARTABASDUS RULES AS EASTERN EMPEROR.
750-1150 A.D.	NUBIA, KNOWN AS "CUSH" IN THE BIBLE, AND "SUDAN" TODAY, HAS A CHRISTIAN GOLDEN AGE. A "BAQT" AGREEMENT ENABLED CHRISTIANS AND MOSLEMS TO LIVE TOGETHER IN PEACE.

751 A.D.	THE MOSLEM ARMIES DEFEAT THE CHINESE ARMY AT THE BATTLE OF THE TALAS RIVER.
762 A.D.	THE ARAB EMPIRE MOVES ITS CAPITAL FROM DAMASCUS TO BAGHDAD AND LOOSES INTEREST IN WESTERN EUROPE.
775-780 A.D.	LEO IV RULES AS EASTERN EMPEROR.
780-797 A.D.	CONSTANTINE VI RULES AS EASTERN EMPEROR.
797-802 A.D.	IRENE RULES AS EASTERN EMPEROR.
800 A.D.	POPE LEO III SEPARATES FROM THE EASTERN EMPIRE AND DECLARES HIMSELF SUPREME BISHOP OF THE WEST.
802-811 A.D.	NICEPHORUS I RULES AS EASTERN EMPEROR.
802 A.D.	KHMER EMPIRE IS FOUNDED.
811 A.D.	STRAURACIUS RULES AS EASTERN EMPEROR.
811-813 A.D.	MICHEL I RULES AS EASTERN EMPEROR.
813-820 A.D.	LEO V RULES AS EASTERN EMPEROR.
820-829 A.D.	MICHAEL II (PHRYGIAN DYNASTY) RULES AS EASTERN EMPEROR.
821-823 A.D.	THOMAS RULES AS EASTERN EMPEROR.
829-839 A.D.	EGBERT, KING OF ESSEX, WINS ALLEGIANCE OF AND RULES ALL OF ENGLAND. HE IS A SAXON KING.
830 A.D.	THE FORTY-SIXTH YEAR OF JUBILEE.
840 A.D.	DANE SETTLERS FOUND DUBLIN AND LIMERICK.
842-867 A.D.	MICHAEL III RULES AS EASTERN EMPEROR.
845 A.D.	A SEVERE PERSECUTION OF CHRISTIANS IN CHINA BREAKS OUT. THE SMALL CHRISTIAN COMMUNITY THERE IS SERIOUSLY WEAKENED.

851 A.D.	THE CANTERBURY CATHEDRAL IS SACKED BY THE DANES.
855 A.D.	ETHEL WULF OF WESSEX GOES WITH HIS SON ALFRED ON A PILGRIMAGE TO ROME.
858-860 A.D.	ETHEL BALD, SON OF ETHEL WULF, UNITES KENT AND WESSEX.
866-871 A.D.	ETHEL RED I, THIRD SON OF ETHEL WULF, BECOMES KING OF WESSEX AND FIGHTS THE DANES.
867-886 A.D.	BASIK I (MACEDONIAN DYNASTY) RULES AS EASTERN EMPEROR.
869-879 A.D.	CONSTANTINE RULES AS EASTERN EMPEROR.
871-899 A.D.	ALFRED THE GREAT, FOURTH SON OF ETHEL WULF, DEFEATS THE DANES AND FORTIFIES LONDON
878 A.D.	CHRISTIAN PRESENCE STILL EXISTS IN PORT CITIES OF CHINA.
879 A.D.	THE POPE AND THE PATRIARCH OF CONSTANTINOPLE EXCOMMUNICATE EACH OTHER.
880 A.D.	THE FORTY-SEVENTH YEAR OF JUBILEE.
887-912 A.D.	LEO VI RULES AS EASTERN EMPEROR.
899-924 A.D.	EDWARD THE ELDER, SON OF ALFRED, UNITES ENGLAND AND CLAIMS SCOTLAND.
912-913 A.D.	ALEXANDER RULES AS EASTERN EMPEROR.
913-959 A.D.	CONSTANTINE VII PORPHYGENITUS RULES AS EASTERN EMPEROR.
917 A.D.	BULGARIAN CHRISTIANS, AS A GROUP, OFFICIALLY SEPARATE FROM THE AUTHORITY OF ROMAN AND CONSTANTINOPLE.
904 A.D.	MAROZIA, MISTRESS TO POPE SERGIUS III, BECOMES THE MOTHER TO POPE JOHN XI (931-936). SHE IS ALSO AUNT OF

	POPE JOHN XIII (965-972) AND GRAND MOTHER OF POPE BENEDICT IV (973-974).
920-944 A.D.	ROMANUS I LECAPENUS RULES AS EASTERN EMPEROR.
921-931 A.D.	CHRISTOPHER RULES AS EASTERN EMPEROR.
924-940 A.D.	ATHELSTAN, THE GLORIOUS, EDWARD'S SON, RULES MERCIA AND WESSEX
925-945 A.D.	STEPHEN RULES AS EASTERN EMPEROR.
930 A.D.	THE FORTY-EIGHTH YEAR OF JUBILEE.
940 A.D.	IKHSHIDIDS FIGHTS ABBASIDS AT LEJJUN NEAR MEGIDDO WITH NO VICTOR.
940-946 A.D.	EDMUND I, THIRD SON OF EDWARD, RULES MERCIA AND WESSEX.
946 A.D.	IKHSHIDIDS DEFEATS HAMDANIDS AT LEJJUN AND AKSAL NEAR MEGIDDO.
c950 A.D.	THE CANTERBURY CATHEDRAL IS REBUILT.
955-959 A.D.	EDWY THE FAIR, ELDEST SON OF EDMUND, RULES WESSEX.
959-963 A.D.	ROMANUS II RULES AS EASTERN EMPEROR.
959-975 A.D.	EDGAR THE PEACEFUL, SECOND SON OF EDMUND, RULES ALL ENGLAND.
963-969 A.D.	NICEPHORUS II PHOCAS RULES AS EASTERN EMPEROR.
975 A.D.	THE BYZANTINES DEFEAT FATIMIDS AT MOUNT TABOR NEAR MEGGIDO.
976-1016 A.D.	ETHEL RED II, SECOND SON OF EDGAR RULES ENGLAND, MARRYING EMMA OF NORMANDY.
976-1025 A.D.	BASIL II RULES AS EASTERN EMPEROR.
980 A.D.	THE FORTY-NINTH YEAR OF JUBILEE.
987 A.D.	CATHOLIC MONKS REPORT THAT THEY CAN NOT FIND ANY CHRISTIANS IN CHINA.

c1000 A.D.	THE CHRISTIANS OF BRITAIN LAUNCH AN EVANGELISTIC EFFORT TO CONVERT THE VIKINGS. THEY ALSO OUTLAW THE PRESENCE OF CATHOLIC PRIESTS IN BRITAIN. CHRISTIANS WHO DISAGREED RELIGIOUSLY WITH ROMAN (PAPAL) AUTHORITY OVER THE CHURCH WERE NUMEROUS IN ITALY, SPAIN, GAUL, AND GERMANY, AND SUFFERED OCCASIONAL LOCAL PERSECUTIONS.
1016 A.D.	EDMUND II, SON OF ETHEL RED II, RULES LONDON.
1016-1035 A.D.	CANUTE, THE DANE, MARRIES EMMA, GIVES WESSEX TO EDMUND.
1022 A.D.	DISAGREEMENT WITH CATHOLIC RELIGIOUS RULE OFTEN TREATED AS A CAPITAL OFFENSE.
1025-1028 A.D.	CONSTANTINE VIII (IX) RULES AS EASTERN EMPEROR.
1028-1034 A.D.	ROMANUS III ARGYRUS RULES AS EASTERN EMPEROR.
1030 A.D.	THE FIFTIETH YEAR OF JUBILEE.
1034-1041 A.D.	MICHAEL IV, THE PAPHLAGONIAN, RULES AS EASTERN EMPEROR.
1035-1040 A.D.	HAROLD I, OF CANUTE, RULES ENGLAND.
1041-1042 A.D.	MICHAEL V CALAPHATES RULES AS EASTERN EMPEROR.
1042-1066 A.D.	EDWARD, SON OF ETHEL RED II, RULES ENGLAND.
1042 A.D.	ZOE AND THOEDORA RULE IN THE EAST.
1042-1055 A.D.	CONSTANTINE IX MONOMCHUS RULES IN THE EAST
c1050 A.D.	MOSLEM SELJUK TURKS COME FROM CENTRAL ASIA, PASS THROUGH PERSIA, AND STRENGTHEN BAGHDAD.

1055-1056 A.D.	THEODORA RULES THE EASTERN EMPIRE.
1056-1057 A.D.	MICHAEL VI STRATIOTICUS RULES AS EASTERN EMPEROR.
1057-1050 A.D.	ISAAC I COMNENOS RULES AS EASTERN EMPEROR.
1059-1067 A.D.	CONSTANTINE X (IX) DUCAS RULES AS EASTERN EMPEROR.
c1062 A.D.	MOSLEM SELJUK TURKS FROM PERSIA AND BAGHDAD CROSS THE EUPHRATES RIVER AND THEN INVADE ASIA MINOR AND ARMENIA.
1066 A.D.	HAROLD II, EDWARD'S BROTHER-IN-LAW, TAKES THE THRONE OF ENGLAND, BUT WILLIAM OF NORMANDY, A FRENCH CATHOLIC, CONQUERS ENGLAND.
1066-1087 A.D.	WILLIAM I OF NORMANDY RULES ENGLAND.
1066-1534 A.D.	THE BRITISH ISLES, WITH MUCH RESISTANCE, ENDURES CATHOLIC RULE.
1068-1071 A.D.	ROMANUS IV DIOGENES RULES AS EASTERN EMPEROR.
1071 A.D.	THE BYZANTINE ARMY IS CRUSHED AT MANZIKERT.
1071-1078 A.D.	MICHAEL VII DUCAS RULES AS EASTERN EMPEROR.
1078-1081 A.D.	NICEPHORUS III BONTANIATES, NICEPHORUS BYRENNIUS, AND NICEPHORUS BASILACIUS RULE AS EASTERN EMPERORS.
1080 A.D.	FIFTY-FIRST YEAR OF JUBILEE.
1080-1081 A.D.	NICEPHORUS MELISSENUS RULES AS EASTERN EMPEROR.
1081-1118 A.D.	ALEXIUS I COMNENUS (COMMNENI DYNASTY) RULES AS EASTERN EMPEROR.

1087-1100 A.D.	WILLIAM II, THIRD SON OF WILLIAM I, RULES ENGLAND.
1099 A.D.	THE FIRST OF MANY CATHOLIC CRUSADES LAUNCHED TO TURN BACK THE TURKISH MOSLEMS.
1100-1135 A.D.	HENRY I, YOUNGEST SON OF WILLIAM I, RULES ENGLAND.
1113 A.D.	MAUDUD DEFEATS THE CRUSADERS AT MOUNT TABOR NEAR MEGGIDO.
1118-1143 A.D.	JOHN II COMENUS RULES AS EASTERN EMPEROR.
1130 A.D.	FIFTY-SECOND YEAR OF JUBILEE.
1135-1154 A.D.	STEPHEN OF BLOIS, SON OF A DAUGHTER OF WILLIAM I RULES ENGLAND.
1143-1180 A.D.	MANUEL I RULES AS EASTERN EMPEROR.
1150-1200 A.D.	CATHOLIC WRITERS CLAIM NON-CATHOLIC CHRISTIANITY "NOT ONLY MENACED THE CHURCH'S (CATHOLIC) EXISTENCE, BUT UNDERMINED THE VERY FOUNDATION OF CHRISTIAN (CATHOLIC) SOCIETY" THROUGHOUT GERMANY, FRANCE, AND SPAIN. NUMEROUS NON-CATHOLIC CHRISTIANS WERE BURNED AT THE STAKE.
1154-1189 A.D.	HENRY II, SON OF A DAUGHTER OF HENRY I, RULES ENGLAND.
1172 A.D.	TURKISH MAMLUKS ATTACK NORTHERN NUBIA, BURNING TOWNS, DESTROYING CHURCH BUILDINGS AND SCATTERING PEOPLE.
1180 A.D.	FIFTY-THIRD YEAR OF JUBILEE
1180-1183 A.D.	ALEIUS II RULES AS EASTERN EMPEROR.
1182 A.D.	SALADIN DEFEATS THE DABURIYANS AT DABURIYA AND THEN DEFEATS

	THE CRUSADERS AT FORBELET NEAR MEGIDDO.
1183-1185 A.D.	ANDRONICUS I RULES AS EASTERN EMPEROR.
1183-1191 A.D.	ISAAC RULES AS EMPEROR OF CYPRUS.
1183 A.D.	SALADIN AND THE CRUSADERS FIGHT AT AYN JALUT NEAR MEGIDDO, BUT THERE IS NO CLEAR VICTOR.
1185-1195 A.D.	ISAAC II (ANGELI DYNASTY) RULES AS EASTERN EMPEROR.
1187 A.D.	SALADIN DEFEATS THE CRUSADERS AT MOUNT TABOR, DABURIYA, ZARIN AND AL-FULA NEAR MEGGIDO.
1189-1199 A.D.	RICHARD THE LION HEARTED, A CRUSADER, SON OF HENRY II, RULES ENGLAND. THIS IS THE TIME OF ROBINHOOD.
1195-1203 A.D.	ALEXIUS III RULES AS EASTERN EMPEROR.
1199-1216 A.D.	JOHN, SON OF HENRY II, RULES ENGLAND.
1203-1204 A.D.	ISAAC II (RESTORED) WITH ALEXIUS IV RULES AS EASTERN EMPEROR.
1204 A.D.	ALEXIUS V DUCAS MURTZUPHLUS RULES AS EASTERN EMPEROR.
1204-1222 A.D.	THEODORE I LASCARIS (LASCARID DUNASTY) RULES AS EASTERN EMPEROR.
1206-1227 A.D.	MONGOLIANS UNDER GENGHIS KHAN CONQUER CHINA, AFGHANISTAN, AND MUCH OF IRAN (PERSIA). THE DESCENDANTS OF MAGOG STRETCH THEIR EMPIRE FROM SHANGHAI TO BUDAPEST. THE CAPITOL CITY WAS KHANBALIK (LATER KNOWN AS PEKING AND THEN BEIJING).

1209 A.D.	THE POPE ORDERS A CRUSADE AGAINST CHRISTIANS IN SOUTHERN FRANCE WHO DENY HIS AUTHORITY.
1215 A.D.	FOURTH LATERN COUNCIL PROVIDES SPECIAL LAWS AND PUNISHMENT FOR CHRISTIANS WHO DISAGREE WITH CATHOLIC LEADERSHIP.
1215 A.D.	ENGLISHMEN REVOLT AND FORCE JOHN TO SIGN THE MAGNA CARTA. THIS GRANTED FREE MEN DUE PROCESS OF LAW. NOBLES WERE GIVEN RIGHTS THAT THE KING COULD NOT TAKE AWAY.
1216-1272 A.D.	HENRY III, SON OF JOHN, BEGINS TO RULES ENGLAND AT NINE YEARS OF AGE.
1217 A.D.	THE MOSLEMS DEFEAT THE CRUSADERS AT MOUNT TABOR NEAR MEGIDDO.
1222-1254 A.D.	JOHN III DUCAS VATATZES RULES AS EASTERN EMPEROR.
1230 A.D.	FIFTY-FOURTH YEAR OF JUBILEE.
1252 A.D.	INNOCENT IV AUTHORIZES TORTURE OF CHRISTIANS TO GET CONFESSIONS AND INFORMATION ABOUT THOSE WHO DO NOT FOLLOW CATHOLIC VIEWS.
1254-1258 A.D.	THEODORE II LASCARIS RULES AS EASTERN EMPEROR.
1258-1261 A.D.	JOHN IV LASCARIS RULES AS EASTERN EMPEROR.
1259-1282 A.D.	MICHAEL VIII PALEOLOGUS (PALEOLOGI DYNASTY) RULES AS EASTERN EMPEROR.
1260 A.D.	MAMLUKES DEFEATS THE MONGOLS AT 'AYN JALUT NEAR MEGIDDO.
1263 A.D.	MAMLUKES DEFEATS THE HOSPITALLERS AT MOUNT TABOR NEAR MEGIDDO.

1264 A.D.	THE HOSPITALLERS AND TEMPLARS DEFEAT A MAMLUK ARMY AT LEJJUN NEAR MEGIDDO.
1265 A.D.	SULTAN BAYBARS OF EGYPT SENDS EXPEDITIONS INTO NUBIA, KILLING PEOPLE, AND MAKING SLAVES.
1272-1307 A.D.	EDWARD I, SON OF HENRY III, RULES ENGLAND.
1276 A.D.	MAMLUK ARMIES CONQUER THE NUBIAN IMPERIAL CITY OF DONGOLA; CHANGE ITS NAME TO "DUNQULAH" AND PLACE SHEKANDA ON THE THRONE. HE REQUIRED ALL NON-MOSLEMS TO CONVERT TO ISLAM, PAY A HEAD TAX (JIZYA), OR BE KILLED.
1280 A.D.	THE FIFTY-FITH YEAR OF JUBILEE.
1279 A.D.	KHUBILAI KHAN ESTABLISHES HIS MONGOLIAN ADMINISTRATION AND BECOMES EMPEROR OF ALL OF CHINA. MONGOLIANS (THE SONS OF MAGOG) BECOME THE RULING CLASS OF CHINA.
1280 A.D.	THE FIFTY-FITH YEAR OF JUBILEE.
1281 A.D.	KHUBILAI KHAN TRIES TO CONQUER JAPAN WITH 150,000 SOLDIERS. A STORM CALLED "KAMIKAZE" DESTROYS HIS FLEET AND SAVES JAPAN.
1282-1328 A.D.	ANDRONICUS II RULES AS EASTERN EMPEROR.
1300 A.D.	TURKISH MUSLIMS, WHO HAD SETTLED IN ASIA MINOR, BEGIN FORMING THE OTTOMAN EMPIRE.
1307-1327 A.D.	EDWARD II, SON OF EDWARD I, RULES ENGLAND, BUT IS EVENTUALLY DEPOSED BY PARLIAMENT.
1327-1377 A.D.	EDWARD III, SON OF EDWARD II, RULES ENGLAND.
1328-1341 A.D.	ANDRONICUS III RULES AS EASTERN EMPEROR.

1330 A.D.	THE FIFTY-SIXTH YEAR OF JUBILEE.
1341-1391 A.D.	JOHN V (RESTORED) RULES AS EASTERN EMEROR.
1347-1352 A.D.	THE BLACK DEATH (BUBONIC PLAGUE) KILLS 1/3 OF EUROPE. (OVER 23,000,000 PEOPLE)
1351 A.D.	ENGLAND PASSES A LAW THAT FORBIDS THE POPE TO INTERFERE IN THE CHOOSING OF CHURCH OFFICIALS.
1353 A.D.	ENGLAND PASSES A LAW PROHIBITING LEGAL APPEALS TO THE POPE OR ANY OTHER COURT OUTSIDE ENGLAND.
1377-1400 A.D.	RICHARD II, GRANDSON OF EDWARD III, RULES ENGLAND UNTIL HE IS DEPOSED.
1378-1417 A.D.	THE CATHOLIC CHURCH IS DIVIDED BETWEEN TWO POPES. ONE RESIDES IN ROME, THE OTHER IN AVIGNON, FRANCE.
1380 A.D.	THE FIFTY-SEVENTH YEAR OF JUBILEE.
1390 A.D.	JOHN VII RULES AS EASTERN EMPEROR.
1391-1425 A.D.	MANUEL II RULES AS EASTERN EMPEROR.
1399-1413 A.D.	HENRY IV, OF THE HOUSE OF LANCASTER, RULES ENGLAND.
1413-1422 A.D.	HENRY V, SON OF HENRY IV, RULES ENGLAND.
1422-1461AND 1470-1471A.D.	HENRY VI, SON OF HENRY V, RULES ENGLAND UNTIL DEPOSED IN 1461. HE REGAINS THE THRONE IN 1470, BUT IS THEN IMPRISONED IN THE TOWER OF LONDON WHERE HE DIES (TIME OF THE WAR OF THE ROSES).
1425-1448 A.D.	JOHN VIII RULES AS EASTERN EMPEROR.
1430 A.D.	THE FIFTY-EIGHTH YEAR OF JUBILEE.
1434-1499 A.D.	PORTUGAL EXPLORES AFRICA AND INDIA.

1438 A.D.	TYPE CASTING IS INVENTED IN GERMANY. THE FIRST PRINTING PRESS BEGINS OPERATION.
1449-1453 A.D.	CONSTANTINE XI (XIII) DRAGASES RULES AS EASTERN EMPEROR.
1453 A.D.	CONSTANTINOPLE FALLS TO OTTOMAN CANNONS.

CHAPTER NINE
A CHRISTIAN CHRONOLOGY OF HISTORY
(FALL OF THE EASTERN EMPIRE – 1858 A.D.)
A TIME LINE OF HUMAN HISTORY
FROM A CHRISTIAN PROSPECTIVE
Compiled by "God's Friend"

1453 A.D.	FALL OF CONSTANTINOPLE
1455 A.D.	FIRST BIBLE PRINTED ON A PRINTING PRESS.
1461-1470 A.D. AND 1471-1483	EDWARD IV, GREAT-GRANDSON OF EDWARD III, RULES ENGLAND. IMPRISONS HENRY VI IN TOWER OF LONDON IN 1471, WHERE HENRY DIES.
1480 A.D.	THE FIFTY-NINTH YEAR OF JUBILEE.
1484 A.D.	THE LAST KNOWN CHRISTIAN KING IN SUDAN, JOEL, IS REMOVED FROM THE THRONE IN DATAWO. MISSIONARIES REPORT THE PEOPLE OF SUDAN "ARE NEITHER CHRISTIAN, MOSLEM, OR JEWS, BUT THEY LIVE IN THE DESIRE OF BECOMING CHRISTIAN." (Voice of the Martyrs- Restricted Nations: Sudan)
1485-1509 A.D.	HENRY VII UNITES LANCASTER AND YORK BY MARRIAGE, AND RULES ENGLAND.
1492 A.D.	COLUMBUS DISCOVERS AMERICA ALL JEWS ARE EXPELLED FROM SPAIN UNDER PENALTY OF DEATH, NEVER TO RETURN.
1492-1522 A.D.	SPAIN EXPLORES CENTRAL AND SOUTH AMERICA AND SAILS AROUND THE WORLD.

1494 A.D.	POPE ALEXANDER I DIVIDES THE WORLD BETWEEN SPAIN AND PORTUGAL AND THE TWO COUNTRIES SIGN THE TREATY OF TORDESILLAS. THOMAS TORQUEMADA IS MADE INQUISITOR-GENERAL OF ALL SPAIN.
1495 A.D.	ALL JEWS ARE EXPELLED FROM PORTUGAL. LEONARDO DAVINCI BEGINS PAINTING "THE LAST SUPPER."
1504 A.D.	FUNJ PEOPLES MOVE INTO SUDAN AND ESTABLISH THE SULTANATE OF SINNAR.
1506 A.D.	POPE JULIUS II STARTS BUILDING ST. PETER'S CATHEDRAL AND AUTHORIZES THE SALE OF INDULGENCES TO FINANCE IT.
1508-1509 A.D.	MICHELANGELO BEGINS PAINTING THE CEILING OF THE SISTINE CHAPEL. THE FIRST NEGRO SLAVES ARE BROUGHT TO AMERICA.
1509-1547 A.D.	HENRY VIII, SON OF HENRY VII, RULES ENGLAND.
1512 A.D.	CATHOLICS ADOPT THE NAME, "CHURCH OF MALIGNANTS," FOR CHRISTIANS OUTSIDE THE CATHOLIC CHURCH. COPERNICUS CHALLENGES CATHOLIC DOCTRINE, SAYING THE EARTH AND OTHER PLANETS REVOLVE AROUND THE SUN.
1514 A.D.	CARDINAL XIMENES PUBLISHES THE FIRST POLYGLOT BIBLE IN HEBREW, CHALDEE, GREEK, AND LATIN.
1516 A.D.	ERASMUS PUBLISHES HIS GREEK NEW TESTAMENT.
1517 A.D.	MARTIN LUTHER PUBLISHES 95 OBJECTIONS TO CATHOLIC PRACTICES AND PROTESTS THE SALE OF INDULGENCES. EGYPT IS CONQUERED BY THE OTTOMAN TURKS.

1519 A.D.	ZWINGLI IS CONVERTED WHILE PASTOR AT ZURICH, AND BEGINS THE SWISS REFORMATION. HORSES ARE BROUGHT TO NORTH AMERICA BY CORTEZ.
1521 A.D.	THE AZTECS SURRENDER TO THE SPANISH. AT THE DIET OF WORMS CHARLES V ANNOUNCES WAR AGAINST LUTHER AND CHRISTIANS DEFYING THE POPES AUTHORITY.
1524 A.D.	FRANCE BEGINS TO EXPLORE AMERICA (CANADA).
1526 A.D.	TYNDALE'S TRANSLATION OF THE BIBLE IS PUBLISHED. CHARLES V. EMPEROR OF SPAIN, AMERICA, SICILY, NAPLES, AND THE NETHERLANDS, SACKS ROME AND TAKES THE POPE PRISONER.
1530 A.D.	THE SIXTIETH YEAR OF JUBILEE. LUTHER'S TRANSLATION OF THE BIBLE IS PUBLISHED.
1534 A.D.	HENRY VIII BREAKS FROM THE CATHOLIC CHURCH AND ESTABLISHES HIMSELF AS HEAD OF THE CHURCH OF ENGLAND. HE KEEPS MUCH OF THE STRUCTURE OF THE CATHOLIC CHURCH. THE ARCHBISHOP OF CANTERBURY BECOMES ADMINISTRATIVE HEAD OF THE CHURCH OF ENGLAND.
1536 A.D.	JOHN CALVIN BEGINS A REFORM MOVEMENT IN GENEVA. THE AUTHORITY OF THE POPE IS DECLARED VOID IN ENGLAND.
1546-1555 A.D.	WAR BETWEEN THE CATHOLIC AND LUTHERAN PRINCES OF GERMANY ENDS WITH THE PEACE OF AUGSBURG THAT PERMITTED EACH PRINCE TO

	CHOOSE THE RELIGION ALLOWED IN HIS DOMAIN. THIS GAVE NO RELIEF TO MANY CHRISTIANS.
1547-1553 A.D.	EDWARD VI, SON OF HENRY VIII, RULES ENGLAND. HE RULED UNDER REGENTS. HE NAMED LADY JANE GREY HIS SUCCESSOR, BUT SHE RULED ONLY 9 DAYS BEING REPLACED BY MARY I WHO HAD HER BEHEADED.
1553-1558 A.D.	BLOODY MARY BECOMES QUEEN OF ENGLAND, MARRIES PHILIP II, KING OF SPAIN, AND TRIES TO FORCE ENGLAND TO BE CATHOLIC.
1558-1603 A.D.	ELIZABETH I BECOMES A RALLYING POINT FOR PROTESTANTS, AND THEN, AS QUEEN OF ENGLAND, SHE REESTABLISHED THE CHURCH OF ENGLAND, AND SOME TOLERANCE FOR NON-CATHOLIC, NON-CHURCH OF ENGLAND GROUPS. MARY IS EXECUTED IN 1587.
1572 A.D.	THE INCAS SURRENDER TO THE SPANISH. CATHOLICS IN FRANCE KILL OVER 20,000 NON-CATHOLIC CHRISTIANS FOR FEAR THEY WILL COME TO POWER.
1558 A.D.	DEFEAT OF SPANISH ARMADA BREAKS THE BACK OF CATHOLIC NAVAL POWER.
1598 A.D.	HENRY IV OF FRANCE GRANTS NON-CATHOLIC CHRISTIANS THE SAME RIGHTS AS CATHOLIC CHRISTIANS (THE EDICT OF NANTES). HENRY IV WAS ONE OF THE CHRISTIANS PERSECUTED IN 1572. HE RECEIVED HIS THRONE ONLY AFTER PROMISING TO BE A CATHOLIC.

1603-1625 A.D.	JAMES I, SON OF BLOODY MARY, ALLY OF ELIZABETH I, BECOMES NON-CATHOLIC KING OF ENGLAND.
1607 A.D.	ENGLAND ESTABLISHES HER FIRST AMERICAN COLONY.
1608 A.D.	FRANCE SETTLES QUEBEC, FORBIDDING NON-CATHOLICS THE RIGHT TO GO THERE.
1610 A.D.	HENRY IV OF FRANCE IS ASSASSINATED FOR HIS PART IN THE EDICT OF NANTES.
1615 A.D.	KING JAMES AUTHORIZES AN ENGLISH TRANSLATION OF THE BIBLE.
1620 A.D.	NON-CATHOLIC, NON-CHURCH OF ENGLAND, CHRISTIANS, WANTING RELIGIOUS FREEDOM, SETTLE AMERICA, ARRIVING IN NEW ENGLAND ABOARD THE MAYFLOWER. ONE OF THOSE PILGRAMS WAS MARY SINGLETON. THEY WERE FOLLOWED BY NUMEROUS OTHERS OF SIMILAR RELIGIOUS BELIEFS. ONLY TWO BRITISH COLONIES, GEORGIA (A PENAL COLONY) AND MARYLAND (A CATHOLIC COLONY), ARE EXCEPTIONS.
1624 A.D.	THE DUTCH ESTABLISH COLONIES IN NORTH AMERICA CALLED, "NEW NEATHERLANDS."
1625-1649 A.D.	CHARLES I, KING OF ENGLAND, SCOTLAND, AND IRELAND, BEGAN HIS RULE BY OFFENDING THE ENGLISH PUBLIC BY MARRYING A CATHOLIC. HE WAS LATER CONVICTED OF TREASON AND BEHEADED BY LEADERS OF THE ENGLISH PARLIAMENT.
1628 A.D.	CHARLES I WAS FORCED TO AGREE TO A PETITION OF RIGHTS. TAXES COULD NOT BE RAISED WITHOUT PARLIAMENT'S APPROVAL.

1630 A.D.	THE SIXTY-FOURTH YEAR OF JUBILEE.
1629-1640 A.D.	CHARLES I GOVERNS WITHOUT CALLING PARLIAMENT INTO SESSION.
1640 A.D.	ATTEMPTING TO FORCE THE SCOTS TO BE MEMBERS OF THE CHURCH OF ENGLAND, CHARLES NEEDS WAR FUNDS AND CALLS PARLIAMENT INTO SESSION TO RAISE TAXES. NON-CATHOLIC, NON-CHURCH OF ENGLAND CHRISTIANS DOMINATE PARLIAMENT AND PASS LAWS PROTECTING THEMSELVES, INCLUDING FREEDOM FROM RELIGIOUS OR POLITICAL PERSECUTION. THIS LAYS THE GROUND WORK FOR RELIGIOUS FREEDOM THROUGHOUT THE BRITISH EMPIRE. THE EMPIRE WAS TO SPAN THE GLOBE AND INCLUDE SUCH DISTANT PLACES AS GREAT BRITAIN, IRELAND, SCOTLAND, NORMANDY IN FRANCE, THE AMERICAN COLONIES, THE BRITISH INDIES, NEWFOUNDLAND, AUSTRALIA, CANADA, SOUTH AFRICA, KENYA, UGANDA, TANGANYIKA, ZANZIBAR, CEYLON, MALTA, CAPE OF GOOD HOPE, NEW ZEALAND, BURMA, MALAYA, NEW GUINEA, PAKISTAN, CYPRUS, GIBRALTAR, BRITISH SOMALI LAND, RHODESIA, SARAWAK, SINGAPORE, FIJI, THE BRITISH SOLOMON ISLANDS, BORNEO, INDIA, EGYPT, HONG KONG, AND MANY MORE. ENGLAND'S EMPIRE GREW TO CONTROL A FOURTH OF THE WORLD. THEIR POLICIES INFLUENCE MUCH OF THE REST OF THE WORLD. THIS IS THE BEGINNING OF THE ELIMINATION

	OF FORCED STATE RELIGION. IT ENDS 1260 YEARS OF CORRUPT, "CHRISTIAN" STATE CHURCHES.
1642-1649 A.D.	KING CHARLES IGNORED SOME OF THE PASSED LAWS. NON-CATHOLIC, NON-CHURCH OF ENGLAND CHRISTIANS FOUGHT FOR THEIR RIGHTS OF SELF-GOVERNMENT AND RELIGIOUS FREEDOM, WINNING AND BEHEADING CHARLES, HEAD OF THE CHURCH OF ENGLAND. CHARLES WAS ALSO UNPOPULAR BECAUSE HE WANTED TO INTER-MARRY HIS LINEAGE WITH CATHOLIC EUROPEAN ROYALTY. OLIVER CROMWELL LEADS THE LIBERATING ARMY.
1652-1658 A.D.	OLIVER CROMWELL RULES ENGLAND AS LORD PROTECTOR.
1658-1659 A.D.	RICHARD CROMWELL, SON OF OLIVER, RULES ENGLAND. HE RESIGNED ON MAY 5, 1659.
1660-1685 A.D.	CHARLES II, SON OF CHARLES I, RULES ENGLAND.
1662-1690 A.D.	ENGLAND ESTABLISHES TRADE COLONIES IN INDIA.
1664 A.D.	THE DUTCH LOOSE NEW NEATHERLANDS TO ENGLAND.
1673-1683 A.D.	POLAND SMASHES THE OTTOMAN TURKS AT THE BATTLE OF CHOCZIM AND VIENNA.
1674 A.D.	FRANCE ESTABLISHES A TRADE COLONY IN INDIA.
1680 A.D.	THE SIXTY-THIRD YEAR OF JUBILEE.
1685 A.D.	LOUIS XIV OF FRANCE ABOLISHES THE EDICT OF NANTES.
1685-1689 A.D.	JAMES II, SON OF CHARLES I, RULES ENGLAND, BUT IS DEPOSED.

1689 A.D.	UNWILLING TO ENDURE A CATHOLIC KING (THE HEIR APPARENT), PARLIAMENT ASKED WILLIAM OF ORANGE (A NON-CATHOLIC CHRISTIAN), KING OF THE NETHERLANDS, TO COME RULE ENGLAND. THE AGREEMENT WORKED OUT RESULTED IN THE ESTABLISHMENT OF A CONSTITUTIONAL MONARCHY AND CONTINUED RELIGIOUS FREEDOM.
1689-1702 A.D.	WILLIAM III (WILLIAM OF ORANGE) AND HIS WIFE, MARY II, DAUGHTER OF JAMES II, RULE ENGLAND.
1689-1763 A.D.	THE FRENCH AND INDIAN WARS IN AMERICA RESULT IN ENGLAND GAINING CONTROL OF CANADA AND LAND WEST OF THE THIRTEEN AMERICAN COLONIES.
1692 A.D.	THE CHURCH OF ENGLAND BECOMES THE ESTABLISHED CHURCH OF MARYLAND AND THE SALARIES OF THEIR CLERGY ARE PAID BY TAXES UNTIL THE END OF THE REVOLUTIONARY WAR.
1702-1714 A.D.	ANNE, SECOND DAUGHTER OF JAMES II, RULES ENGLAND.
1714-1727 A.D.	GEORGE I OF THE HOUSE OF HANOVER RULES ENGLAND.
1727-1760 A.D.	GEORGE II, SON OF GEORGE I, RULES ENGLAND.
1730 A.D.	SIXTY-FOURTH YEAR OF JUBILEE.
1735 A.D.	ZAHIR AL-UMAR DEFEATS THE NABLUS-SAQR ALLIANCE AT AL-RAWDAH NEAR MEGIDDO.
1742 A.D.	AN ITALIAN MISSIONARY DESCRIBES THE RELIGION ON A NILE ISLAND IN SUDAN AS, "THERE ARE STILL

	SOME CHRISTIANS, ALTHOUGH THEY HAVE ENDURED MANY TROUBLES, DISTURBANCES AND WARS FROM TURKS, TO FORCE THEM TO EMBRACE MOHAMMEDANISM. THEY EVEN AT THE COST OF THEIR LIVES, HAVE ALWAYS PERSEVERIED AS CHRISTIANS"(Voice of Martyrs-Restricted Nations: Sudan).
1760-1820 A.D.	GEORGE III, GRANDSON OF GEORGE II, RULES ENGLAND. CONSIDERED DERANGED AFTER 8010.
1763 A.D.	THE ENGLISH DRIVE THE FRENCH FROM INDIA AND CANADA.
1765 A.D.	THE ENGLISH KING IMPOSES THE STAMP ACT ON THE AMERICAN COLONIES.
1771-1773 A.D.	ZAHIR AL-UMAR DEFEATS LEJJUN AT LEJJUN NEAR MEGIDDO.
1773 A.D.	THE BOSTON TEA PARTY IS LED BY SAMUEL ADAMS, A COUSIN OF JOHN ADAMS.
1775-1783 A.D.	THE AMERICAN REVOLUTIONARY WAR TAKES PLACE. THIS TURNS THE THIRTEEN AMERICAN COLONIES INTO THE UNITED STATES OF AMERICAN.
1776 A.D.	THE UNITED STATES DECLARATION OF INDEPENDENCE RECOGNIZES THAT GOD RULES ABOVE GOVERNMENTS AND RECOGNIZES INDIVIDUAL'S GOD GIVEN RIGHTS THAT GOVERNMENTS HAVE NO RIGHT TO INTERFERE WITH. IT IS WRITTEN BY A COMMITTEE THAT INCLUDED THOMAS JEFFERSON AND JOHN ADAMS. JOHN ADAMS IS THE SEVEN TIMES GREAT GRANDFATHER OF BILL SINGLETON. HE WAS ALSO THE FATHER OF JOHN QUINCY ADAMS.

1780 A.D.   THE SIXTY-FITH YEAR OF JUBILEE.
1781 A.D.   RICHARD STOCKTON, THE FATHER OF
             RICHARD STOCKTON (STOCKTON, CA.
             WAS NAMED AFTER HIM), DIRECTED
             HIS CHILDREN IN HIS LAST WILL AND
             TESTAMENT, "WITH THE LAST WORD
             OF THEIR FATHER, I THINK PROPER
             HERE, NOT ONLY TO SUBSCRIBE
             TO THE ENTIRE BELIEF OF THE
             GREAT LEADING DOCTRINE OF THE
             CHRISTIAN RELIGION... BUT ALSO IN
             THE HEART OF A FATHER'S AFFECTION,
             TO CHARGE AND EXHORT THEM TO
             REMEMBER THAT THE FEAR OF THE
             LORD IS THE BEGINNING OF WISDOM."
1784 A.D.   JOHN WESLEY ARRIVES IN NEW
             YORK AND STARTS THE METHODIST
             EPISCOPAL CHURCH IN AMERICA. THE
             ORGANIZATION IS NOT ACCORDING
             TO BIBLE TEACHING. WESLEY TEACHES
             THAT THE BIBLE SHOULD BE THE
             ONLY AUTHORITY. HE CALLS PEOPLE
             TO BECOME "DOWN RIGHT BIBLE
             CHRISTIANS."
1786 A.D.   ALEXANDER CAMBELL IS BORN IN
             NORTH IRELAND. HIS COMMUNITY IS
             PREDOMINANTLY ANGLO-SCOTTISH
             PROTESTANT. HIS FATHER IS A
             PRESBYTERIAN SCHOOL TEACHER AND
             HE LATER FOLLOWS IN HIS FATHER'S
             OCCUPATION.
1787 A.D.   THE UNITED STATES CONSTITUTION
             IS ESTABLISHED AS THE HIGHEST
             HUMAN LAW FOR THE UNITED
             STATES. IT RECOGNIZES THAT HUMAN
             GOVERNMENTS ARE BELOW GOD IN
             AUTHORITY. IT ALSO RECOGNIZES THE

	INDIVIDUAL'S FREEDOM OF RELIGION. JOHN ADAMS HELPS AUTHOR IT.
1788 A.D.	ENGLAND ESTABLISHES AUSTRALIA AS A PENAL COLONY. GEORGE WASHINGTON, THE FIRST PRESIDENT OF THE UNITED STATES, ISSUES A NATIONAL DAY OF THANKSGIVING PROCLAMATION STATING, "IT IS THE DUTY OF ALL NATIONS TO ACKNOWLEDGE THE PROVIDENCE OF ALMIGHTY GOD, TO OBEY HIS WILL, TO BE GRATEFUL FOR HIS BENEFITS, AND HUMBLY IMPLORE HIS PROTECTION AND FAVOR...." GEORGE WASHINGTON CHOOSES JOHN ADAMS AS HIS VICE-PRESIDENT.
1789-1799 A.D.	THE FRENCH REVOLUTION AND REIGN OF TERROR BEGINS IN WHICH FRANCE LOOSES MANY OF HER BEST MINDS, BUT GAINS SOME FREEDOM FOR THE COMMON MAN.
1793 A.D.	FREE ENGLISH SETTLERS BEGIN TO ARRIVE IN AUSTRALIA.
1795 A.D.	JAMES HUTTON LAYS THE EARLY BASIS FOR "UNIFORMITARIANISM" IN EVOLUTIONARY GEOLOGY. HE SAYS THAT IN GEOLOGY ALL THINGS HAVE ALWAYS PRECEDED THE SAME. OUR PLANET IS THE RESULT OF GRADUALLY DEVELOPING PROCESSES UNINFLUENCED BY A GREAT CATASTROPHE (SEE 63-68 A.D.). THIS MISUNDERSTANDING OF OUR PLANET'S HISTORY FULFILLS THE PROPHESY OF 2 PETER 3:3-10 AND OFFERS THE BASIS FOR BAD SCIENCE THAT CAN MISINTERPRET GEOLOGY TO SUPPORT EVOLUTIONARY THEORY.
1799-1815 A.D.	THE NAPOLEONIC WARS RAGE IN EUROPE.

1799 A.D.	NAPOLEON DEFEATS THE OTTOMANS AT MOUNT TABOR NEAR MEGIDDO.
1804 A.D.	THE PRESBYTERIAN SYNODS BEGIN MARKING SOME PREACHERS AS HERETICS RESULTING IN A GROUP OF PREACHERS, INCLUDING BARTON W. STONE, FORMING AN INDEPENDENT SYNOD. THEY DECLARE THEIR TOTAL ABANDONMENT OF ALL AUTHORITATIVE CREEDS, EXCEPT THE BIBLE. IN LESS THAN A YEAR, 15 CONGREGATIONS ARE ESTABLISHED. THE INDEPENDENT (SPRINGFIELD) SYNOD DECIDES ITS OWN EXISTENCE IS AN ADDITION TO BIBLE ORGANIZATION AND DISSOLVES ITSELF. THIS GROUP EXPRESSES A SINCERE AND HONEST DESIRE TO GIVE UP EVERYTHING OF HUMAN ORIGIN IN RELIGION AND TAKE ONLY THE BIBLE. THIS BECOMES THE MARK OF THE AMERICAN RESTORATION MOVEMENT. THOMAS JEFFERSON, THE THIRD PRESIDENT OF THE UNITED STATES, WRITES, "I CONSIDER THE DOCTRINES OF JESUS, AS DELIVERED BY HIM, TO CONTAIN THE OUTLINES OF THE SUBLIMEST SYSTEM OF MORALITY THAT HAS EVER BEEN TAUGHT..."
1807 A.D.	THOMAS CAMBELL, FATHER OF ALEXANDER, COMES TO AMERICA AND BEGINS CIRCUIT PREACHING FOR THE CHARTERS PRESBYTERY.
1808 A.D.	THOMAS CAMBELL IS DISMISSED BY THE PRESBYTERIAN SYNOD BECAUSE OF CHARGES THAT HE TAUGHT THERE WAS NOTHING BUT HUMAN AUTHORITY FOR CREEDS AND

CONFESSIONS OF FAITH. HE FEELS
THAT THE HOLY SCRIPTURES, DIVINELY
INSPIRED, ARE ALL SUFFICIENT. HE
BEGINS PREACHING TO GATHERINGS
AND COINS THE MOTTO: "WHERE THE
BIBLE SPEAKS, WE SPEAK, WHERE THE
BIBLE IS SILENT, WE ARE SILENT."

1809 A.D. ALEXANDER CAMBELL JOINS
HIS FATHER IN AMERICA AFTER
GRADUATING FROM GLASGOW
UNIVERSITY. JAMES MADISON, THE
FOURTH PRESIDENT OF THE UNITED
STATES AND A LEADER IN WRITING
THE CONSTITUTION, SAYS, "WE HAVE
ALL BEEN ENCOURAGED TO FEEL
THE GUARDIANSHIP AND GUIDANCE
OF THAT ALMIGHTY BEING, WHO'S
POWER REGULATES THE DESTINY OF
NATIONS...."

1811 A.D. JOHN QUINCY ADAMS, SIXTH
PRESIDENT OF THE UNITED STATES
WRITES, "SO GREAT IS MY VENERATION
FOR THE BIBLE, AND SO STRONG
MY BELIEF, THAT WHEN DULY READ
AND MEDITATED ON, IT IS OF ALL
BOOKS IN THE WORLD, THAT WHICH
CONTRIBUTES MOST TO MAKE MEN
GOOD, WISE, AND HAPPY."

1813 A.D. ALEXANDER CAMBELL PREACHES FOR
THE BRUSH RUN CHURCH WHICH
JOINS THE REDSTONE ASSOCIATION
OF BAPTIST CHURCHES UPON THE
CONDITION THAT IT CAN TEACH
WHAT IT BELIEVES THE BIBLE TEACHES.
JOHN ADAMS, THE SECOND PRESIDENT
OF THE UNITED STATES, WRITES, "I
HAVE EXAMINED ALL RELIGIONS, AS
WELL AS MY NARROW SPHERE, MY

	STRAIGHTENED MEANS, AND MY BUSY LIFE WOULD ALLOW, AND THE RESULT IS THAT THE BIBLE IS THE BEST BOOK IN THE WORLD..."
1818 A.D.	WALTER SCOTT, AFTER GRADUATION FROM EDINBURGH UNIVERSITY, LANDS IN NEW YORK AND BECOMES A LATIN TEACHER.
1820-1830 A.D.	GEORGE IV, ELDEST SON OF GEORGE III, RULES ENGLAND.
1820 A.D.	ALEXANDER CAMBELL HOLDS HIS FIRST DEBATE. IT IS ON THE SUBJECT AND MODE OF BAPTISM. HIS OPPONENT IS JOHN WALKER, A PRESBYTERIAN PREACHER. THIS IS THE FIRST OF MANY DEBATES ON VARIOUS SUBJECTS THAT HAVE AN IMPACT ON THE BELIEF OF MILLIONS.
1821 A.D.	BARTON W. STONE COMES TO REALIZE THAT THE BIBLE TEACHES BAPTISM BY IMMERSION OF PENITENT BELIEVERS FOR THE REMISSION OF SINS. JOHN QUINCY ADAMS, THE SIXTH PRESIDENT OF THE UNITED STATES, DECLARES, "THE HIGHEST GLORY OF THE AMERICAN REVOLUTION WAS THIS; IT CONNECTED IN ONE INDISSOLUBLE BOND THE PRINCIPLES OF CIVIL GOVERNMENT WITH THE PRINCIPLES OF CHRISTIANITY."
1821 A.D.	A TURKISH ARMY INVADES SUDAN, UNIFYING THE NORTHERN PART OF SUDAN. ETHNIC GROUPS WERE FORCED FROM THEIR TRADITIONAL LANDS AND THE EXPORT OF SUDANESE SLAVES TO EGYPT GREW.
1823 A.D.	ALEXANDER CAMPBELL BEGINS PUBLISHING THE "CHRISTIAN BAPTIST".

1824 A.D.	ALEXANDER CAMPBELL AND BARTON W. STONE MEET. CAMPBELL HAD LEFT THE PRESBYTERIAN CHURCH AND BECOME A PREACHER IN THE REFORMED BAPTIST CHURCH. STONE ALSO HAD BEEN PERSECUTED BY ORGANIZATIONS THAT WANTED HIM TO FOLLOW THEIR CREEDS INSTEAD OF THE BIBLE.
1825 A.D.	JAMES MONROE, FIFTH PRESIDENT OF THE UNITED STATES, SAYS IN A SPEECH, WHILE TALKING OF GOD'S OVERRULING PROVIDENCE, "EXCEPT THE LORD KEEP THE CITY, THE WATCHMAN WAKETH IN VAIN..."
1826 A.D.	BARTON STONE BEGINS PUBLISHING THE "CHRISTIAN MESSENGER".
1827-1829	WALTER SCOTT HOLDS MEETINGS ACROSS THE WESTERN RESERVE AND SPARKS A REVIVAL THAT MOVES MANY TO BECOME CHRISTIANS BASING THEIR RELIGION ON THE BIBLE ONLY. DURING HIS LIFE WALTER SCOTT PERSONALLY BAPTIZED OVER 1200 INTO CHRIST.
1830 A.D.	THE SIXTY-SIXTH YEAR OF JUBILEE.
1830-1837 A.D.	WILLIAM IV, THIRD SON OF GEORGE III, RULES ENGLAND.
1830 A.D.	ALEXANDER CAMBELL BECOMES EDITOR OF THE "MILLENNIUM HARBINGER."
1830-1872 A.D.	SIR CHARLES LYELL BART PUBLISHES ELEVEN EDITIONS OF "PRINCIPLES OF GEOLOGY." HE TAKES THE UNIFORMITARIAN POSITION WHICH GREATLY INFLUENCES CHARLES DARWIN.
1832 A.D.	WALTER SCOTT BEGINS PUBLISHING "THE EVANGELIST."

1837-1901 A.D.	VICTORIA, LAST OF THE HOUSE OF HANOVER, RULES ENGLAND.
1837 A.D.	LEOPOLD VON BUCH COINS THE TERM, "UNIFORMITARIANISM," FOR THE VIEW IN GEOLOGY THAT DENIES THE CATASTROPHE THAT CAME WITH NOAH'S FLOOD.
1840 A.D.	AN EARTH QUAKE ON MOUNT ARARAT APPEARS TO HAVE BROKEN NOAH'S ARK IN HALF, LETTING THE STERN DROP A THOUSAND FEET OR MORE DOWN THE MOUNTAIN SIDE.
1841 A.D.	WILLIAM HENRY HARRISON, THE NINTH PRESIDENT OF THE UNITED STATES, STATES, "SOUND MORALS, RELIGIOUS LIBERTY, AND A JUST SENSE OF RELIGIOUS RESPONSIBILITY ARE ESSENTIALLY CONNECTED WITH ALL TRUE AND LASTING HAPPINESS..."
1845 A.D.	ANDREW JACKSON, THE SEVENTH PRESIDENT OF THE UNITED STATES, FOUNDER OF THE DEMOCRATIC PARTY, AND RELATIVE OF THE SINGLETONS, WROTE IN HIS WILL, "THE BIBLE IS TRUE. UPON THAT SACRED VOLUME I REST MY HOPE OF ETERNAL SALVATION, THROUGH THE MERITS OF OUR BLESSED LORD AND SAVIOR, JESUS CHRIST..."
1845 A.D.	JAMES KNOX POLK, THE ELEVENTH PRESIDENT OF THE UNITED STATES, DECLARES, "I FERVENTLY INVOKE THE AID OF THAT ALMIGHTY RULER OF THE UNIVERSE IN WHOSE HANDS ARE THE DESTINIES OF NATIONS..."
1849 A.D.	ZACHARY TAYLOR, THE TWELFTH PRESIDENT OF THE UNITED STATES, SPEAKING OF THE BIBLE, WROTE, "IT

WAS FOR THE LOVE OF TRUTHS OF
THIS GREAT BOOK THAT OUR FATHERS
ABANDONED THEIR NATIVE SHORES
FOR THE WILDERNESS. ANIMATED
BY LOFTY PRINCIPLES, THEY TOILED
AND SUFFERED TILL THE DESERT
BLOSSOMED AS A ROSE..."

c1852 A.D.   JAMES ABRAM GARFIELD, LATER TO BE
THE TWENTIETH PRESIDENT OF THE
UNITED STATES, SAYS, "IT IS A HABIT
OF MINE TO READ A CHAPTER IN THE
BIBLE EVERY EVENING..."

1853 A.D.   FRANKLIN PIERCE, THE FOURTEENTH
PRESIDENT OF THE UNITED STATES,
ACKNOWLEDGED HIS, "DEPENDENCE
UPON GOD AND HIS OVERRULING
PROVIDENCE..."

1858 A.D.   CHARLES DARWIN PRESENTS THE
THEORY OF EVOLUTION IN, ON THE
ORIGIN OF SPECIES. THIS BECOMES
THE RELIGION OF MANY WHO WANT
TO DENY THE AUTHORITY OF GOD, OR
THE GOD GIVEN RIGHTS AND DIGNITY
OF MAN.

1861-1865 A.D.   THE AMERICAN CIVIL WAR IS WAGED.
THE GREAT RESTORATION MOVEMENT
IS PUT ON HOLD WHILE FOR 3 ½ YEARS
BROTHER SLAUGHTERS BROTHER.
AMERICA LEAVES GOD'S WORK TO BE
ENGULFED IN SATAN'S WORK, BUT
GOD USES THIS TO BEGIN A WORK
TO OUTLAW RACIAL BASED PHISICAL
SLAVERY. THE AMERICAN CIVIL WAR
IS VERBALLY FOUGHT OVER STATES'
RIGHTS. ALMOST 700,000 AMERICANS
LOOSE THEIR LIVES.

CHAPTER TEN
A CHRISTIAN CHRONOLOGY OF HISTORY
(THE AMERICAN CIVIL WAR – 1917A.D.)
A TIME LINE OF HUMAN HISTORY
FROM A CHRISTIAN PROSPECTIVE
Compiled by "God's Friend"

1861-1865 A.D.	THE AMERICAN CIVIL WAR IS WAGED. THE GREAT RESTORATION MOVEMENT IS PUT ON HOLD WHILE FOR 3 ½ YEARS BROTHER SLAUGHTERS BROTHER. AMERICA LEAVES GOD'S WORK TO BE ENGULFED IN SATAN'S WORK, BUT GOD USES THIS TO BEGIN A WORK TO OUTLAW RACIAL BASED PHISICAL SLAVERY. THE AMERICAN CIVIL WAR IS VERBALLY FOUGHT OVER STATES' RIGHTS. ALMOST 700,000 AMERICANS LOOSE THEIR LIVES.
1861 A.D.	ABRAHAM LINCOLN, THE SIXTEENTH PRESIDENT OF THE UNITED STARES, DECLARES, "IT IS FIT AND BECOMING IN ALL PEOPLE, AT ALL TIMES, TO ACKNOWLEDGE AND REVERE THE SUPREME GOVERNMENT OF GOD..."
1862 A.D.	MARTIN VAN BUREN, EIGHTH PRESIDENT OF THE UNITED STATES, STATED, DURING HIS FINAL ILLNESS, "THE ATONEMENT OF JESUS CHRIST IS THE ONLY REMEDY AND REST FOR MY SOUL..."

1862 A.D.	LINCOLN PROCLAIMS SLAVES IN SECEDED STATES FREE. THIS IS A POLITICAL MOVE THAT EVENTUALLY LEADS TO THE FREEING OF ALL SLAVES IN THE UNITED STATES. HE ALSO IS BAPTIZED INTO THE CHURCH OF CHRIST. HE IS BAPTIZED BY A PREACHER IN THE MOVEMENT THAT HAD BEEN PARTIALLY FORMED BY STONE, SCOTT, AND CAMBELL, THE RESTORATION MOVEMENT. ABOUT THIS TIME ANDREW JOHNSON, THE SEVENTEENTH PRESIDENT OF THE UNITED STATES, AND LINCOLN'S VICE PRESIDENT, STATES, "OUR MOTTO: 'LIBERTY AND UNION, ONE AND INSEPARABLE, NOW AND FOREVER... CHRIST FIRST, OUR COUNTRY NEXT!'"
1865 A.D.	THE THIRTEENTH AMENDMENT TO THE CONSTITUTION IS PASSED AFTER LINCOLN'S DEATH. IT ENDS SLAVERY IN THE U.S.A.
1866 A.D.	DAVID LIPSCOMB, A RESTORATION PREACHER, REVIVES THE "GOSPEL ADVOCATE" (IT IS STILL A MAJOR CHRISTIAN PUBLICATION TODAY). IN IT HE TEACHES THERE ARE THREE IDEAS OF THE RELATION OF THE CHURCH TO WORLD POWERS:

1) THE CHURCH SHOULD FORM ALLIANCES WITH WORLD POWERS AND USE THEM.
2) POLITICAL GOVERNMENTS ARE OF DIVINE ORIGIN AND SHOULD BE SUSTAINED BY THE CHURCH.

3) THE CHURCH AND THE CIVIL
GOVERNMENTS ARE TWO
SEPARATE AND DISTINCT
SYSTEMS. THE CHURCH IS
PERFECT AND NEEDS NO
HUMAN HELP. GOD ALLOWS
THOSE WHO REFUSE TO SUBMIT
TO THE DIVINE GOVERNMENT
TO FORM GOVERNMENTS
OF THEIR OWN. WHILE THE
CHRISTIAN IS TO HAVE NO PART
IN THIS GOVERNMENT, HE WILL
QUIETLY SUBMIT TO IT WHERE
ITS LAWS DO NOT CONFLICT
WITH THE TEACHINGS OF THE
BIBLE.

VIEW 3 WAS SUPPORTED BY LIPSCOMB
AND BECAME WIDELY ACCEPTED,
ESPECIALLY IN THE SOUTH
FOLLOWING THE CIVIL WAR. I BELIEVE
THIS TEACHING TO BE TRAGIC AND
TO BE BLAMED FOR THE CURRENT
LACK OF POLITICAL INPUT OF THE
CHURCHES OF CHRIST. THEY ARE A
POLITICAL GIANT BARELY BEGINNING
TO WAKE UP. OUR SOCIETY SUFFERS
BECAUSE IT HAS BEEN DENIED
THEIR GOD TRAINED WISDOM AND
DIRECTION. (THAT IS NOT TO SAY
MEN LIKE GEORGE HOUSE, FORMER
STATE OF CALIFORNIA CONGRESSMAN
AND SPECIAL PROSECUTOR KEN
STARR, BOTH PRODUCTS OF THE
RESTORATION MOVEMENT CHURCHES
OF CHRIST, HAVE NOT HAD THEIR
IMPACT ON U.S. POLITICS). MANY
HONORABLE MEN WITH GREAT

MENTAL ABILITY WITHIN THE
RESTORATION MOVEMENT HAVE
PURPOSEFULLY AVOIDED SECULAR
POLITICAL INVOLVEMENT. A MANY
TIMES GREAT GRANDFATHER OF MINE
(JOHN ADAMS) HELPED SHAPE THIS
NATION SO THAT CHRIST AND HIS
FOLLOWERS WOULD HAVE A PLACE
UNDER THE SUN THAT WELCOMED
THEIR PARTICIPATION IN SECULAR
GOVERNMENT. IF CHRISTIANS
CAN GIVE TO THEIR FAMILY AND
NEIGHBORS A BETTER, FREER PLACE
TO LIVE, WHERE EXPRESSING THE
LOVE OF JESUS IN YOUR LIFE IS
NOT A CRIME, THEN THEY SHOULD
CHERISH THAT OPPORTUNITY
TO PARTICIPATE IN IMPERFECT
SECULAR GOVERNMENT. THE GREED
FOR POWER AND AUTHORITY HAS
USUALLY RESULTED IN GOVERNMENTS
RESENTING THE SUPERIOR PLACE
OF GOD'S GOVERNMENT IN HUMAN
LIVES, RESULTING IN ALMOST
UNBEARABLE PERSECUTION FOR
THOSE WHO ORDERED THEIR LIVES
CORRECTLY. LET US GIVE TO GOD
WHAT IS GOD'S AND TO CAESAR WHAT
IS CAESAR'S. IF CAESAR IS REASONABLE,
EXERCISE YOUR INFLUENCE IN THE
AFFAIRS OF CAESAR SO THAT YOU CAN
DO YOUR GIVING IN AN ATMOSPHERE
OF PEACE AND HARMONY. IF IT BE
POSSIBLE, AS MUCH AS LIETH IN US,
WE MUST LIVE PEACEABLY WITH ALL
MEN. THROUGH OUR INFLUENCE OF
CAESAR WE MAKE THE KEEPING OF
THIS COMMANDMENT POSSIBLE AND

AVOID MUCH SORROW. IN PASSING
LET IT ALSO BE NOTED THAT THE
PERFECTLY ORGANIZED GOVERNMENT
OF GOD LOVED US AND LET US
PARTICIPATE. OUR IMPERFECTIONS
AND REBELLIONS AGAINST CHRIST,
HAVE AT TIMES, MADE THAT
GOVERNMENT MISERABLE TO LIVE
UNDER AND THE JUST RECIPIENT OF
CHRISTIAN RESISTANCE AS CHRISTIANS
ANSWERED TO THE HEAD AND NOT
TO IMPERFECT, ARROGANT OFFICIALS.
THE NUREMBERG TRIALS STAND AS
A GREAT SECULAR DECLARATION OF
THIS REQUIREMENT TO ANSWER TO
GOD ABOVE HUMAN COMMANDS.

1867 A.D.   CANADA BECOMES A SELF-GOVERNING
NATION OF THE BRITISH EMPIRE.

1868 A.D.   JAMES BUCHANAN, THE FIFTEENTH
PRESIDENT OF THE UNITED STATES,
WRITES TO HIS BROTHER, "I TRUST IN
GOD THAT, THROUGH THE MERITS
AND ATONEMENT OF HIS SON, WE
MAY BOTH BE PREPARED FOR THE
INEVITABLE CHANGE."

1871 A.D.   KING WILLIAM I OF PRUSSIA UNITES
THE GERMAN STATES AND BECOMES
GERMAN KAISER (EMPEROR).

1874 A.D.   R. M. BISHOP, AN ELDER OF A
RESTORATION MOVEMENT
CONGREGATION IN CINCINNATI, IS
ELECTED GOVERNOR OF OHIO.

1876 A.D.   ULYSSES S. GRANT, THE EIGHTEENTH
PRESIDENT OF THE UNITED STATES,
WRITES, "HOLD FAST TO THE BIBLE
AS THE SHEET ANCHOR OF YOUR
LIBERTIES; WRITE ITS PRECEPTS IN
YOUR HEARTS, AND PRACTICE THEM

	IN YOUR LIVES." SIR JAMES BRINGS BACK TO LONDON A PIECE OF NOAH'S ARK FROM MOUNT ARARAT.
1877 A.D.	RUTHERFORD BIRCHARD HAYES, THE NINETEENTH PRESIDENT OF THE UNITED STATES, DECLARES, "I BELIEVE ALSO IN THE HOLY SCRIPTURES AS THE REVEALED WORD OF GOD TO THE WORLD FOR ITS ENLIGHTENMENT AND SALVATION."
1880 A.D.	JAMES ABRAM GARFIELD, A PREACHER IN THE RESTORATION MOVEMENT, IS ELECTED PRESIDENT OF THE UNITED STATES. R. M. GANO OF DALLAS, A PROMINENT RESTORATION PREACHER, IS URGED BY THE "GREENBACKERS" TO RUN FOR GOVERNOR OF TEXAS. GANO REFUSED. THE "CHRISTIAN PREACHER" WROTE, "BROTHER GANO COULD DO MORE GOOD PREACHING THE GOSPEL THAN TEN CONGRESSMEN COULD MAKING LAWS, EVEN IF THEY ALWAYS MADE GOOD ONES. THE GOSPEL OF CHRIST IS SUPERIOR TO THE GREENBACK GOSPEL..." SIMILARLY O. A. BURGESS, ANOTHER RESTORATION PREACHER IS URGED TO RUN ON THE REPUBLICAN TICKET FOR GOVERNOR OF INDIANA, BUT REFUSES. RESTORATION PREACHERS WHO RAN FOR OFFICE, BUT WERE DEFEATED INCLUDED D. R. DUNGAN, A CANDIDATE FOR GOVERNOR OF IOWA, AND J.M. PICKENS, A CANDIDATE FOR GOVERNOR OF ALABAMA. SIR CHARLES LYELL BART PUBLISHES THE STATEMENT, "NO CAUSES WHATEVER HAVE FROM THE EARLIEST

TIME TO WHICH WE CAN LOOK BACK,
TO THE PRESENT, EVER ACTED BUT
THOSE NOW ACTING AND THAT THEY
NEVER ACTED WITH DIFFERENT
DEGREES OF ENERGY FROM THAT
WHICH THEY NOW EXERT." THIS
STATEMENT BECOMES A CENTRAL
PRINCIPLE OF THE EVOLUTIONARY
THEORY. IT DENIES NOAH'S FLOOD.

1881-1885 A.D.   CHESTER ALAN ARTHUR, THE SON
OF A BAPTIST PREACHER, BECOMES
THE TWENTY-FIRST PRESIDENT OF
THE UNITED STATES. HE EARNED THE
NICKNAME, "GENTLEMAN BOSS", FOR
HIS SUCCESS IN RUNNING AN HONEST
GOVERNMENT.

1881 A.D.   MOHAMMED AHMED DECLARES
HIMSELF A "REDEEMER" CHOSEN OF
GOD TO RESTORE SUDAN TO THE
"TRUE RELIGION" OF ISLAM. HE LEADS
RESISTANCE TO BRITISH INFLUENCE
AND THEIR EFFERT TO ABOLISH
SLAVERY.

1882 A.D.   REFLECTING ON HIS EARLIER WORK,
CHARLES DARWIN COMMENTED, "I
WAS A YOUNG MAN WITH
UNFORMED IDEAS. I THREW OUT
QUERIES, SUGGESTIONS, WONDERING
ALL THE TIME OVER EVERYTHING; AND
TO MY ASTONISHMENT THE IDEAS
TOOK LIKE WILDFIRE. PEOPLE MADE A
RELIGION OF THEM."

1883 A.D.   TURKISH COMMISSION SEES AND
REPORTS THE PRESENCE OF NOAH'S
ARK ON ARARAT.

1884 A.D.   A. MCGARY BEGINS PUBLISHING
THE "FIRM FOUNDATION," A GOSPEL
PUBLICATION WITH A DEDICATED

FOLLOWING. HIS FATHER HAD
FOUGHT WITH SAM HOUSTON'S
POORLY EQUIPPED AND GREATLY
OUT NUMBERED ARMY AGAINST
SANTA ANNA. WHEN HOUSTON'S
ARMY SUDDENLY TURNED AND
DEFEATED THE MEXICAN ARMY, A.
MCGARY'S FATHER HAD BEEN THE ONE
THAT GUARDED THE BEDRAGGLED
MEXICAN CAPTIVE THAT TURN OUT
TO BE SANTA ANNA. MCGARY GREW
UP PLAYING WITH SAM HOUSTON'S
CHILDREN. WHEN MCGARY RETURNED
FROM THE CIVIL WAR HIS FATHER'S
HOMESTEAD HAD BEEN PILLAGED
BY UNION SOLDIERS. WHEN HE
PASSED SOME UNION SOLDIERS ON
A ROAD, HE SAW THEY WERE RIDING
HIS FATHER'S HORSES. HE PULLED
A GUN AND TOOK THEM BACK. HE
LATER BECAME SHERIFF OF MADISON
COUNTY. HE WAS KNOWN FOR
BOLD, FEARLESS ACTIONS. WHEN
CHALLENGED BY THE KU-KLUX KLAN,
HE BOLDLY ANNOUNCED THAT, "YOU
KNOW WHERE I LIVE, MY DOOR IS
ALWAYS UNLOCKED, YOU CAN COME
ANY TIME, BUT YOU BETTER BRING A
WHEELBARROW TO CARRY YOUR BOYS
HOME IN." HE BECAME A RESTORATION
GOSPEL PREACHER, BUT HIS SERMONS
AS WELL AS HIS PUBLICATIONS FIT HIS
CHARACTER.

1885 A.D, STEPHEN GROVER CLEVELAND, THE
TWENTY SECOND AND TWENTY
FOURTH PRESIDENT OF THE UNITED
STATES URGED, "LET US NOT TRUST
TO HUMAN EFFORT ALONE, BUT

	HUMBLY ACKNOWLEDGE THE POWER AND GOODNESS OF ALMIGHTY GOD WHO PRESIDES OVER THE DESTINY OF NATIONS, AND WHO HAS AT ALL TIMES BEEN REVEALED IN OUR COUNTRY'S HISTORY."
1885 A.D.	IN SUDAN, AHMED DIES OF TYPHUS AND ABDULLAH AL-Ta-AISHI TAKES HIS PLACE IN THE FIGHT TO FORCE ISLAM ON ALL IN SUDAN AND CONTINUE THE SLAVE TRADE, RAIDING AND DESTROYING CHRISTIAN COMMUNITIES.
1887 A.D.	PRINCE NURIE OF BABYLON SEES NOAH'S ARK.
c1890 A.D.	BENJAMIN HARRISON, THE TWENTY THIRD PRESIDENT OF THE UNITED STATES, WROTE, "IT IS A GREAT COMFORT TO TRUST GOD…"
1892 A.D.	IRA J. CHASE, A RESTORATION GOSPEL PREACHER, BECOMES GOVERNOR OF INDIANA. IN A SUPREME COURT DECISION, (CHURCH OF THE HOLY TRINITY VS. UNITED STATES), THE U.S. SUPREME COURT STATES, "OUR LAWS AND OUR INSTITUTIONS MUST NECESSARILY BE BASED UPON AND EMBODY THE TEACHINGS OF THE REDEEMER OF MANKIND…"
1897 A.D.	WILLIAM MCKINLEY, THE TWENTY FIFTH PRESIDENT OF THE UNITED STATES, STATES OF THE BIBLE, "THE MORE CLOSELY WE OBSERVE ITS DIVINE PRECEPTS, THE BETTER CITIZENS WE WILL BECOME AND THE HIGHER WILL BE OUR DESTINY AS A NATION."

1899 A.D.	ABDULLAH AL-TA-AISHI IS KILLED BY THE BRITISH AND SUDAN HAS SOME RELEASE FROM THE CRUEL ARAB PLUNDERING OF CHRISTIAN COMMUNITIES.
1901-1910 A.D.	EDWARD VII, SON OF VICTORIA, RULES ENGLAND.
1902 A.D.	GEORGE HERROPEAN VISITS THE ARK AND CLIMBS ON IT.
c1903 A.D.	THEODORE ROOSEVELT, THE TWENTY-SIXTH PRESIDENT OF THE UNITED STATES, DECLARES, "A THOROUGH KNOWLEDGE OF THE BIBLE IS WORTH MORE THAN A COLLEGE EDUCATION."
1907 A.D.	"STEALTH BANKERS" CREATE THE FEDERAL RESERVE TO CONTROL THE U.S. MONEY SUPPLY.
1909 A.D.	W. H. TAFT, THE 27TH PRESIDENT OF THE UNITED STATES, PUBLICLY ASKED FOR THE "AID OF ALMIGHTY GOD" IN THE PERFORMANCE OF HIS JOB.
1910-1936 A.D.	GEORGE V, SECOND SON OF EDWARD VII, FIRST OF THE HOUSE OF WINDSOR, RULES ENGLAND.
1912-1915 A.D.	ALFRED WEGENER PRESENTS AN EVOLUTION SUPPORTIVE THEORY OF CONTINENTAL DRIFT THAT ENDED UP BEING REJECTED AT THAT TIME. THOSE WHO TRUSTED IN HIS LOGIC STAGED A GOLD RUSH TO SOUTH AMERICA, BUT FOUND NO GOLD. THE MINERAL DEPOSITS OF AFRICA AND SOUTH AMERICA PROVED TO BE DIFFERENT.
c1913 A.D.	WOODROW WILSON, THE TWENTY-EIGHTH PRESIDENT OF THE UNITED STATES, ASSERTS, "A MAN HAS DEPRIVED HIMSELF OF THE BEST THERE IS IN THE WORLD WHO

	HAS DEPRIVED HIMSELF OF THIS, A KNOWLEDGE OF THE BIBLE."
1914-1920 A.D.	AUSTRIA, SUPPORTED BY GERMANY, BEGINS WORLD WAR I. ALLIED FORCES ARE ENGLAND, FRANCE, RUSSIA, BELGIUM, SERBIA, MONTENEGRO, GREECE, ITALY, AND THE UNITED STATES. THE OPPOSING CENTRAL POWERS ARE GERMANY, AUSTRIA-HUNGARY, BULGARIA, AND TURKEY. BEFORE THE END OF 1915, SERBIA AND MONTENEGRO FALL. ITALY DID NOT ENTER THE CONFLICT UNTIL MID 1915. GREECE AND THE UNITED STATES DID NOT ENTER UNTIL 1917. THE RUSSIAN REVOLUTION ELIMINATED RUSSIA AS A USEFUL ALLY BEFORE THE U.S. ENTERED THE WAR. 10,000,000 ARE KILLED AND 20,000,000 ARE WOUNDED. MOST OF THE CASUALTIES WERE FROM EUROPEAN NATIONS. 1915, 1916, 1918, RUSSIAN AVIATORS SEE NOAH'S ARK, AND THEN THEIR ARMY VISITS IT EACH YEAR MAPPING AND PHOTOGRAPHING THE ARK
1917 A.D.	COMMUNIST REVOLUTION BEGINS IN RUSSIA. THEY DENY THE EXISTENCE OF GOD AND GOD GIVEN RIGHTS AND HUMAN DIGNITY. THE STATE IS VIEWED AS HAVING ULTIMATE AUTHORITY. THE RELIGION IS ATHEISTIC EVOLUTION AND THERE IS TREMENDOUS PERSECUTION FOR PRACTICING CHRISTIANS. THE STATE TRIES TO TAKE THE BIBLE AWAY FROM THE PEOPLE. THE RELIGION OF EVOLUTION IS USED AS THE FOUNDATION FOR ITS FIRST GOVERNMENTAL EXPERIMENT.

CHAPTER ELEVEN
A CHRISTIAN CHRONOLOGY OF HISTORY
(COMMUNIST RULE IN RUSSIA – 1953 A.D.)
A TIME LINE OF HUMAN HISTORY
FROM A CHRISTIAN PROSPECTIVE
Compiled by "God's Friend"

1917-1924 A.D.	IN ORDER TO SECURE CONTROL OVER THE LIVES OF THE PEOPLE OF THE SOVIET UNION, THE COMMUNIST PARTY KILLS 62,000,000 SOVIET CITIZENS.
1917-1924 A.D.	LENIN RULES THE SOVIET UNION.
1918 A.D.	ALLENBY DEFEATS THE OTTOMANS AT MEGIDDO.
1921 A.D.	WARREN GAMALIEL HARDING, THE TWENTY-NINTH PRESIDENT OF THE UNITED STATES, ANNOUNCES, "I HAVE ALWAYS BELIEVED IN THE INSPIRATION OF HOLY SCRIPTURES."
1923-1929 A.D.	THE SOVIET UNION, UNDER COMMUNISM, EXPERIENCES WIDE SPREAD CIVIL WAR AND FAMINE.
1924-1938 A.D.	STALIN BEGINS SHARING CONTROL OF THE SOVIET UNION WITH SEVEN COMRADES. FIVE ARE EXECUTED AND ONE IS EXILED, LEAVING STALIN IN CONTROL. THIS GODLESS FAITH SYSTEM SPREADS RUTHLESSNESS AMONG FRIENDS. YOU CAN TRACE ITS BETRAYALS BY THE CORPSES.

1925 A.D.
A TENNESSEE LAW FORBIDS THE TEACHING OF EVOLUTION IN THE PUBLIC SCHOOLS. JOHN THOM SCOPES, A SCIENCE TEACHER, VIOLATES THE LAW. ABOUT THE ONLY TESTIMONY HEARD BY THE JURY IS THE TESTIMONY OF TWO STUDENTS WHO SAY HE TAUGHT EVOLUTION. THE DEFENSE DOES PRESENT INFORMATION ABOUT "NABRASKA MAN" OUTSIDE THE HEARING OF THE JURY. SCOPES IS FOUND GUILTY. "THE NEBRASKA MAN" IS LATER FOUND TO BE A FRAUD. SINCE THEN ADVOCATES FOR EVOLUTION AND THEIR SPIN DOCTORS HAVE GROSSLY MISREPRESENTED THE CASE.

c1926 A.D.
JOHN CALVIN COOLIDGE, THE THIRTIETH PRESIDENT OF THE UNITED STATES, POINTS OUT THAT, "THE FOUNDATIONS OF OUR SOCIETY AND OUR GOVERNMENT REST SO MUCH ON THE TEACHINGS OF THE BIBLE, THAT IT WOULD BE DIFFICULT TO SUPPORT THEM IF FAITH IN THESE TEACHINGS WOULD CEASE TO BE PRACTICALLY UNIVERSAL IN OUR COUNTRY..."

1929-1932 A.D.
THERE IS AN ECONOMIC CRASH IN THE UNITED STATES.

1930 A.D.
THE SIXTY-EIGHTH YEAR OF JUBILEE.

1932 A.D.
MAO LEADS IN THE CREATION OF CHINESE COMMUNIST REPUBLIC OF JIANGXI. A UKRAINE FAMINE KILLS 3,000,000. THE SOVIET UNION PUTS MILLIONS IN PENAL COLONIES AND USES THEM AS SLAVE LABOR.

1933 A.D.	THE NAZI PARTY COMES TO POWER IN GERMANY. THEY BELIEVE IN THE THEORY OF EVOLUTION. THEY JUSTIFY ARYAN RACIAL DOMINANCE AND UTILIZATION OF OTHER RACES AS CATTLE. THE CONCEPT OF GOD GIVEN RIGHTS AND DIGNITY FOR NON–ARYANS IS REJECTED. NATURAL SELECTION MEANS THEY ARE DESTINED TO RULE AND OTHERS SERVE OR BECOME EXTINCT.
1934 A.D.	CHIANG KAI- SHEK LEADS A CHINESE NATIONALIST ARMY THAT FORCES THE COMMUNIST OUT OF THE JIANGXI AREA. 100, 000 COMMUNIST RELOCATE TO SHAANXI PROVINCE.
1935 A.D.	FRANKLIN D. ROOSEVELT, THE 32ND PRESIDENT OF THE UNITED STATES, DECLARES "WE CANNOT READ THE HISTORY OF OUR RISE AND DEVELOPMENT AS A NATION, WITHOUT RECKONING WITH THE PLACE THE BIBLE HAS OCCUPIED IN SHAPING THE ADVANCES OF THE REPUBLIC... WHERE WE HAVE BEEN THE TRUEST AND MOST CONSISTENT IN OBEYING ITS PRECEPTS, WE HAVE ATTAINED THE GREATEST MEASURE OF CONTENTMENT AND PROSPERITY..."
1936-1938 A.D.	GERMANY TAKES THE RHINELAND, AUSTRIA, AND CZECHOSLOVAKIA.
1936-1952 A.D.	GEORGE VI, SECOND SON OF GEORGE V, BECOMES KING OF ENGLAND AFTER HIS BROTHER, EDWARD THE VIII, ABDICATED THE THRONE TO MARRY A COMMONER.
1937 A.D.	JAPAN ATTACKS CHINA. THE NATIONALIST AND THE COMMUNIST

	CHINESE AGREE TO JOIN AND FIGHT THE JAPANESE.
1938-1955 A.D.	STALIN RUTHLESSLY RULES THE SOVIET UNION
1939 A.D.	STALIN AND HITLER AGREE TO DIVIDE POLAND. RUSSIA IS GIVEN HALF OF POLAND, ESTONIA, LATVIA, AND LITHUAINIA. GERMANY INVADES POLAND, RUSSIA INVADES FINLAND, AND WORLD WAR II BEGINS.
1939-1945 A.D.	NAZI CONCENTRATION CAMPS KILL 12,000,000 CIVILIANS. MANY JEWS AND CHRISTIANS, WHO RESIST THE NAZI BELIEF SYSTEM, DIE. MOST OF THE MEMBERS OF THE CHURCHES OF CHRIST IN EASTERN EUROPE ARE EXTERMINATED. MORE DIE IN THE CONCENTRATION CAMPS OF WORLD WAR II THAN DIED ON THE BATTLE FIELDS OF WORLD WAR I. THE NAZI BELIEF SYSTEM IS AN EVIL MOVEMENT GROWING FROM THE ATHEISTIC THEORY OF EVOLUTION. MEN ARE VIEWED AS A DEVELOPING SPECIES OF ANIMALS. THE ARIAN RACE IS VIEWED AS THE GREATEST ACHIEVEMENT OF EVOLUTION WITH THE REST OF MANKIND FOR THEIR USE AS OTHERS USE FARM ANIMALS. FOR GERMANS TO BECOME WORLD RULERS IS MERELY A FULFILLMENT OF DESTINY.
1940 A.D.	FRANCE SURRENDERS TO GERMANY.
1941 A.D.	GERMANY INVADES RUSSIA, PROVING THERE IS NO HONOR AMONG THIEVES. RUSSIA SWITCHES SIDES.
1942 A.D.	U.S. SCIENTISTS CREATE THE FIRST CONTROLLED CHAIN REACTION.

1943 A.D.	HERBERT HOOVER, THE 31 ST PRESIDENT OF THE UNITED STATES, ISSUED A JOINT STATEMENT WITH THE WIVES OF THE 30TH, THE 27TH, THE 26TH, THE 23RD, AND THE 22ND PRESIDENTS OF THE UNITED STATES, (AND OTHER LEADERS), WHICH AFFIRMED THAT, "DEMOCRACY IS THE OUTGROWTH OF THE RELIGIOUS CONVICTION OF THE SACREDNESS OF EVERY HUMAN LIFE. ON THE RELIGIOUS SIDE, ITS HIGHEST EMBODIMENT IS THE BIBLE, ON THE POLITICAL SIDE, THE CONSTITUTION".
1944 A.D.	WESTERN NATIONS AGREE TO A CURRENCY PEGGING SYSTEM, AT BRETTON WOODS, NEW HAMPSHIRE. THIS ESTABLISHES A VALUE FOR MAJOR CURRENCIES AGAINST THE US DOLLAR, WHICH IN TURN IS PEGGED AT $35.00 TO THE TROY OUNCE OF GOLD. THIS IS KNOWN AS THE GOLD STANDARD.
1945 A.D.	U.S. TESTS THE FIRST ATOMIC BOMB, AND THEN DROPS TWO BOMBS ON JAPAN. WORLD WAR II ENDS WITH THE SURRENDER OF JAPAN AND GERMANY.
1947-1950 A.D.	MAO PROCLAIMS THE PEOPLE'S REPUBLIC OF CHINA, AND FIGHTS AGAINST FORCES UNDER CHIANG KAI-SHEK. MAIN LAND CHINA FALLS UNDER COMMUNIST RULE. CHIANG KIA-SHEK IS FORCED TO FALL BACK TO FORMOSA WHERE HIS PEOPLE ESTABLISH NATIONALIST CHINA OR TAIWAN.
1948 A.D.	THE ESTABLISHMENT OF A NEW JEWISH NATION OF ISRAEL LEADS TO THE FIRST ARAB-ISRAELI WAR. WESTERN POWERS DESIRE TO GIVE THE JEWS THEIR OWN LAND, BUT

PALESTINIAN ARABS ALREADY CLAIM THE REGION. THE ISRAELIS DEFEAT ARAB FORCES AT ZARIN, MEGIDDO, MISHMAR, HAEMEK, AND LEJJUN. TITO BREAKS WITH THE SOVIET UNION, BUT CZECHOSLOVAKIA REMAINS COMMUNIST.

1950-2014+ A.D. THE COMMUNIST PARTY OF CHINA RULES WITH AN IRON HAND, KILLING OVER 38,000,000 PEOPLE TO STAY IN CONTROL. THEIR GREED FOR POWER COSTS MORE LIVES THAN MOST ANY OTHER RUTHLESS HUMAN EFFORT IN HISTORY, AND IS ONLY SURPASSED BY THE RUTHLESS COMMUNIST EFFORT FOR CONTROL OF THE SOVIET UNION. THEY ESTABLISH SLAVE LABOR CAMPS, TRY TO BAND THE BIBLE, AND SELL PRISONER BODY PARTS. THEIR EFFORT TO BAND THE BIBLE FAILS, AND HOUSE CHURCHES SPRING UP THROUGH OUT THEIR EMPIRE. THEY THEN TRY TO CONTROL CHRISTIANITY BY OUTLAWING SERVICES THAT ARE NOT HELD IN PUBLIC FACILITIES. THEY ESTABLISH A GOVERNMENT AGENCY TO APPOINT THE PREACHERS PERMITTED TO PREACH AT THE PERMITTED SERVICES. THE PREACHERS ARE NORMALLY UNBELIEVERS, MEMBERS OF THE COMMUNIST PARTY. THEY ALSO DENY GOVERNMENT SERVICES (HOUSING, MEDICAL CARE, AND FOOD) TO FAMILIES WITH MORE THAN ONE CHILD. SINCE IT IS CUSTOM FOR THE SON TO STAY WITH HIS PARENTS AND HELP THEM IN THEIR OLD AGE, AND

	THE DAUGHTER TO LEAVE HER HOME AND HELP HER HUSBAND'S PARENTS, A GREAT IMBALANCE OF YOUNG MEN DEVELOPS.
c1950 A.D.	HANS GRIMM, A SURVIVOR OF THE GERMAN CONCENTRATION CAMPS, A NON-CATHOLIC, NON-GREEK ORTHODOX MEMBER OF THE CHURCHES OF CHRIST OF EASTERN EUROPE, WRITES A HISTORY OF HIS PEOPLE. THEIR TRADITIONS AND ORIGINS WENT BACK TO THE TIME BEFORE CONSTANTINE. HE WAS DELIGHTED TO DISCOVER THAT THE RESTORATION MOVEMENT ON THE AMERICAN WESTERN FRONTIER HAD PRODUCED THE SAME, IDENTICAL BELIEF SYSTEM AND FELLOWSHIP IN AMERICA. HIS INITIAL CONTACT WITH THE AMERICAN CHURCHES OF CHRIST CAME THROUGH OTTIS GATEWOOD, AN ORGANIZER OF THE COLD WAR BIBLE PRINTING AND SMUGGLING RING IN CZECHOSLOVAKIA
1950-1953 A.D.	NORTH KOREA, BACKED BY COMMUNIST CHINA, INVADES SOUTH KOREA. UNITED NATIONS FORCES, LED BY U.S. FORCES, DRIVES THEM OUT OF SOUTH KOREA. GEN. MACARHTUR WANTS TO INVADE RED CHINA, BUT PRESIDENT TRUMAN FIRES HIM INSTEAD.

CHAPTER TWELVE
A CHRISTIAN CHRONOLOGY OF HISTORY
(END OF KOREAN CONFLICT – 1997 A.D.)
A TIME LINE OF HUMAN HISTORY
FROM A CHRISTIAN PROSPECTIVE
Compiled by "God's Friend"

1950-1953 A.D.	NORTH KOREA, BACKED BY COMMUNIST CHINA, INVADES SOUTH KOREA. UNITED NATIONS FORCES, LED BY U.S. FORCES, DRIVES THEM OUT OF SOUTH KOREA. GEN. MACARHTUR WANTS TO INVADE RED CHINA, BUT PRESIDENT TRUMAN FIRES HIM INSTEAD. QUEEN ELIZABETH II ASCENDS TO THE THRONE OF ENGLAND WITH FIRST WIDESPREAD USE OF TELEVISION.
1952 A.D.	HARRY S. TRUMAN, 33RD PRESIDENT OF THE UNITED STATES, ADMONISHES, "THE FUNDAMENTAL BASIS OF THIS NATION'S LAWS WERE GIVEN BY MOSES ON THE MOUNT. THE FUNDAMENTAL BASIS OF OUR BILL OF RIGHTS COMES FROM THE TEACHINGS WE GET FROM EXODUS AND ST. MATTHEW, FROM ISAIAH AND ST. PAUL. I DON'T THINK WE EMPHASIZE THAT ENOUGH THESE DAYS. IF WE DON'T HAVE A PROPER FUNDAMENTAL MORAL BACKGROUND, WE WILL FINALLY END UP WITH A TOTALITARIAN GOVERNMENT WHICH

	DOES NOT BELIEVE IN RIGHTS FOR ANYBODY EXCEPT THE STATE!"
c1953 A.D.	IKE EISENHOWER IS PRESIDENT OF THE UNITED STATES.
1953-1961 A.D.	WITH THE SUPPORT OF PRESIDENT EISENHOWER THE PHRASE, "UNDER GOD," IS ADDED TO THE UNITED STATES PLEDGE OF ALLEGIANCE. CONSISTENT WITH THE DECLARATION OF INDEPENDENCE, THIS RECOGNIZES GOD'S RANK ABOVE THE NATION'S GOVERNMENT.
1954 A.D.	STALIN DIES.
1955 A.D.	NIKITA KRUSHCHEV DENOUNCES STALIN AND RULES THE SOVIET UNION. 1956 A.D. PRESIDENT IKE SAYS THE UNITED STATES WILL HELP ENSLAVED PEOPLES THROW OFF COMMUNIST RULE. HUNGARIANS REVOLT. THE U.S. ONLY TALKS. SOVIET TANKS CRUSH A POPULAR REVOLT IN HUNGARY. 7,000 ARE KILLED FIGHTING TANKS WITH STONES AND BOTTLES OF GASOLINE. THOUSANDS BECOME REFUGEES FLEEING TO AUSTRIA. POLISH WORKERS RIOT. ADILI STEVENSON RUNS FOR THE SECOND TIME AGAINST IKE FOR THE PRESIDENCY OF THE UNITED STATES. TO ME HE SEEMED TO BE ONE OF THE BEST CANDIDATES EVER FIELDED BY THE DEMOCRATIC PARTY. HE STATES THAT THERE ARE TWO DANGEROUSLY DISHONEST MEN IN AMERICAN POLITICS, RICHARD NIXON AND JOHN KENNEDY. OF THE TWO HE DECLARES KENNEDY THE MOST DANGEROUS BECAUSE HE IS ALSO RICH.

1956-1964 A.D.
A COUP SPONSORED BY RUSSIA PUTS
PRO-COMMUNISTS IN CHARGE OF
SYRIA. RUSSIA PUTS UP TWO SPUTNIKS
AND BEATS THE U.S. INTO SPACE. IN
THE U.S., LITTLE ROCK CENTRAL HIGH
SCHOOL IS INTEGRATED.

1957 A.D.
NIKITA KHRUSHCHEV TOURS THE U.S.
HE BOASTS THAT, WITHOUT FIRING A
SHOT, COMMUNISM WILL BURY THE
U.S., AND BY 1995 WILL MARCH IN
AS CONQUERORS. HE SAYS WE WILL
FORGET ABOUT FOREIGN AFFAIRS,
AND BECOME SO INVOLVED IN SPORTS
THAT WE WILL NOT REALIZE WHAT IS
HAPPENING.

1959 A.D.
THE SEGUNDO, CA. CHURCH OF
CHRIST AND THE STOCKTON, CA.
CENTRAL CHURCH OF CHRIST BEGIN
AN ETHIOPIAN MISSION OUTREACH.
SEGUNDO SUPPORTS THE BOB GOWEN
FAMILY AND THE CENTRAL CHURCH
SUPPORTS THE CARL THOMPSON
FAMILY. EMPEROR HAILE SELASSIE
REQUIRES THAT THE CHURCH BUILD
A PROGRAM THAT WILL BE OF SERVICE
TO HIS COUNTRY. THE CHURCH
BEGINS A SCHOOL FOR THE DEAF. THIS
SERVICE ENLARGED AND THE CHURCH
NOW PROVIDES TRAINING FOR MANY
DEAF STUDENTS. THEY RUN ALL THE
TRAINING FOR THE DEAF IN ETHIOPIA
TO THE CURRENT TIME. A DAUGHTER
OF THE EMPEROR GAVE THE CHURCH
A 99 YEAR LEASE ON COMPOUNDS FOR
THE FIRST DEAF SCHOOL.

1960 A.D.
JOHN F. KENNEDY, DURING HIS
INAUGURAL ADDRESS, PROCLAIMS,
"THE RIGHTS OF MAN COME NOT

1961 A.D.

FROM THE GENEROSITY OF THE STATE, BUT FROM THE HAND OF GOD..." KENNEDY IS THE FIRST CATHOLIC PRESIDENT OF THE UNITED STATES. CUBA SLIPS INTO COMMUNIST HANDS. KENNEDY DENIES FREEDOM FORCES PROMISED AIR SUPPORT AT THE BAY OF PIGS AND CUBAN PATRIOTS ARE SLAUGHTERED BY TANKS. AFTER THIS CASTRO THREATENS THAT THE COMMUNISTS WILL BRING THE U.S. DOWN THROUGH DRUGS. KENNEDY PROVIDES THE NATION WITH THE FAMOUS QUOTE, "ASK NOT WHAT YOUR COUNTRY CAN DO FOR YOU, BUT WHAT YOU CAN DO FOR YOUR COUNTRY."

1961-1963 A.D.

DURING THIS TIME PERIOD MARSHALL KEEBLE HELD A MEETING AT THE UNIVERSITY CHURCH OF CHRIST IN ALBUQUERQUE, N.M. I ATTENDED IT. HE WAS A GREAT GOSPEL PREACHER WHO BAPTISED TENS OF THOUSANDS OF PEOPLE INTO CHRIST. HE TOLD A STORY ABOUT A SHOT-GUN BAPTISM HE ONCE PARTICIPATED IN. IT HAPPENED DURING A MEETING HE HELD IN THE DEEP SOUTH. THE MEETING LASTED FOR SEVERAL DAYS (NORMALLY A WEEK OR TWO). AT THE BEGINNING OF THE MEETING HE WAS TOLD BY REPRESENTATIVES OF THE LOCAL KLU KLUX KLAN THAT HE SHOULD NOT HOLD THE MEETING. HE POLITELY TOLD THEM HE HAD TO PREACH THE GOSPEL IN ORDER TO BE OBEDIENT TO JESUS. THEY THREATENED HIM AND TOLD HIM

IF HE CONTINUED THERE WOULD
BE A LYNCHING. OF COURSE HE
CONTINUED. ON ONE OF THE LAST
DAYS OF THE MEETING, AFTER THE
PEOPLE HAD GATHERED, A NUMBER
OF WHITE, HOODED INDIVIDUALS
ENTERED THE CHURCH BUILDING
AND LINED UP ALONG THE BACK OF
THE BUILDING IN FRONT OF THE
EXIT. THEY WERE CARRYING A ROPE
WITH A HANGMAN'S NOOSE ON ONE
END. THEY WERE ALSO ALL CARRYING
SHOTGUNS OR RIFLES. MARSHALL
WENT AHEAD AND PREACHED HIS
SERMON WONDERING IF IT WOULD
BE HIS LAST. AT THE END OF THE
SERMON ONE OF THE HOODED,
ARMED INDIVIDUALS MADE HIS
WAY TO THE PULPIT. HE STEPPED IN
FRONT OF MARSHALL AND LAID HIS
SHOTGUN ACROSS THE PODIUM.
LEANING ON THE PODIUM HE LOUDLY
PROCLAIMED TO THE AUDIENCE, "THIS
GUY HAS BEEN TELLING YOU THE
TRUTH. LINE-UP. YOU'RE ALL GOING
TO BE BAPTISED!" MARSHALL KEEBLE
THANKED GOD FOR A SHOTGUN
BAPTISM INSTEAD OF A SHOTGUN
LYNCHING.

1962 A.D. THE THEORY OF CONTINENTAL
DRIFT IS REVIVED WITH THE
THEORIES OF SEA FLOOR SPREADING
AND MAGNETIC REVERSAL. IT IS
DISCOVERED THAT THE EARTH
IS CRACKED INTO TWENTY-ONE
PLATES AND CRACKED DOWN THE
MIDDLE OF THE ATLANTIC WITH
MAGNETIC STRIPES ON BOTH SIDES

OF THE ATLANTIC CRACK. RUSH TO SUPPORT THE THEORY OF EVOLUTION IGNORES THE FACT THAT GEOLOGICAL SURVEYS OF NORTH AMERICAN AND EUROPEAN ROCK FORMATIONS SHOW NO MAGNETIC REVERSALS IN ALL OF GEOLOGICAL TIME. THEY DO SHOW A CATACLYSMIC SKIP IN POLE LOCATIONS ABOUT TWO THIRDS OF THE WAY BACK IN THE MIGRATION RECORD. THE CRUST MOVED SUDDENLY 5,000 MILES TO THE EAST IN RELATIONSHIP TO THE CORE. THIS SUGGESTS AN ACCORDION LIKE FOLDING OF THE ATLANTIC OCEAN BOTTOM CRUST INSTEAD OF MAGNETIC REVERSAL. THE AVERAGE WIDTH OF THE STRIPES IS THE SAME AS THE AVERAGE THICKNESS OF OCEAN BOTTOM CRUST (SEE 2524-2523B.C.).

1962-1973 A.D. THE UNITED STATES BECOMES INVOLVED IN THE VIETNAM WAR. COMMUNIST NORTH VIETNAM INVADES SOUTH VIETNAM. PRESIDENT KENNEDY BEGINS AMERICAN INVOLVEMENT. PRESIDENT JOHNSON INCREASES INVOLVEMENT. U.S. LEADERS ARE NOT WILLING TO LET AMERICAN OR SOUTH VIETNAM FORCES INVADE THE NORTH TO BRING THE WAR TO A CLOSE. PRESIDENT NIXON, PROMISING THE SOUTH VIETNAMESE CONTINUED US ARMS AND SUPPORT, DISENGAGES U.S. TROOPS. AFTER DISENGAGEMENT, CONGRESSMAN CHURCH GETS A LAW PASSED THAT FORBIDS THE USE OF AMERICAN AIR POWER IN SOUTHEAST ASIA.

1963 A.D.	PRESIDENT KENNEDY IS ASSASSINATED.
1963-1969 A.D.	L.B. JOHNSON IS PRESIDENT OF THE UNITED STATES.
1964-1982 A.D.	BREZHENEV LEADS THE SOVIET UNION.
1964-1967 A.D.	BILLY CURL WORKS AS AN ETHIOPIAN MISSIONARY SUPPORTED BY THE SAN FRANCISCO UP-TOWN CHURCH OF CHRIST.
1965 A.D.	PRESIDENT JOHNSON QUOTES THE PRAYER OF KING SOLOMON FROM THE BIBLE AND APPLIES IT TO HIMSELF, "GIVE ME NOW WISDOM AND KNOWLEDGE THAT I MAY GO OUT AND COME IN BEFORE THIS PEOPLE."
1967 A.D.	THE ISRAELIS DEFEAT THE ARABS AT THE RAMAT DAVID AIRFIELD...A BATTLE NEAR MEGIDDO.
1967-1974 A.D.	JANE FONDA IS AN AMERICAN LEADER OF THE MOVEMENT TO TURN COUNTRIES OF SOUTHEAST ASIA OVER TO COMMUNISM. SHE PREACHES THE VIRTUES OF NORTH VIETNAM AND EARNS THE NAME, "HANOI JANE."
1968-1971 A.D.	JOHN ED CLARK AND DON LAZZARESCHI BECOME LEADERS IN THE CHURCH OF CHRIST ETHIOPIAN MISSION OUT REACH. A PREACHER SCHOOL IS HELD TO TEACH TWELVE NATIVE PREACHERS FROM THE KAMBATTA AREA. BROTHER BEHAILU, BROTHER EROMO, AND BROTHER ARTIE REED SELECTED THE CANDIDATES. BROTHER EROMO AND BROTHER BEHAILU HAD BECOME NATIVE LEADERS IN THE ADDIS ABABA CHURCH. THE OUTREACH HAS OVER 3,000 IN REGULAR ATTENDANCE IN 101 CONGREGATIONS.

1969 A.D.	GAAFAR MOHAMMED NUMERI LEADS A MILITARY COUP IN SUDAN
1970 A.D.	A MILITARY COUP FRIENDLY TO SOUTH VIETNAM AND THE U.S. TAKES PLACE IN CAMBODIA. THE CAMBODIAN KING, NORODOM SIHANOUK, RUNS TO COMMUNIST CHINA AND NORTH KOREA FOR PROTECTION.
1970 A.D.	IN JULY SUDANESE GOVERNMENT TROUPS ENTER A CHRISTIAN WORSHIP SERVICE AT BANZA NEAR THE SUDAN-CONGO BORDER. THEY TIE THE WORSHIPERS TO THE PEWS, MEN WOMEN AND CHILDREN, AND THEN SHOOT THEM. THEY THEN SET THE BUILDING IN WHICH THEY WERE MEETING ON FIRE. SOME OF THE WOUNDED CHILDREN TRY TO ESCAPE THE FIRE, BUT ARE CAUGHT AND THROWN BACK INTO THE BLAZING BUILDING.
1971-1977 A.D.	FOUR MORE PREACHER TRAINING SCHOOLS ARE HELD AT ADDIS ABABA TRAINING 150 PREACHERS.
1971 A.D.	NIXON ABANDONS THE GOLD STANDARD, DIRECTLY PEGGING MAJOR CURRENCIES TO THE US DOLLAR.
1972 A.D.	STEPHEN JAY GOULD AND NILES ELDRIDGE DEVELOP A THEORY CALLED "PUNCTUATED EQUILIBRIUM" TO HELP JUSTIFY THE FOSSIL RECORD'S FAILURE TO SUPPORT THE THEORY OF EVOLUTION. THEY STRUGGLE TO KEEP EVOLUTION BELIEVABLE.
1973-1977 A.D.	NIXON RESIGNS AS PRESIDENT AND GERALD FORD LEADS THE UNITED STATES.

1973 A.D.	FOLLOWING THE SECOND MAJOR DEVALUATION OF THE US DOLLAR, THE FIXED-RATE CURRENCY EVALUATION MECHANISM IS DISCARDED TO BE REPLACED BY A FLOATING RATE SUBJECT TO THE FORCES OF SUPPLY AND DEMAND.
1973 A.D.	ISRAEL DEFEATS SYRIA AT THE RAMAT DAVID AIRPORT.
1974-1977 A.D.	NORTH VIETNAM LAUNCHES A MAJOR OFFENSIVE. SOUTH VIETNAM FORCES DROP BACK TO SAIGON, LEAVING A LARGE AMOUNT OF WAR SUPPLIES BEHIND. SOUTH VIETNAM ASKS TO BE RE-SUPPLIED, BUT THE U.S. REFUSES. SOUTH VIETNAM, LAOS, AND CAMBODIA FALL INTO COMMUNIST HANDS. NORTH VIETNAM, RUSSIAN TRAINED AND BACKED FORCES TAKE LAOS AND SOUTH VIETNAM. COMMUNIST CHINESE TRAINED AND BACKED KHMER ROUGH FORCES TAKE CAMBODIA. RUSSIAN BACKED COMMUNIST FORCES SEIZE POWER IN ETHIOPIA AND OTHER EAST AFRICAN NATIONS. OVER 50,000,000 PEOPLE BECOME COMMUNIST SLAVES FOR THE FIRST TIME. THE NORTH VIETNAMESE EXECUTE HUNDREDS OF THOUSANDS OF SOUTH VIETNAMESE. MANY FROM SOUTH VIETNAM AND LAOS ARE SHIPPED TO SLAVE CAMPS IN EASTERN EUROPE AS PAYMENT FOR RUSSIAN HELP DURING THE VIETNAMESE CONFLICT. (I HAVE BEEN ABLE, THROUGH PERSONAL VISITS AND COMMUNICATIONS, TO LEARN OF THE TREATMENT OF BOTH CAMBODIANS

AND ETHIOPIANS DURING THEIR ENSLAVEMENT BY THE COMMUNIST. SINCE MY PERSONAL INFORMATION IS VERY SURE ABOUT THE TREATMENT OF THESE POPULATIONS, I WILL MAINLY TALK OF THEIR TREATMENT.)

1974-1978 A.D. THE KHMER ROUGH EXECUTE OR STARVE TO DEATH MILLIONS OF KHMER PEOPLE (4 T0 6 MILLION- OVER ½ OF 1975 CAMBODIAN POPULATION). IT IS A CAPITAL OFFENSE TO BE CAUGHT WITH FOOD STORES. IT IS A CAPITAL OFFENSE TO BE EDUCATED, WEAR GLASSES, OR BE CAUGHT OVER 10 KM FROM YOUR HOME. CHILDREN ARE SEPARATED FROM THEIR PARENTS AFTER FIVE YEARS OF AGE. THEY ARE MADE TO WORK IN LEACH INFESTED MUD BOGS. PARENTS ARE NOT ALLOWED EVEN TO SEE THEIR CHILDREN AT NIGHT OR DOCTOR THEIR FESTERING SORES. FOUR AND FIVE YEAR OLDS ARE ALLOWED TO SEE THEIR MOTHERS AT NIGHT, BUT DURING THE DAY THEY WORK CLEANING MANURE FROM TICK INFESTED CATTLE PENS. HUSBANDS AND WIVES ARE KEPT SEPARATE. THE KHMER ROUGH STEAL EVERYTHING.

FRIENDS OF AMERICA TORTURED IN
A CAMP SOUTH OF PHENOM PENH
DURING THE KHMER ROUGH

THE KHMER ROUGH KEPT DETAILED RECORDS ON THE ABUSE THEY INFLICTED ON THE PRISONERS. WHEN I LOOKED AT THE RECORDS IT SEEMED MOST WERE TAKING A YEAR AND A HALF TO DIE. THE ABUSE INCLUDED DRILLING HOLES IN THEIR SKULLS WITH OUT MEDICATIONS WHILE THEY WERE ALIVE. MOST WERE BURIED IN GRAVES OF ABOUT EIGHT HUNDRED.

IN CAMBODIA THOSE WHO MISS
WORK TOO MUCH ARE PERIODICALLY
EXECUTED. CAMBODIA IS A LARGE
SLAVE CAMP. THOSE THE KHMER
ROUGH BECOME ANGRY WITH ARE
CHAINED TO TREES AND SLOWLY
STARVED TO DEATH. THE COMMUNITY
IS PERIODICALLY MARCHED BY AS
THEY STARVE SO THE VILLAGERS CAN
RECEIVE AN OBJECT LESSON. SOME
OF THE SOLDIERS ARE RUTHLESS,
FORCING MOTHERS TO KILL THEIR
OWN BABIES AND LAUGHING
ABOUT IT.
ETHIOPIA IS NO BETTER. ONE
THIRTEEN YEAR OLD GIRL IS
ARRESTED AND BEATEN EVERY DAY
FOR THIRTY DAYS BECAUSE SHE
WILL NOT DENY HER FAITH IN JESUS.
TEENAGERS THAT SEEM RECEPTIVE
TO INDOCTRINATION ARE SHIPPED
AWAY FOR SIX MONTHS OF INTENSE
INDOCTRINATION. WHEN THEY
RETURN THEY ARE GIVEN GUNS AND
TOLD TO SHOOT WHOEVER IS NOT
ACCEPTING THE INDOCTRINATION.
THE RELIGIOUS GROUPS ARE PLAYED
AGAINST ONE ANOTHER. AT TIMES
THE COPTIC STATE CHURCH IS
OUTLAWED. AT OTHER TIME ALL
OTHER CHURCHES ARE OUTLAWED.
DEMERA, A LAWYER AND GOOD
CHRISTIAN BROTHER, IS SELECTED TO
BE THE LEGAL REPRESENTATIVE FOR
THE ADDIS ABABA COMMUNIST URBAN
LEAGUE, THE LARGEST COMMUNIST
ORGANIZATION IN ETHIOPIA. THE
CHURCH OF CHRIST GROWS TO BE

OVER 300 CONGREGATIONS WITH
OVER 50,000 IN ATTENDANCE. OF
THE SOLDIERS BEING USED TO KEEP
ETHIOPIA COMMUNIST, THE CUBANS
ARE THE MOST PITIABLE. THE RUSSIAN
DISRESPECT THEM. THE ETHIOPIANS
DISRESPECT THEM. THEY SEEM TO STAY
DRUNK ALL THE TIME. THEY HAVE NO
FUTURE. IN BATTLE THEY ARE PUT IN
FRONT OF THE RUSSIANS AND IF THEY
BACK UP THE RUSSIANS SHOOT THEM.
THE ETHIOPIANS ARE USED SIMILARLY
IN FRONT OF THE CUBANS, BUT THE
ETHIOPIANS THEY ARE FIGHTING
WILL OFTEN LET THEM GO BY AND
SHOOT THE CUBANS AND RUSSIANS.
AFTER THE FIGHTING IS OVER THE
ETHIOPIANS ARE ACCEPTED BY THE
POPULACE. AS THE RUSSIAN BACKED
COMMUNIST FORCES SEIZE POWER IN
ETHIOPIA, HUNDREDS OF THOUSANDS
ARE EXECUTED. EMPEROR HAILE
SELASSIE IS ASSASSINATED. DURING
THE FIRST YEAR IT IS ESTIMATED
THAT OVER 200,000 ARE EXECUTED BY
FIRING SQUAD IN THE FIELD ACROSS
FROM THE DEAF SCHOOL IN ADDIS
ABABA. THE CHURCH CONTINUES TO
OPERATE THE DEAF SCHOOLS. THE
COMMUNIST TRY TO ORGANIZE THE
WORKERS TO CREATE PROBLEMS,
BUT THE CHRISTIAN WORKERS
REFUSE TO COMPLAIN AGAINST
THE SCHOOL. THE GOVERNMENT
REQUIRES FATHERS TO MAKE ONE
PROPAGANDA MEETING EACH SUNDAY
AND MOTHERS AND CHILDREN
MAKE OTHERS. THE GOAL IS TO

INDOCTRINATE IN COMMUNISM AND
BREAK DOWN FAMILY LOYALTY. WIVES
AND CHILDREN ARE ENCOURAGED
TO INFORM ON FATHERS AND
HUSBANDS. THE GOVERNMENT
NATIONALIZES NINE TENTHS OF
THE FARM LAND. A FARMER IS TO
CONTINUE TO FARM ALL HIS LAND,
BUT COME HARVEST TIME HE GETS
TO HARVEST ONLY ONE TENTH OF
HIS LAND. THE GOVERNMENT GETS
TO HARVEST THE REST. THEY TRY TO
FORCE THE CHRISTIAN SCHOOLS TO
HIRE COMMUNIST INDOCTRINATORS.
THEY TRY TO FORCE THE CHURCH TO
LET THEM HAVE SIGNATURE RIGHTS
IN THE CHURCH BANK ACCOUNT.
IT BECOMES A CAPITAL OFFENSE TO
HAVE MORE THAN A WEEK'S WORTH
OF FOOD. IF YOU DO NOT MAKE THE
SUNDAY PROPAGANDA MEETINGS YOU
DO NOT RECEIVE PERMISSION TO BUY
YOUR NEXT WEEKS FOOD SUPPLY.

1976-1978 A.D.   THE U.N.'S WORLD HEALTH
ORGANIZATION, IN THEIR
PUBLICATION, SAY THEY CAN MAKE A
VIRUS THAT FITS THE DESCRIPTION OF
THE AIDS VIRUS. THEY THEN SUGGEST
THAT THEY DO IT.

1977-1981 A.D.   JIMMY CARTER IS PRESIDENT OF
THE UNITED STATES. HE CONSIDERS
HIMSELF A "BORN AGAIN CHRISTIAN."
IN EXPLAINING THAT TERM HE
SAYS, "WE BELIEVE THAT THE FIRST
TIME WE'RE BORN, AS CHILDREN
IT'S HUMAN LIFE GIVEN TO US, AND
WHEN WE ACCEPT JESUS AS OUR
SAVIOR, IT'S NEW LIFE...." (QUOTE

GIVEN IN 1976). THE COMMUNIST
CHINESE ESPIONAGE EFFORT OBTAINS
INFORMATION ABOUT THE W-70
NUCLEAR WAR HEAD (FOR LANCE
SHORT RANGE MISSILE WITH POSSIBLE
NEUTRON BOMB ADAPTATION).
THIS TECHNOLOGICAL BREACH
ALONG WITH THE ONE DURING
THE REAGAN ADMINISTRATION
(SEE 1981 A.D.) IS USED BY THE
CLINTON ADMINISTRATION TO
TRIVIALIZE THEIR MASSIVE BREACHES.
THE CARTER ADMINISTRATION
NEGOTIATES A TREATY WITH PANAMA
THAT REQUIRES THE U.S. TO TURN THE
PANAMA CANAL OVER T0 PANAMA BY
2000 A.D. THE US REMAINS A MILITARY
PROTECTORATE WITH THE RIGHT
TO MILITARILY INTERVENE IF CANAL
ACCESS BECOMES A PROBLEM. AN
IN-LAW OF THE KING OF CAMBODIA,
NAREN LOR, RUNS AWAY AND BECOMES
A REFUGEE IN STOCKTON, CA. MARVIN
BLAIR BAPTIZES HER INTO CHRIST.

1978-1981 A.D.

THERE IS A BREAK IN THE KHMER
ROUGH LEADERSHIP. POL POT HAS
MISMANAGED THE RICE CROP AND
ORDERS MILLIONS (ABOUT 1/3RD OF
THE COUNTRY) KILLED. HUN SEN, A
KHMER ROUGH GENERAL, BALKS AT
THIS ORDER AND POL POT ORDERS
HUN SEN KILLED. HUN SEN RUNS
TO VIETNAM, AND RETURNS WITH A
VIETNAMESE ARMY. HE HAS PROMISED
THEM CAMBODIAN LAND FOR THEIR
SERVICE. THREE KHMER ROUGH
GENERALS (LATER REFERRED TO AS
THE CAMBODIAN TRIAD) JOIN WITH

HUN SEN. THE FIGHTING CAUSES
THE KHMER ROUGH TO LOOSE
CONTROL OF THE COUNTRYSIDE.
MANY CAMBODIANS SEIZE THE
OPPORTUNITY TO RUN. THE SINGING
OAKS CHURCH OF CHRIST IN DENTON,
TEXAS BECOMES INVOLVED IN
MINISTERING TO INMATES IN SHERIFF
GEORGE'S COUNTY JAIL. ONE OF
THEM CONTROLS LOCAL MARIJUANA
TRAFFIC AND SHUTS IT DOWN. HE
ALSO INFORMS ON THE HEAVY DRUG
TRAFFICERS WHO REPORTEDLY ARE
MOVING A THOUSAND POUNDS A
WEEK INTO THE AREA FROM MEXICO.
OTT AND BAKER ARE ARRESTED,
BUT AS THEY ARE ARRESTED A TEXAS
RANGER IS KILLED. I AM TOLD A
MEXICAN CARTEL HAS PUT OUT A
CONTRACT ON THE GIRL FRIEND OF
THE INFORMER. I SPEND A NIGHT
MOVING HER TO LUBBOCK AND THE
HOME OF CLYDE THOMSEN. CLYDE
TURNED TWENTY-ONE IN PRISON
DOING LIFE WITHOUT PAROLE. AT
THAT AGE HE HAD KILLED FIVE
PEOPLE, SOME CUSTODY OFFICIERS. HE
WAS THE ONLY ONE I COULD LOCATE
WHO WAS WILLING TO TAKE CARE OF
THE YOUNG LADY. HE WAS CURRENTLY
THE LUBBOCK COUNTY PRISON
CHAPLAIN AND HAD WRITTEN THE
BOOK, <u>THE BEST WAY OUT IS UP</u>. THE
MEXICAN CARTEL THEN TOOK OUT AN
INJUNCTION TO KEEP THE SINGING
OAKS CHURCH FROM EVANGELIZING
OTT AND BAKER. THE GOSPEL OF JESUS

	IS A MAJOR THREAT TO THE EVIL PART OF OUR SOCIETY.
1979-1980 A.D.	SILVER SOARS TO $54/OZ. THE NEW YORK INTERESTS CHANGE THE COMEX TRADING RULES, PERMITTING ONLY SELLING OF SILVER TO THEM, NOT BUYING, PROVING A WILLINGNESS TO "CHEAT" IF THEY AREN'T WINNING. THE HUNT BROTHERS, WILLIAM HERBERT AND NELSON BUNKER, BECOME ONE OF THE BIGGEST BANKRUPTCIES IN U.S. HISTORY. THE NEW YORK TRADERS STEAL THEIR FORTUNE.
1980 A.D.	THE SIXTY-NINTH YEAR OF JUBILEE.
1980-1988 A.D.	RONALD WILSON REAGAN IS THE FORTIETH PRESIDENT OF THE UNITED STATES. HE DECLARES, "THE TIME HAS COME TO TURN TO GOD AND REASSERT OUR TRUST IN HIM FOR THE HEALING OF AMERICA...OUR COUNTRY IS IN NEED OF... A SPIRITUAL RENEWAL..."
1980-1991 A.D.	IRAN AND IRAQ BEGIN A LONG "OFF AND ON "CONFLICT. RUSSIA AND THE U.S. SUPPLY ARMS TO IRAQ AND RUSSIA SUPPLIES ARMS TO IRAN. RUSSIA TRAINS THE OFFICER CORPS OF BOTH ARMIES.
1981 A.D.	ETHIOPIAN CHRISTIANS FEEL SEVERELY PERSECUTED. ZENI TEMIE, A YOUNG TEENAGER, IS SMUGGLED OUT BY HER FAMILY (HER FATHER IS A DOCTOR). THEY FEAR THEY WILL NEVER SEE HER AGAIN, BUT WANT HER TO HAVE A FUTURE. CONGRESSMAN SHUMWAY HELPS HER BECOME A LEGAL IMMIGRANT. I AM HER SCIENCE

141

	TEACHER AND SHE IS ONE OF THE BRIGHTEST STUDENTS I HAVE EVER TAUGHT. SHE BECOMES PART OF THE STORMY WARD FAMILY.
1981-1989 A.D.	RONALD REAGAN IS PRESIDENT OF THE UNITED STATES. HE BUILDS UP THE MILITARY AND REDUCES TAXES. THE CHINESE ESPIONAGE EFFORT OBTAINS INFORMATION ON THE W-88 WAR HEAD (FOR THE TRIDENT II D-5 SUB-LAUNCHED ICBM-8 PER MISSILE). THIS TECHNOLOGICAL BREACH (SEE 1977A.D.), IS LATER USED BY THE CLINTON ADMINISTRATION TO TRIVIALIZE CLINTON'S MASSIVE BREACHES (SEE 1997).
1982-1984 A.D.	THE U.N. HIRES INVESTIGATORS TO DETERMINE IF THEY HAD INTRODUCED THE AIDS VIRUS AND HAD HELPED SPREAD IT THROUGH THE WORLD POPULATIONS. THE INVESTIGATION ANSWERS, "YES." ANDROPOV LEADS THE SOVIET UNION.
1984 A.D.	RONALD REAGAN, THE FORTIETH PRESIDENT OF THE UNITED STATES, INFORMS HIS AUDIENCE, "WITHOUT GOD THERE IS NO VIRTUE BECAUSE THERE IS NO PROMPTING OF THE CONSCIENCE... WITHOUT GOD THERE IS A COARSENING OF THE SOCIETY; WITHOUT GOD DEMOCRACY WILL NOT AND CANNOT LONG ENDURE... IF WE EVER FORGET THAT WE ARE ONE NATION UNDER GOD, THEN WE WILL BE A NATION GONE UNDER."
1984-1985 A.D.	CHERNENKO LEADS THE SOVIET UNION. THE COMMUNIST REGIME IN ETHIOPIA MAKES LARGE FOOD

SHIPMENTS TO RUSSIA AND A
DEVASTATING FAMINE BEGINS
IN ETHIOPIA. SEVERAL MILLION
PEOPLE DIE FROM THE FAMINE. THE
AMERICAN CHURCHES OF CHRIST
SUPPORT A FEEDING CAMP THAT
FEEDS 35,000 A DAY. THEY ARE NOT
ALLOWED TO FEED IN THE AREA
WHERE THEIR CONGREGATIONS ARE
STRONG (THE MISSION EFFORT HAS
RESULTED IN OVER 50,000 MEMBERS IN
THE SOUTHERN PART OF ETHIOPIA.)
THIS RELIEF EFFORT RESULTS IN
THE CHURCH BEING PLANTED IN
THE NORTHERN, MOSLEM PART
OF ETHIOPIA. AT THE END OF THE
FAMINE THE COMMUNIST ROUND
UP BY FORCE MOST HEALTHY YOUNG
PEOPLE BETWEEN 13 AND 23. THEY ARE
SHIPPED TO SERVE THE COMMUNIST
CAUSE IN ACCORDANCE WITH AN
AGREEMENT BETWEEN THE RULING
REGIME AND RUSSIA. A COLONEL
IN THE ETHIOPIAN ARMY AT THE
TIME INFORMS US THAT THE FIRST
GROUP SHIPPED IS THREE HUNDRED
THOUSAND TO ROMANIA AND FOUR
HUNDRED THOUSAND TO CUBA. IT IS
KNOWN THAT THERE ARE FURTHER
SLAVE SHIPMENTS. NUMBERS AND
DESTINATIONS ARE NOT KNOWN TO
ME. NONE OF THESE CHILDREN ARE
EVER EXPECTED TO BE PERMITTED TO
HAVE CONTACT WITH THEIR FAMILIES
AGAIN.

1985-1993 A.D. GORBACHEV LEADS THE SOVIET
UNION.

1986 A.D.	THERE IS A NUCLEAR DISASTER AT CHERNOBYL IN THE UKRAINE, NEAR ROMANIA. SOME FILMS SUGGEST THAT PERHAPS ETHIOPIAN YOUTH WERE USED TO HELP IN THE CLEAN UP. MANY DIE UNOFFICIALLY. THE AREA IS EVACUATED. MUCH FARM LAND IS CONTAMINATED. A TORTURE OF A SUDANESE CHRISTIAN BY GOVERNMENT SECURITY OFFICIALS IN SUDAN DURING MARCH OF 1986 IS RECORDED IN "RESTRICTED NATIONS: SUDAN" ON PAGES 39 AND 40. IT WOULD BE GOOD TO READ SO YOU UNDERSTAND WHAT ACCEPTABLE TREATMENT OF CHRISTIANS IN A MOSLEM NATION IS. <u>VOICE OF THE MARTYRS</u> HAS TEN SMALL, SHORT BOOKLETS THAT DISCUSS MISTREATMENT OF CHRISTIANS IN TEN NATIONS. IT WOULD BE GOOD TO READ THEM ALL. THE U.S. LAUNCHES AN AIR ATTACK AGAINST LIBYA'S MUAMMER GADDAFI. HE HAD BEEN COOPERATING WITH TERRORISTS. LIBYA IS BEING LED TO HATE AMERICA AND LEAN ON THE SOVIET UNION.
1988-1992 A.D.	GEORGE BUSH SR. IS PRESIDENT OF THE UNITED STATES. HE NEGOTIATES A DISARMAMENT TREATY WITH THE SOVIET UNION.
1989-1997 A.D.	HASHEMI RAFSANJANI RULES IRAN. YATOLLAH ALI HOSEINE KHAMENEI IS CONSIDERED THE ULTIMATE RULER OF IRAN.
1991 A.D.	THE HARD CORE COMMUNIST GOVERNMENT IN ETHIOPIA COLLAPSES AND IS REPLACED BY

A SOCIALIST GOVERNMENT. TOP
LEADERS ARE STILL NOT ELECTED
AND ENEMIES OF THE LEADERS ARE
STILL KILLED, BUT NOT OPENLY. THERE
IS AN OPEN MARKET AND TRAVEL
ABOUT THE COUNTRY IS EASY. IRAQ
SEIZES KUWAIT. THE U.S. ORGANIZES
A LIBERATION FORCE AND DRIVES
IRAQ OUT. THE BEST OF IRAQI AIR
POWER IS FLOWN TO IRAN TO ESCAPE
DESTRUCTION.

1991-1998 A.D.   CAMBODIA HAS U.N. SUPERVISED
ELECTIONS. KING SIHANOUK'S PARTY
WINS THE LAST OF THE ELECTIONS IN
THIS TIME PERIOD. HE RETURNS FROM
COMMUNIST CHINA WITH NORTH
KOREAN BODY GUARDS. ALTHOUGH
HUN SEN LOST THE LAST ELECTION,
HE IS PERMITTED TO CO-RULE TO
AVOID WAR. THIS IS INSISTED ON BY
THE CAMBODIAN TRIAD. EACH OF
THESE THREE GENERALS MAINTAINS
A STANDING ARMY OF ABOUT 5,000
MEN, AND CONTROL LAND USE IN
THE COUNTRYSIDE. AFTER A FEW
MONTHS OF SHARED RULE, HUN
SEN'S PARTY LEADERS KILL THEIR
COUNTER PARTS AND ASSUME FULL
CONTROL. ONE ESPECIALLY GOOD
OFFICIAL OF THE SIHANOUK PARTY,
WHO STOOD UP TO DRUG TRAFFICERS,
IS PUBLICLY TORTURED DURING
HIS ASSASSINATION. VILLAGERS ARE
RECRUITED FROM THE COUNTRYSIDE
TO GO TO PHENOM PENH TO RIGHT
THE WRONG. THEY ARE RECRUITED
IN THE NAME OF SAM RAINSEY, BUT
SAM RAINSEY TELLS ME HE AND HIS

PARTY HAS NOTHING TO DO WITH
THE RECRUITMENTS. HE TELLS HIS
PARTY NOT TO GO. THE RECRUITS ARE
PUT UP IN A WAREHOUSE AND GIVEN
NON-FUNCTIONAL RIFLES. EARLY IN
THE MORNING THEY ARE CALLED
OUT BY POLICE AND GUNNED DOWN.
I LATER VISIT THE AREA THAT I WAS
TOLD WAS THE AREA MANY OF THE
RECRUITS CAME FROM. THE AREA WAS
POPULATED WITH SINGLE WOMEN
HEAD OF HOUSEHOLDS HAVING
FINANCIALLY DIFFICULT TIMES. THEIR
FAMILIES WERE VOID OF EVEN OLDER
BOYS TO HELP THEIR MOTHERS WITH
THE FIELD WORK. SEVERAL YEARS
LATER (2008) WE ESTABLISH A CHURCH
CONGREGATION IN THE AREA AND
HELPED WHAT WE COULD THROUGH
THAT CONGREGATION.

THE EARLY POM TA MAY CONGREGATION
(CAMBODIA-2008)

THREE MEN AND TANG SINGLETON ARE FROM KAMPONG CHAM. THE REST IN THIS PHOTO ARE THE MEMBERS OF THE EARLY POM TA MAY CHURCH OF CHRIST. NOTICE THERE ARE NO MEN IN THE GROUP. THESE WOMEN DO EVERYTHING FOR THEIR FAMILIES BY THEMSELVES. THE EARLY WALLS OF THE BUILDING ARE MADE FROM PAPER AND PLASTIC CEMENT BAGS. THERE WAS ONE MAN IN THIS VILLAGE WE TRAINED AS A PREACHER. HE LIVED IN THE CEMENT BAG HOUSE. THE HOMES HAVE NO ELECTRICITY, PLUMBING, OR RUNNING WATER. ONLY A FEW HAVE A WELL.

CHAPTER THIRTEEN
A CHRISTIAN CHRONOLOGY OF HISTORY
(AMERICA IS BETRAYED– 2008 A.D. +)
A TIME LINE OF HUMAN HISTORY
FROM A CHRISTIAN PROSPECTIVE
Compiled by "God's Friend"

1992 A.D.

TED TURNER AND NEW WIFE JANE FONDA SUPPORT THE ELECTION OF BILL CLINTON, A FORMER NORTH VIETNAMESE SYMPATHIZER WHO RECEIVED SOME TRAINING IN RUSSIA. BY NOW TED TURNER'S NEWS BROADCASTING HOLDINGS ARE SOME OF THE MOST POWERFUL IN THE UNITED STATES (SEE 1967 AND 1980 A.D.). BILL CLINTON REPORTEDLY HAS TIES TO MAJOR COCAINE DEALERS AND CLOSE ASSOCIATES SAY HE IS PROTECTING THEM AND LAUNDERING THEIR MONEY THROUGH ARKANSAS STATE AGENCIES. CLINTON HAS PARDONED HIS FRIEND, DAN LASATER, AFTER HE WAS CONVICTED AS A MAJOR DRUG TRAFFICKER. REPORTS SAY THEY ARE LAUNDERING $100,000,000.00 PER MONTH. THE MONEY GOES TO MAKE LOANS TO CLINTON SUPPORTERS THAT THEY DO NOT HAVE TO REPAY. THE DRUG TRAFFICKERS (LASATER ET AL) GET ARKANSAS BONDS FOR THEIR CASH WITH BOND SALES

COMMISSIONS AND ACCUMULATING INTEREST. THE ONLY LOSERS ARE ARKANSAS TAX PAYERS WHEN THE BONDS COME DUE. (SEE DVD: "THE CLINTON CHRONICLES")

1992 A.D.   GEORGE BUSH, THE FORTY FIRST PRESIDENT OF THE UNITED STATES, PRAYS, "THE LORD OUR GOD BE WITH US AS HE WAS WITH OUR FATHERS; MAY HE NOT LEAVE US OR FORSAKE US; SO THAT HE MAY INCLINE OUR HEARTS TO HIM TO WALK IN ALL HIS WAYS... THAT ALL THE PEOPLE OF THE EARTH MAY KNOW THAT THE LORD IS GOD; THERE IS NO OTHER."

1993 A.D.   THE SOVIET UNION DISSOLVES AND DOES NOT FULFILL ITS OBLIGATIONS UNDER THE DISARMAMENT TREATY.

1993 A.D.   CLINTON LEADS THE UNITED STATES TO CONTINUE UNILATERAL DISARMAMENT UNDER THE TREATY. YELTSIN BECOMES THE LEADER OF THE COMMUNIST NATIONS THAT WERE KNOWN AS THE SOVIET UNION. HE IS PRESIDENT OF RUSSIA.

1993 A.D.   CLINTON APPOINTS A RELATIVE, JANET RENO, AS U.S. ATTORNEY GENERAL. SHE FIRES ALL 93 U.S. ATTORNEYS AND STOPS THE INVESTIGATIONS INTO CLINTON'S WHITEWATER SCANDAL. KATHLEEN WILLEY IS SEXUALLY ASSAULTED BY CLINTON IN HIS OFFICE AND CONFIDES IN LINDA TRIPP, A SECRETARY IN THE WHITE HOUSE COUNSEL'S OFFICE. LINDA TRIPP SOMETIMES WORKS WITH VINCENT FOSTER JR. VINCENT FOSTER JR., A LAWYER WORKING FOR CLINTON,

IS PROBABLY MURDERED AND THEN DROPPED IN A PARK NEAR THE WHITE HOUSE. CLINTON DECLARES HIS DEATH A "SUICIDE." ONE OF VINCENT'S BODY GUARDS ENDS UP DEAD A FEW DAYS LATER. CLINTON, FOR THE FIRST TIME IN HISTORY, BEGINS REQUIRING AMERICAN SOLDIERS, WHO PLEDGED THEIR ALLEGIANCE TO THE UNITED STATES, TO ACCEPT COMMANDERS FROM FOREIGN NATIONS WHO DO NOT HAVE THAT ALLEGIANCE, OR BE COURT MARSHALED OUT OF THE MILITARY. THIS IS ILLEGAL, BUT HE DOES IT ANYWAY. ONE OF THE FIRST TOP COMMANDERS THEY ARE REQUIRED TO OBEY IN BOSNIA IS A PERSON WITH ALLEGIANCE TO IRAQ AND SADDAM HUSSEIN.

1994-1998 A.D.   LINDA TRIPP IS SUBPOENAED TO TESTIFY ABOUT THE KATHLEEN WILLEY INCIDENT IN THE PAULA JONES CASE. AFTER HER TESTIMONY THE WHITE HOUSE USES ITS POWER TO SMEAR HER CHARACTER, AND TRANSFERS HER TO THE PUBLIC AFFAIRS OFFICE AT THE PENTAGON. CLINTON THEN HAS AN AFFAIR WITH MONICA LEWINSKY. WHEN HE DECIDES TO COOL THE AFFAIR DOWN HE TRANSFERS MONICA TO THE PENTAGON PUBLIC AFFAIRS OFFICE WHERE MONICA CONFIDES IN LINDA. THE AFFAIR IS DOCUMENTED IN TESTIMONY. CLINTON LIES ABOUT IT UNDER OATH, ATTEMPTING TO OBSTRUCT JUSTICE THROUGH A NUMBER OF MEANS. HE ENDS UP BEING IMPEACHED,

BUT THE SENATE, EXCEPT FOR TWO
BRAVE DEMOCRATS, VOTES DOWN
PARTY LINES. DURING THE HOUSE
IMPEACHMENT PROCEEDINGS
CLINTON APPEARS TO USE THE
ILLEGALL HELD FBI FILES (SEE 1996)
TO TRY TO EMBARRASS REPUBLICAN
LEADERS. TWO MAJORITY LEADERS
RESIGN. AFTER THE IMPEACHMENT
CLINTON DECLARES A VENDETTA
AGAINST THE HOUSE MANAGERS WHO
DID THEIR DUTY AND BROUGHT THE
IMPEACHMENT CASE.

1995 A.D.   MANY VILLAGES IN CENTRAL AFRICA
BECOME UNINHABITED DUE TO AIDS.
THE CLINTON ADMINISTRATION
APPEARS TO BEGIN MANIPULATING
THE GOLD MARKET. THIS MAKES THE
DOLLAR SEEM MUCH STRONGER
THAN IT MERITS AND INTERFERES
WITH NORMAL INTEREST RATE
ADJUSTMENTS.

1996 A.D.   COMMUNIST CHINA APPEARS TO
ILLEGALLY FUNNEL MILLIONS
OF DOLLARS INTO CLINTON'S
REELECTION FUNDS. THEY ALSO
REPORTEDLY PUT A MILLION
DOLLARS INTO HIS PERSONAL LEGAL
DEFENSE FUND. THEY APPEAR ALSO
TO CONTRIBUTE HEAVILY TO AN
APPARENT $1,000,000.00 BRIBE GIVEN
WEBSTER HUBBELL FOR SILENCE.
THEN COMMUNIST CHINA RECEIVES
BASES OF OPERATIONS ON BOTH ENDS
OF THE PANAMA CANAL AND IN LONG
BEACH, CA. CONGRESS PASSES A LAW
BLOCKING THEIR CONTINUED USE
OF THE LONG BEACH PORT OF ENTRY

AFTER THEY ARE CAUGHT BRINGING
IN THOUSANDS OF AUTOMATIC
WEAPONS. OVER A HUNDRED
THOUSAND MEXICAN FELONS ARE
ILLEGALLY NATIONALIZED TO VOTE
IN THE CALIFORNIA SYSTEM AND THE
RIGHT OF AMERICANS TO CHOOSE
THEIR OWN LEADERS IS TAMPERED
WITH. THE BRITISH TURN HONG
KONG OVER TO COMMUNIST CHINA
DESPITE THE CITIZENS' OBJECTIONS.
CHINA DISSOLVES HONG KONG'S
ELECTED LEGISLATURE AND APPOINTS
THEIR OWN. BY THIS TIME ABOUT 50
ASSOCIATES OF BILL CLINTON HAVE
HAD QUESTIONABLE "SUICIDES"
OR FATAL "ACCIDENTS" JUST
BEFORE THEY ARE TO BECOME AN
EMBARRASSMENT FOR BILL CLINTON.
RON BROWN IS IN THE CHAIN OF
COMMAND OF A COMMUNIST
CHINESE AGENT WHO HAS BEEN
GIVEN TOP SECRET CLEARANCE
AT BILL CLINTON'S ORDER (THE
FBI NEVER DID THE BACKGROUND
INVESTIGATION REQUIRED FOR
CANDIDATES FOR TOP SECRET
CLEARANCE). HE HAS HELPED FUNNEL
FUNDS FROM RED CHINA INTO
ACCOUNTS THAT SUPPORT CLINTON.
BROWN IS ALSO A MAIN OPERATIVE TO
GIVE TAXPAYER HELP IN SETTING UP
FOREIGN BUSINESSES FOR CAMPAIGN
CONTRIBUTIONS. BROWN IS CALLED
ON TO TESTIFY IN A CONGRESSIONAL
INVESTIGATION. HE AND CLINTON
HAVE A FALLING OUT AND HE IS
ORDERED TO TAKE A TRIP TO BOSNIA

BEFORE HE TESTIFIES. DURING THE
TRIP RON BROWN DIES IN AN AIR
PLANE CRASH WITH A NUMBER OF
AMERICAN BUSINESSMEN. CLINTON
DECLARES HIS DEATH AN "ACCIDENT"
AND ORDERS NO AUTOPSY. THE
MILITARY DOES AN AUTOPSY AND
FINDS A 45 SLUG THROUGH THE
HEAD AS THE PROBABLE CAUSE FOR
BROWN'S DEATH. A NUMBER OF
MILITARY PERSONNEL KILLED IN THE
"ACCIDENT", HAVE DRAWN WEAPONS
AS THOUGH THEY ARE TRYING TO
DEFEND BROWN. CHARLES MEISSNER,
THE IMMEDIATE SUPERVISOR OF
JOHN HUANG, THE COMMUNIST
CHINA AGENT, IS ALSO KILLED IN
THE PLANE CRASH. ONE OF THE
MILITARY ATTENDANTS SURVIVES
THE CRASH AND WALKS AROUND
FOR OVER AN HOUR BEFORE RESCUE
UNITS ARRIVE. AS THE UNITS BEGIN
TO OFFER HER AID, A HELICOPTER OF
SPECIAL FORCE TROOPS ARRIVE AND
INSIST SHE GOES TO THE HOSPITAL
WITH THEM. SHE DIES OF A BROKEN
NECK BEFORE SHE REACHES THE
HOSPITAL. CLINTON CLAIMS STORM
CONDITIONS CONTRIBUTED TO
THE CRASH. MILITARY PERSONNEL
CLAIM THERE WERE NO STORM
CONDITIONS. A GUIDANCE BEACON
IS MISSING AND THE GROUND CREW
SARGENT REVEALING THE MISSING
GUIDANCE BEACON AND NO STORM
CONDITIONS ENDS UP DEAD.
THE LEAD MILITARY INCIDENT
INVESTIGATOR QUESTIONS CLINTON'S

CLAIM IT IS AN "ACCIDENT". CLINTON
SENDS AN ENVOY TO TALK TO THE TOP
MILITARY OFFICER RESPONSIBLE FOR
THE PLANE CRASH INVESTIGATION.
AFTER THE ENVOY LEAVES, THE
OFFICER IS FOUND WITH A 45 SLUG
THROUGH HIS HEART. CLINTON
DECLARES THIS DEATH A "SUICIDE"
AND DEMOTES AND DRIVES THE
AUTOPSY PARTICIPATING PERSONNEL
FROM THE MILITARY. CLINTON
STILL PUBLICLY MAINTAINS THAT
BROWN'S DEATH IS ACCIDENTAL.
ABOUT A MONTH AFTERWARDS
BROWN'S SECRETARY IS FOUND IN HER
WASHINGTON, D.C. OFFICE NAKED
AND DEAD. THIS SCANDAL BECOMES
KNOWN AS "CHINAGATE." IN THIS
SAME YEAR IT IS LEARNED THAT THE
WHITE HOUSE ILLEGALLY HAS IN
ITS POSSESSION FBI BACK GROUND
FILES ON MORE THAN 900 LEADING
REPUBLICANS. THESE FILES CONTAIN
RAW, UNVERIFIED INFORMATION
TO INCLUDE RUMORS AND GOSSIP.
THE SUDANESE GOVERNMENT HAS
A FALLING OUT WITH OSAMA BIN
LADEN AND HAS HIM MOVE HIS
MAIN TERRORIST BASE FROM THEIR
COUNTRY TO AFGHANISTAN. CLINTON
TURNS DOWN AN OPPORTUNITY TO
ARREST HIM.

1997 A.D.
RUSSIA WORKS ON BUILDING A
NUCLEAR POWER PLANT IN IRAN
GIVING THEM POTENTIAL NUCLEAR
WEAPONS CAPABILITIES. SEYED
MOHAMMAD KHATAMI BECOMES
THE PRESIDENT (RULER) OF IRAN.

AYATOLLAH ALI HOSEINE KHAMENEI
CONTINUES TO BE THE ULTIMATE
RULER OF IRAN.

1997-1999 A.D. U.S. ATTORNEY GENERAL RENO
BLOCKS INVESTIGATIONS INTO
CHINAGATE (A CHINESE ESPIONAGE
SCANDAL INVOLVING CLINTON,
CAMPAIGN CONTRIBUTIONS, AND THE
COMMERCE DEPARTMENT) BY KEN
STARR. JUDICIAL WATCH, A PRIVATE
FUNDED ORGANIZATION SUPPORTED
BY VOLUNTARY CONTRIBUTIONS,
BECOMES THE NATION'S BEST
PROTECTION. THE HEAD OF THE
F.B.I. AND HER OWN HEAD OF
INVESTIGATIONS NOTIFY RENO IN
WRITING OF HER OBLIGATION, UNDER
LAW, TO TURN THE SCANDAL OVER
TO AN INDEPENDENT COUNSEL.
SHE REFUSES. JUDICIAL WATCH'S
INVESTIGATION RESULTS IN OVER
FIFTY PERSONS CLOSELY ASSOCIATED
WITH THE CLINTON ADMINISTRATION
AND INVOLVED IN CHINAGATE EITHER
PLEADING THE 5TH AMENDMENT
OR SEEKING POLITICAL ASYLUM IN
COMMUNIST CHINA. COMMUNIST
CHINA BEGINS A MASSIVE MILITARY
BUILD UP CONTRIBUTING TO AN
ASIAN ECONOMIC CRASH (THE HONG
KONG STOCK MARKET LOOSES OVER
HALF ITS VALUE). ATTORNEY GENERAL
RENO BEGINS BLOCKING F.B.I.
EFFORTS TO INVESTIGATE CHINESE
ESPIONAGE AT THE DEPARTMENT OF
ENERGY (THIS APPEARS TO PERMIT
THE MAJOR SUSPECT TO CONTINUE
TO SUPPLY INFORMATION TO

COMMUNIST CHINA FOR THREE
EXTRA YEARS). THE COMMUNIST
CHINESE STEAL LEGACY CODES
(COMPUTER CODES WITH 50 YEARS OF
U.S. NUCLEAR TESTING KNOWLEDGE
AND DESIGN INFORMATION),
WARHEAD SIMULATION TECHNOLOGY
(ENABLES ONE TO DEVELOP AND
MAINTAIN NUCLEAR WEAPONS
WITHOUT ACTUAL TESTING),
ELECTROMAGNETIC TECHNOLOGY
(USEFUL IN SPACE-BASED ANTI-
SATELLITE AND ANTIMISSILE SYSTEMS),
ANTISUBMARINE TECHNOLOGY
(SPACE-BASED RADAR TO DETECT
SUBMERGED SUBMARINES), MISSILE
NOSE CONE TECHNOLOGY (IMPROVES
THE RELIABILITY OF BALLISTIC
MISSILES), AND OVER 200 PAGES
OF OTHER COX REPORT NUCLEAR
INFORMATION THE CLINTON
ADMINISTRATION SAYS CANNOT BE
MADE PUBLIC. IT APPEARS THAT THE
CHINESE ALSO OBTAIN PLANS FOR
THE FOLLOWING U.S. WAR HEADS:
W-87 WARHEAD (FOR PEACE KEEPER
SILO-BASED ICBM-10 PER MISSILE), W-78
WARHEAD (FOR MINUTEMAN MARK
12A SILO-BASED ICBM-3 PER MISSILE),
W-76 WARHEAD (FOR TRIDENT IC-4 SUB
LAUNCHED ICBM-8 PER MISSILE), W-62
WARHEAD (MINUTEMAN III SILO-BASED
ICBM-3 PER MISSILE), W-56 WARHEAD
(FOR MINUTEMAN II SILO-BASED
ICBM-1 PER MISSILE), THE NEUTRON
BOMB (NEVER DEPLOYED ENHANCED
RADIATION WEAPON-KILLS PEOPLE,
BUT LEAVES STRUCTURES STANDING),

AND REENTRY VEHICLES (HEAT SHIELD PROTECTING WARHEADS AS THEY REENTER EARTH'S ATMOSPHERE). CLINTON ALSO ORDERED MASSIVE AMOUNTS OF NUCLEAR INFORMATION DECLASSIFIED, AND STOPPED FBI BACKGROUND CHECKS FOR WORKERS AND VISITORS AT THE WEAPONS LABS. HE LEAKED CLASSIFIED INFORMATION TO THE MEDIA, SWITCHED EXPORT LICENSE AUTHORITY FOR SATELLITES AND MILITARY-RELATED TECHNOLOGY TO AN AGENCY, COMMERCE MINDED AND NOT MILITARY SECURITY MINDED. HE GRANTED WAIVERS, ALLOWING MISSILE TECHNOLOGY TRANSFERS TO COMMUNIST CHINA, RELAXED SECURITY-BASED TRADE RESTRICTIONS, AND PERMITTED STATE OF THE ART COMPUTER SALES THAT WERE DIVERTED TO COMMUNIST CHINA'S MILITARY BUILDUP. CLINTON USES TECHNOLOGICAL BREACHES DURING THE CARTER AND REAGAN ADMINISTRATIONS TO TRIVIALIZE THE BREACHES DURING HIS ADMINISTRATION (SEE 1977 AND 1981 A.D.). TOP MILITARY CHINESE GENERALS BEGIN BOASTING THAT THE Y2K PROBLEM WILL ELIMINATE THE U.S. TECHNOLOGICAL ADVANTAGE. THEY ALSO SAY THE U.S. IS THE MAIN OBSTACLE TO THE ACCOMPLISHMENT OF COMMUNIST CHINA'S EXPANSION GOALS. THE CLINTON ADMINISTRATION BEGINS TO USE VOCABULARY THAT INDICATES THEIR WILLINGNESS TO LET COMMUNIST

CHINA SEIZE TAIWAN. THERE IS A
TREATY THAT WOULD REQUIRE THE
U.S. TO WITHDRAW FROM PANAMA
BY THE END OF 1999 WHILE STILL
GUARANTEEING ACCESS. PANAMA
TRIES TO NEGOTIATE A TREATY
THAT WOULD GUARANTEE THAT
U.S. TROOPS WOULD STAY THERE
BEYOND 1999 (SEE 1976 AND 1996 A.D.).
THE CLINTON ADMINISTRATION
SABOTAGES THIS EFFORT. BY THE
END OF THIS PERIOD OVER 70
ASSOCIATES WHO HAVE BECOME A
POLITICAL EMBARRASSMENT FOR
BILL CLINTON HAVE OFFICIALLY
COMMITTED "SUICIDE" OR HAD
A FATAL "ACCIDENT." NOT ONLY
CAN YOU FOLLOW THE CLINTON
ADMINISTRATION'S SCANDALS BY
FOLLOWING THE MONEY, BUT THE
MORE OBVIOUS TRAIL IS THE CORPSE
TRAIL. CLINTON SEEMS TO FOLLOW
STALIN'S USE OF POLITICAL ALLIES.
AT THE BEGINNING OF THIS PERIOD
COMMUNIST CHINA COULD NOT
DELIVER NUCLEAR WAR HEADS FROM
THEIR HOMELAND TO TARGETS IN
THE U.S. BY THE END OF THIS PERIOD
THEY CAN AND HAVE TARGETED U.S.
CITIES WITH THEIR MISSILES. CHINESE
GENERALS WRITE THAT IN WAR YOU
SHOULD DESTROY YOUR ENEMY'S
ECONOMY PRIOR TO ACTUAL COMBAT,
SO THAT HE CAN NOT FINANCE HIS
FIGHT AGAINST YOU.

1998 A.D.　THE MISSION WORK IN ETHIOPIA
BEGINS TRAINING A HUNDRED NEW
PREACHERS A YEAR. THERE ARE OVER

600 CONGREGATIONS WITH OVER
60,000 CHRISTIANS IN ATTENDANCE.
WAR IS RAGING ALONG THE
NORTHERN BOARDER OF ETHIOPIA
AND OVER FLOWING INTO SUDAN
AND SOMALIA. CAMBODIA HAS A
GENERAL ELECTION WITH MANY
IRREGULARITIES. THE THREE GROUPS
RUNNING FOR ELECTION ARE PARTIES
HEADED BY KING SIHANOUK, HUN
SEN, AND SAM RAINSY. THE SIHANOUK
AND HUN SEN PARTIES AGREE TO TRY
TO SHARE POWER (SEE 1996 - 1998 A.D.).
THE SAM RAINSY PARTY REFUSES TO
SHARE POWER "WITH SUCH ELECTION
HYPOCRISY."

1999 A.D.   THE CLINTON ADMINISTRATION
LEADS NATO TO BOMB KOSOVO
AND SERBIA. THIS INFURIATES
RUSSIA, CHINA, AND SERBIA.
YELTSIN, PRESIDENT OF RUSSIA,
BEGINS INTERRUPTING SPEECHES
ON UNRELATED SUBJECTS TO RAGE
AGAINST CLINTON AND THE U.S. MOST
OF THE BOMBING IS CONDUCTED
FROM HIGH ELEVATIONS AND IT
DAMAGES CIVILIAN TARGETS, KILLING
MANY CIVILIANS. THE CHURCH OF
CHRIST MEETING PLACE IN BELGRADE
IS DESTROYED. THIS GROUP OF
CHRISTIANS PLAYED A MAJOR ROLE IN
THE BIBLE SMUGGLING OPERATIONS
DURING THE COLD WAR BETWEEN
RUSSIA AND THE U.S. AN ESTIMATED
11,000 ANTIPERSONNEL EXPLOSIVE
DEVICES FROM NATO CLUSTER BOMBS
ARE LEFT AS BOOBY TRAPS SCATTERED
ACROSS KOSOVO (THE CLUSTER

BOMBS HAVE A KNOWN RATE OF
FAILURE TO INITIALLY DETONATE AND
THIS FIGURE CAN BE OBTAINED BY
APPLYING THAT KNOWN RATE TO THE
NUMBER OF BOMBS DROPPED). WHEN
ONE BLOWS UP, KILLING BRITISH
SOLDIERS AND CIVILIANS, CLINTON
BLAMES IT ON SERB PLANTED MINES.
AFTER NATO FORCES ENTER KOSOVO
TO REPLACE THE SERB POLICE FORCES,
GERMAN NATO FORCES FIND A MASS
GRAVE. RETURNING ALBANIANS
MASSACRE 17 SERB FARMERS, AND
THERE IS A LOT OF EVERYBODY
BLAMING EVERYBODY ELSE. DRUG
TRAFFIC THROUGH KOSOVO
EXPLODES. THE ALBANIANS DO NOT
DISARM ACCORDING TO THE TREATY.
RUSSIA BEGINS REPLACING OLDER
MISSILES WITH TOPOL-M MISSILES. SHE
BUILDS UP MILITARY SUPPORT UNITS.
RUSSIA ALSO BEGINS TO INCREASE
MISSILE PRODUCTION PROGRAMS
WITH A GENERAL BUILD UP OF NAVAL
FORCES. THE RUSSIAN PARLIAMENT
FAILS TO RATIFY THE START II TREATY
WITH THE U.S. WEEKLY THE U.S. AND
BRITAIN ARE ALSO BOMBING IRAQ
MISSILE PLACEMENTS. IRANIAN NEWS
AGENCIES CONTINUALLY REFER TO
THE "CRIMES" OF BILL CLINTON AND
PRIME MINISTER TONY BLAIR AGAINST
THE IRAQI PEOPLE. THEY SAY THE
AIR RAIDS OVER IRAQ ARE AGAINST
INTERNATIONAL LAW, WITHOUT PRIOR
U.N. KNOWLEDGE OR SANCTION. THE
U.S. PASSES OIL SANCTIONS AGAINST
IRAN AND LIBYA (SEE 597 B.C., 57 A.D.,

AND 96 A.D.). THERE DEVELOPS A MOVE
IN THE CAMBODIAN GOVERNMENT
TO RETURN CAMBODIA TO A FORM
OF COMMUNISM. CAMBODIA FORMS
ALLIANCES WITH COMMUNIST CHINA
AND VIETNAM. A LARGE NUMBER
OF LEGISLATORS RESIGN, AND URGE
THE PEOPLE TO SUPPORT THE SAM
RAINSY PARTY. THEY THEN RUN OFF
TO THAILAND. THE CAMBODIAN
GOVERNMENT BEGINS A DRIVE TO
DISARM THE CAMBODIAN PEOPLE. AT
THE END OF JULY CLINTON ORDERS
ALL U.S. TROOPS TO LEAVE PANAMA.
THIS WOULD REQUIRE COMMUNIST
CHINESE COOPERATION FOR
AMERICAN SHIPPING TO GO FROM
NEW YORK TO LOS ANGELES, OR
THAT SHIPPING TO EITHER GO ALL
THE WAY AROUND THE WORLD OR
BRAVE THE ANTARCTIC SEAS SOUTH
OF SOUTH AMERICA. DAMAGE TO THE
RESERVOIR PROVIDING WATER TO THE
CANAL'S LOCKS COULD DISABLE THE
CANAL FOR TWO TO THREE YEARS
AFTER THE RESERVOIR REPAIR. U.S.
ARMY COLONEL DAVID FRANZ AND
FORMER C.I.A. AGENT LARRY HARRIS
SAY DEBRIEFINGS OF TERRORISTS
INDICATE IRAQ, IRAN, LIBYA, SUDAN
AND OTHER COUNTRIES ARE NOW
OPERATING UNDER THE RELIGIOUS
NOTION THAT THE ADVENT OF THE
YEAR TWO THOUSAND SIGNALS THEIR
LAST CHANCE TO FULFILL THEIR
SACRED MORAL DUTY TO DESTROY
THE UNITED STATES, WHICH THEY
CONSIDER "THE GREAT SATAN."

AGENTS OF THESE COUNTRIES BELIEVE
THEY WILL OBTAIN A SPECIAL PLACE IN
HEAVEN IF THEY ANNIHILATE ENOUGH
AMERICAN CITIZENS. THEY BELIEVE
THEY CAN REDUCE THE AMERICAN
POPULATION BY TWO THIRDS IN
A SHORT PERIOD OF TIME. C.I.A.
INFORMATION INDICATES THERE ARE
OVER 100 TERRORIST "CELL" TEAMS
SECRETED THROUGH OUT MAJOR
U.S. CITIES, EACH IN POSSESSION
OF DOZENS OF VIALS OF DEADLY
ANTHRAX AND BUBONIC PLAGUE
BACTERIA. THEY INTEND TO SPRAY
THESE DEADLY BIOLOGICAL AGENTS
INTO THE AIR WITH SPECIAL SPRAYING
DEVICES CALLED "VENTURIS." THE
CELLS ARE SUPPOSEDLY TARGETING
120 LARGE AMERICAN CITIES DURING
CHRISTMAS RUSH TIME. THEY EXPECT
TO ACCOMPLISH THEIR SLAUGHTER
IN LESS THAN TWO WEEKS. (SEE 597-587
B.C.-EZE. 38, 39, 57-58 A.D., 62-63 A.D.,
96-97 A.D.-REV. 20:7-9). THE CLINTON
ADMINISTRATION KNOWS ABOUT
THIS WELL IN ADVANCE, BUT DOES
NOT DEVELOP ONE PROGRAM FOR
TEACHING AMERICAN CITIZENS HOW
TO SURVIVE. INSTEAD THEY TRAIN
FEDERAL AGENTS ON HOW TO CLEAN
UP THE DEAD AND DYING, HOW TO
SEIZE CONTROL OF KEY INDUSTRIES
AND UTILITIES, HOW TO ENFORCE
CURFEWS AND LIMIT CIVILIAN
TRAVEL. ON SEPT.2 CONGRESS MAKES
IT A FELONY TO EXPORT GAS MASKS
THAT PROTECT AGAINST BIOLOGICAL
WARFARE. BUBONIC PLAGUE IS

NORMALLY TREATABLE WITH
STREPTOMYCIN, BUT NOT PENICILLIN.
THE PREFERRED TREATMENT FOR
ANTHRAX IS PENICILLIN. BOTH ARE
TREATABLE WITH TETRACYCLINE.
IT BECOMES PUBLIC KNOWLEDGE
THAT JOHN HUANG HAS TURNED
STATES EVIDENCE IN CHINAGATE.
BEFORE IT BECOMES KNOWN HE
TAPES HIS CHINA CONTACT TELLING
HIM NOT TO DIVULGE CLINTON
OR A HIGH RANKING COMMUNIST
GENERAL'S ROLL IN THE SCANDAL. THE
LIVES OF HIM AND HIS FAMILY ARE
THREATENED IF HE DOES AND HE IS
PROMISED A PRESIDENTIAL PARDON
IF HE DOESN'T. HE ASKS ABOUT THE
SURETY OF THE PARDON AND IS TOLD
CLINTON KNOWS WHAT IS GOING ON
AND WOULDN'T DARE GO BACK ON
HIS WORD. AS THIS INFORMATION
BECOMES KNOWN, THE WHITEHOUSE
REVISITS TULSA AND RENO ATTEMPTS
TO DISCREDIT THE F.B.I. IT APPEARS A
MOVE IS IN THE MAKING TO REPLACE
THE TOP COMMAND POSITIONS OF
THE F.B.I.

2000 A.D.
THE MUCH FEARED Y2K TECHNOLOGY
PROBLEM DOES NOT MATERIALIZE.
SUDAN'S GOVERNMENT IS
SUPPORTING SLAVE TRADERS WHO
RAID CHRISTIAN VILLAGES, PILLAGING,
KILLING, AND ENSLAVING SURVIVORS.
THEIR DECLARED GOAL IS AFRICAN
CONQUEST FOLLOWED BY WORLD
CONQUEST IN THE NAME OF ALLAH.
GEORGE BUSH IS ELECTED PRESIDENT
OF THE UNITED STATES. SOME CLAIM

THE CLINTON ADMINISTRATION HAS
DISPOSED OF OVER 80% OF THE U.S.
GOLD RESERVES MANIPULATING A LOW
GOLD PRICE AND STRONG DOLLAR.
THE NASDAQ ENTERS A VICIOUS BEAR
MARKET. J.P. MORGAN AND CHASE,
MAJOR U.S. BANKING CONCERNS,
HAVE ENDED UP LEVERAGED 650 TIMES
THEIR NET WORTH. THEIR POSITIONS
ARE SHORT GOLD AND LONG LOW
INTEREST RATES, MADE PROFITABLE BY
A DECLINING PRICE OF GOLD. (THEY
PROVIDED CLINTON'S SECRETARY OF
TREASURY, WHO IS CLAIMED TO HAVE
PARTICIPATED IN THE MANIPULATIONS
THAT COST THE U.S. MOST OF HER
GOLD RESERVES). THE DEUTSCHE
BANK, BUNDES BANK, IMF AND GOLD
SWAPS SEEM TO PLAY A ROLE IN THE
DISAPPEARANCE OF THE U.S. GOLD
RESERVES. THE BUNDESBANK GAINS
OWNERSHIP OF ABOUT 1700 TONS
OF U.S. GOLD. LATER THE DEUTSCHE
BANK HELPS CLINTON OBTAIN REAL
ESTATE HE SHOULD NOT QUALIFY
TO BUY. CLINTON IS LEAVING THE
U.S. BANKING SYSTEM ON THE VERGE
OF COLLAPSE. CLINTON SPENDS
THE LAST FEW MONTHS OF HIS
ADMINISTRATION GETTING ISRAEL
AND THE PALESTINIANS TO DISCUSS
THE FATE OF JERUSALEM. THIS SUBJECT
HAS BEEN A SOURCE OF WAR FOR OVER
A 1000 YEARS AND SHOULD BE A SURE
WAY TO CAUSE CONFLICT, STIRRING
UP MOSLEM HATRED TOWARD THE
U.S. AND ISRAEL. BOB BERARD OPENS
UP A MISSION IN PHNOM PENH AND,

WITH CHOEU LORK, ESTABLISHES THE
PHNOM PENH CHURCH OF CHRIST.

2001 A.D. GEORGE BUSH ASSUMES THE DUTIES
OF THE PRESIDENT OF THE UNITED
STATES. THE DOW FOLLOWS THE
NASDAQ INTO A BEAR MARKET.
GOLD ENTERS A BULL MARKET. THE
CONFLICT IN THE MIDDLE EAST
ESCALATES. DURING THE SUMMER
SAMOL SETH AND BILL SINGLETON
TRAVEL THROUGH CAMBODIA
VISITING DENOMINATIONAL
CHURCHES, VILLAGE GROUPS AND
RELATIVES OF THE SINGLETONS.
OVER 100 ARE BAPTIZED INTO CHRIST.
AMONG THOSE BAPTIZED ARE ANH
PAULEY (BROTHER-IN-LAW TO BILL
SINGLETON) AND HIS FAMILY. DURING
THIS TRIP BILL SINGLETON AND SAMOL
SETH ALSO VISIT IN BATTDAMBANG
IN THE HOME OF GENERAL CHEM
(ONE OF THE TRIAD GENERALS – IT IS
THOUGHT THAT GENERAL CHEM MAY
BE BROTHER TO SIAMONI CHEM, A
REFUGEE HELPED BY BILL SINGLETON
IN AMERICA). THE CHRISTIAN FAITH
IS SPREADING RAPIDLY IN CAMBODIA.
THERE IS AN INADEQUATE SUPPLY OF
BIBLES AND GOOD BIBLE TEACHING
FOLLOW-UP. KIM VORARITSKUL OF
THE KHON KAEN THAILAND BIBLE
INSTITUTE OFFERS TO TRAIN 4 OR 5
CAMBODIANS IN THE THAI SCHOOL IF
THEY CAN READ AND SPEAK FLUENT
THAI. VORARITSKUL IS TRAINING
ABOUT 30 PREACHERS EVERY SIX
MONTHS FOR THAILAND. LAOS HAS
BASICALLY OUTLAWED CHRISTIANITY,

ARRESTING WORSHIPERS, AND
INCARCERATING THEM IN RE-
TRAINING INSTITUTIONS UNTIL THEY
DENOUNCE THE CHRISTIAN FAITH.
THEY ARE BEING GUIDED BY CHINESE
ADVISORS. THE KINGS PARTY (CLOSELY
ASSOCIATED WITH COMMUNIST
CHINA) HAS ESTABLISHED MOSLEM
TRAINING CAMPS ACROSS CAMBODIA.
WE CONTACT TRUMAN SCOTT AND
ASK FOR THE SUNSET INTERNATIONAL
BIBLE INSTITUTE TO ESTABLISH A
SCHOOL OF PREACHING IN CAMBODIA.
HE SEEMS POSITIVE ABOUT IT AND
FOLLOWS UP WITH PLANNING
DISCUSSIONS WITH TRUITT ADAIR.
SAM RAINSY REPORTS THAT HUN SEN
HAS KILLED SEVERAL OF HIS PARTY'S
CANDIDATES AND ARRESTED OTHERS.
THERE IS AN ELECTION IN CAMBODIA
SCHEDULED FOR FEBRUARY OF 2002.
WHILE WE WERE IN PHNOM PENH
A BOMB DESTROYED A HOTEL THAT
PROVIDED INCOME FOR THE KING'S
PARTY. INVESTIGATIONS POINTED
TO MEMBERS OF HUN SEN'S PARTY.
BIN LADIN'S AL-QAIDA TERRORIST
MOSLEM GROUP HAS MEMBERS BOARD
AND SEIZES U.S. FLIGHTS. THEY SLAM
THE AIRPLANES INTO THE WORLD
TRADE CENTER AND THE PENTAGON.
12 TONS OF GOLD USED FOR THE
NEW YORK GOLD TRADE IS BURIED
AT THE BOTTOM OF THE WORLD
TRADE CENTER RUBBLE. MOST OF
THE PEOPLE RUNNING THE U.S. BOND
MARKET ARE KILLED. ANTHRAX
SPORE BEGINS TO BE MAILED TO

LEADING NEWS PERSONALITIES AND
U.S. CONGRESSMEN. AS THE YEAR
ENDS THE U.S. BOND MARKET BEGINS
SHOWING STRESS SIGNS. RUSSIA,
CHINA, AND ISRAEL EXPERIENCE
BULL STOCK MARKETS WHILE THE
U.S. AND THE REST OF THE WORLD
HAVE ENTERED BEAR MARKETS. THE
U.S. HAS FINANCED THE RUSSIAN
ECONOMY REBOUND. RUSSIA AND
CHINA CONTINUE TO BUILD THEIR
MILITARIES FOR EXPECTED CONFLICT
WITH THE U.S. CHINESE GENERALS
HAVE WRITTEN THAT BEFORE YOU
INVADE OR BEGIN A WAR WITH
YOUR ENEMY, YOU FIRST DESTROY
HIS ECONOMY. J.P. MORGAN/CHASE
BANK COMPLEX, A CLINTON AID, IN
DISPOSING OF THE U.S. GOLD WEALTH,
IS HEDGED 712 TIMES ITS NET WORTH
AGAINST GOLD AND RISING INTEREST
RATES. THEY ARE SET TO BE A TRIGGER
FOR U.S. ECONOMIC COLLAPSE. ENRON
ENTERS BANKRUPTCY CHARGING
OFF 2.6 BILLION IN UNSECURED DEBT
TO JP MORGAN/CHASE. J.P. MORGAN
SEEMS TO GET RID OF MOST OF ITS
GOLD DERIVATIVES WITH THE ENRON
COLLAPSE. RECORDS ARE SHREDDED
AND FEW WILL EVER KNOW FOR SURE
WHAT HAPPENED. ARGENTINA ENTERS
BANKRUPTCY CHARGING OFF SEVERAL
BILLION MORE TO THE SAME BANK
COMPLEX. THAT IS LEVERAGED OUT
WITH LIABILITIES OVER 20 TRILLION
AND A NORMAL NET PROFIT OF LESS
THAN 6 BILLION PER YEAR. THEIR

2002 A.D.

TENTACLES STRETCH THROUGHOUT THE U.S. BANKING SYSTEM. SAM SIAM, MOSES, AND BILL SINGLETON WORK TOGETHER PIECING OUT BUDDHA'S RELATIONSHIP WITH DANIEL. SAM SIAM HAS BEEN A CHAINGMAI THAILAND TRAINED BUDDHIST MONK. MOSES WAS FORMERLY A LEADER OF BUDDHIST MONKS AND TRAINED TWELVE YEARS IN CAMBODIA'S BUDDHIST UNIVERSITY SYSTEM. SAM AND MOSES BOTH CURRENTLY PREACH ABOUT JESUS. GOD HAS PROVIDED UNDERSTANDING ABOUT HIS PREPARATION OF THE PEOPLES OF ASIA FOR MASS AND RAPID EVANGELISM TO THE CHRISTIAN FAITH. HE HAS BLESSED US WITH A MARVELOUS TOOL FOR THE CONVERSION OF THE BUDDHIST WORLD. HE HAD BUDDHA ORDER THEM TO LEAVE THEIR OLD WAYS AND JOIN US WHEN WE COME. WHY THE CHRISTIAN MOVEMENT HASN'T UNCOVERED THIS BEFORE NOW IS BEYOND ME EXCEPT FOR GOD'S TIMING. WHAT A WONDER GOD HAS PROVIDED FOR OUR TIMES!!! MOSES TRAVELS CAMBODIA DURING JANUARY AND FEBRUARY BAPTIZING OVER 150 INTO CHRIST. THE ELECTION IN FEBRUARY INCREASES SAM RAINSY CONTROL OF LOCAL POLITICS TO OVER 20%, THE KING'S POWER DROPS TO AROUND 20%. IN THE U.S. THE FOREIGN CURRENCY EXCHANGE MARKET IS OPENED UP TO ENABLE SMALL BUSINESSES AND INDIVIDUALS

TO PARTICIPATE. PAULEY STARTS
TEACHING HIS COMMUNITY IN HIS
HOME. BILL SINGLETON, MOSES, AND
BILL SMITH OF "WORLD RADIO", START
A RADIO PROGRAM THAT EXPLAINS SI-
A-MEETREY TO THE BUDDHIST WORLD.
THE FOLLOWING IS AN EXPLANATION
OF THE SI-A-MEETREY FINDINGS:

BUDDHA (SIDDHARHA GAUMTATA) 563-483 B.C.
PROPHESIES OF BUDDHA'S ANCESTORS
AND DISTANT RELATIVES

In 2513 B.C. Noah exited the Ark. He told his sons that the descendants of Japheth (Europeans and Mongolians) would extend their territories and live in the house of Shem. He said that the descendants of Shem (Southern Asians, and Jews) would have a special relationship with God. In contrast, Ham was warned that the descendants of one of his sons (Canaan) would be the lowest of slaves. Siddhartha was of the Aryan race, descended from Shem. Some of the other descendants of Shem were used by God to write the Bible.

Moses wrote the first five books of the Old Testament (1500-1461 B.C.) He told of the coming great Jewish prophet, king. Anyone who did not listen to him would be called to account before God.

King David wrote the book of Psalms (1064-1024 B.C.) and prophesied that the great king, prophet, Messiah that was to come from his lineage would, in his death, have his hands and feet pierced. The guards would divide his garments and cast lots for his raiment. This Messiah's soul was not to be left in the grave, and his body was not to see decay. The Messiah was to be seated at the right hand of God and given rule and authority.

Isaiah, another descendant of Shem, prophesied (740-712 B.C.) that the coming great one would be called wonderful counselor, mighty God, prince of peace. His power was to be in his mouth and the words he spoke. He would be despised, forsaken and a man of sorrow. He was to be born of a virgin, and do miracles, healing the sick. Lead like a lamb to the slaughter, he would be slain for our iniquities. A book was to be given to lead people out of darkness and gloom. People from all nations were to flow into His kingdom.

THE RELATIONSHIP OF DANIEL AND BUDDHA

It was with this great prophetic background that Daniel (Belteshazzar) was carried into captivity by the Babylonians (627 B.C.). When Daniel interpreted Nebuchadnezzar's dream, revealing that the Medes and Persians were to conquer Babylon, he was elevated to chief administrator of the empire. He also revealed that the Medes and Persians were to be conquered by the Greeks, and the Greeks by the Romans. During the Roman rule, God was to set up his own kingdom (the church) that was to grow and fill the earth.

God used Daniel as a great prophet. Measuring from Ezra's return to Jerusalem, Daniel revealed the great promised one was to come in 26 A.D. (the year Jesus began his ministry) and leave 3 ½ years later (when Jesus was crucified, resurrected, and ascended into heaven). After that a prince (Titus) was to destroy Jerusalem.

The Medes and Persians conquered Babylon in 538 B.C. Shortly thereafter they elevated Belteshazzar to be chief administrator of their empire. His writings dated the coming of the Messiah about 500 years in the future.

Siddhartha Gautama was born on the edge of the Persian Empire, in northwestern India in 563 B.C. The tribal lands of the Magi were nearby to the northeast of Nepal. Nepal was the land ruled by Buddha's father. The Magi sent leaders at Jesus birth to seek the great promised king. Matthew records their meeting with Mary and Jesus, the new born King of Kings. They honored Jesus as the great promised one.

In 534 B.C., at the age of 29, Buddha left the protection of his father's castle to explore the world and seek truth. This was shortly after Daniel began to administer the region near his home. Darius, the Persian emperor, had recently issued a decree that in every part of the empire people were to fear and reverence the God of Daniel.

Near this time Siddhartha began his schooling under Alarak Kalamaganta and Uttakak Ramabotra, studying until he obtained the ancient equivalent of a doctor's degree in religious thought. The chief administrator of the dominate government in that region was Belteshazzar, who had predicted a great world savior in 500 years.

In 531 B.C. Buddha began his own special ministry. Buddha always claimed to be a mere man and recognized that sin offered a significant problem for himself and other mortal men. Buddha's teachings contained that same concept of a great coming savior, "Sira-Adia-Meetrey." This name is a grouping of titles that mean the "the highest, greatest god, the creator of everything, the first and the last, and the Lord of Mercies, the one with love and ever enduring patience for us.

I believe this great God was originally dated by Buddha to come in about 500 years. At first Buddha's teachings were passed by word of mouth among followers. Raja Ashoka (274-232 B.C.) became a supporting member of the Buddhist faith and commissioned an evangelistic outreach to Tibet, China, and Southeast Asia. Manuscripts were made. Unfortunately the Buddhist manuscripts were shipped from Sri Lanka to Southeast Asia and in route the ship sank. It took a long time to find, salvage, and restore the manuscripts. After the smudged ink manuscripts were recovered from the ocean bottom and restored, they were made to read 5000 years to the coming of Si-A-Meetrey. This keeps many who reverence the teachings of Buddha from understanding the true wisdom taught by Buddha. Despite this, the current Buddhist manuscripts still teach that the Buddhist religion should have only lasted 500 years (stated in a discussion about lady monks).

Buddha taught that Sira-Adia-Meetrey (Si-A-Meetrey) is the Prince of Peace, Lord of Lord, King of Kings. Jesus is the Prince of Peace, Lord of Lords, King of Kings. Buddha taught that Si-A-Meetrey is the Way. Jesus is the Way. Buddha taught that Si-A-Meetrey is the Truth. Jesus is the Truth. Buddha taught that Si-A-Meetrey is to be represented by a lion. Jesus is the Lion of Judah of the Davidic lineage. Buddha taught that

Si-A-Meetrey is the only one who can ever forgive sins. Jesus' blood is the only source for the forgiveness of sins. Si-A-Meetrey is the First and the Last. Jesus is the First and the Last, the Alpha and the Omega, the Beginning and the End.

Buddha taught his followers to seek and obey "Dhamma", which is the Word and the Way. Jesus is the Word and the Way. Buddha said "Dhamma" is light. Jesus is the light of the World. Buddha taught that the conquering armies of Si-A-Meetrey will come from the "west" using as weapons love, peace, kindness, and mercy. The missionaries of Jesus have come to that part of the world from the "west" with love, peace, kindness, and mercy.

BUDDHA'S RECOGNITION OF HIS NEED FOR CHRIST

Near his death (483B.C.) Buddha (the Enlightened One) told his followers, "Regardless of how many laws you kept, or even if you pray five times a day, you can not be free from your sins. Even though you burn yourself, even though I become a hermit or am reborn another 10 times, I also shall not be saved." (Manuscript, "Praising in the Temple," Chiengmai, Thailand). Buddha taught that he was not a "god," but only a man, a truth seeker. But on his death bed Buddha taught that there would be a future Messiah, "Lord of Mercies," who would be able to free men of their sins. Buddha said, "He is Lord of Mercies. His name shall be called the King of Kings, the Lord of Lords. He is all knowing, all wise. He knows all that is in the human heart. He is Lord of all the angels and of all humans. No one is greater than He." (Sutrapridot 3:107). Buddha continued to teach of the Lord of Mercies, that "...His side has a wound where he was pierced, and his forehead has many scars. He will carry you to heaven where you will find the triune God. Thus give up following the old ways. A spirit from heaven will come and dwell in your heart."(Manuscript, "Praising in the Temple," Chiengmai, Thailand).
Jesus fulfilled all of these things. The awesomeness of the revealed Christ should call all peoples to submit to His rule. He is the only one under heaven through whom we can be saved.

PLAN OF SALVATION

Believe; Repent; Confess your belief in Jesus as the Christ, the son of God; Be baptized for the forgiveness of your sins; and Offer your body a living sacrifice for Jesus.

MANY ITEMS ON THIS PAGE WERE PROVIDED BY AND ALL ITEMS WERE EDITED FOR ACCURACY BY SETHA VIRYAK BANDITOR (FORMER CHIEF PRIEST OF BUDDHIST MONKS) AND PRA-AKRATO (FORMER BUDDHIST PRIEST).

SETHA VIRYAK BANDITOR (FORMER CHIEF PRIEST OF BUDDHIST MONKS): "If you truly believed Buddha, you would believe Jesus; for he wrote of Jesus."

PRO-AKRATO (FORMER BUDDHIST PRIEST): "Right now Jesus calls us to Him. Buddha told us when we find Jesus to give up the old way and follow the Lord. If you are truly Buddhist, you will listen to Buddha's last words on his death bed."

BENG HENG (FORMER BUDDHIST MONK): "If you fully understand the Buddhist faith, you will become a Christian."

A Vital Connection

I am convinced that all who want to please Jesus (Si-A-Meetrey), that all who want to please Buddha, and that all who want to see Cambodia(YOUR HOMELAND) lifted up and prosper should work diligently to shape the religious organization in Cambodia(YOUR HOMELAND) to conform to the pattern of the New Testament Church. Jesus (Si-A-Meetrey) has said he wants that in all the world. Buddha said when the followers of Si-A-Meetrey come to our land we should join and help them accomplish this task. The New Testament church is a lot different from a lot of "Christian Organizations." In The New Testament church the local people remain in control of their local congregations answering only to Jesus. The congregations are used to teach the people to become love motivated toward their neighbors. All things are to be done through faith expressing itself in love. If we do this our people will continually be lead to love and help one another. That would be a wonderful thing. These church centers of influence where people get together to encourage one another in good works need to be set up in each village. To encourage this I am attaching instructions on how to set up a church of Christ in your community. Please read the rest of this paper through carefully and set up an organization according to the pattern in your village.

2003 A.D.
THE LEAD BUDDHIST AND MOSLEMS OF POUTHISAT PROVINCE ASK FOR A HEARING OF THE GOSPEL AND EXPLANATION OF THE SI-A-MEETREY INFORMATION. THEY GATHER ALMOST 3000 OF THEIR LEADERS FOR THE HEARING AND 387 ARE BAPTIZED. BILL SINGLETON, SAMOL SETH (MOSES) AND BILL SMITH HAVE BEEN BROADCASTING THE COMMAND OF BUDDHA TO LEAVE THE OLD WAYS AND BECOME A CHRISTIAN WHEN THE CHRISTIANS COME. NOW THE PEOPLE OF CAMBODIA ARE BEGINNING TO RESPOND. THE HEAD MOSLEM CLERIC OF POUTHISAT PROVINCE IS AMONG THOSE BAPTIZED. HE GOES HOME AND BAPTISES A 600 MEMBER MOSQUE. THERE IS NO ONE TO HELP TEACH AND FOLLOW UP AND THIS CREATES PROBLEMS. FOR FOUR MONTHS MOSLEM COMMUNITIES BEGIN STRUGGLING, TRYING TO HOLD CHRISTIAN SERVICES WITHOUT GUIDANCE. LARGE NUMBERS ARE ALSO BAPTIZED IN OTHER PROVINCES. EARLY IN THE YEAR, BOB BERARD, AT THE REQUEST OF BILL SINGLETON, VISITS KOH DACH AND BAPTIZES OVER

30 MEETING AT PAULEY'S HOME. BY SPECIAL REQUESTS THE BUDDHISTS OF KAMPONG THOM PROVINCE RECEIVE TWO SPECIAL MEETINGS WHERE LARGE GROUPS GATHERED BY THE BUDDHIST LEADERS OF THAT PROVINCE HEAR A ONE DAY GOSPEL AND SI-A-MEETREY EXPLANATION. OVER TWO HUNDRED ARE BAPTIZED AT EACH OF THE MEETINGS. BOB BERARD CONTINUES TO PROVIDE TEACHING FOR THE KOH DACH CHURCH. IN AUGUST BOB BERARD, THE MISSIONARY LEADING THE PHNOM PENH CHURCH OF CHRIST AND PREACHER'S SCHOOL, IS KILLED IN A TRAFFIC ACCIDENT WHILE TRYING TO BRING SUNDAY BIBLE LESSONS TO DISTANT CHURCHES OF CHRIST (KOH DACH IN KAMPONG CHAM PROVINCE AND TANGKOK IN KAMPONG THOM PROVINCE). SUNSET BIBLE INSTITUTE SERIOUSLY BEGINS CONSIDERING THE SET-UP OF A CAMBODIAN SCHOOL FOR PREACHERS. WE HAVE BEEN ASKING FOR THIS SINCE 2001. THE COUSIN-IN-LAW OF THE KING OF CAMBODIA OFFERS HER PHNOM PENH HOME AND A CAR AND DRIVER TO FACILITATE THIS. THE THREE STAR GENERAL THAT ADVISES THE CAMBODIAN DEFENSE MINISTER, SI SUN TECH, COMES TO STOCKTON, CA. TO DISCUSS HELPING EVANGELIZE THE MILITARY. HE HAD BEEN HELPED BY CHRISTIANS IN STOCKTON WHEN HE RAN FROM THE KHMER ROUGH. THE HEAD OF VOCATIONAL EDUCATION AROUND

BATTAMBANG, A ONE STAR GENERAL
AT KAMPONG THOM, AND THE HEAD
OF PROFESSIONAL EDUCATION IN THE
NORTHERN HALF OF THE COUNTRY
BECOME CHRISTIANS. THE HEAD OF
VOCATIONAL EDUCATION IN THREE
PROVINCES NEAR BATTDAMBANG,
AND THE HEAD OF PROFESSIONAL
EDUCATION IN THE NORTHERN HALF
OF CAMBODIA ARE BOTH RELATIVES
OF SAMOL SETH.

THOSE GATHERED BY
THE MOSLEM AND BUDDHIST LEADERS OF
POUTHISAT TO HEAR AN EXPLANATION OF
SI-A-MEETREY AND
A GOSPEL PRESENTATION

GENERAL PRUM PHENG, COMMANDER
OF THE CAMBODIAN ARMY'S FIRST
DIVISION ASKS FOR A GOSPEL
PRESENTATION FOR HIS 3,000-4,000
TROOPS. THIS IS NEVER ACCOMPLISHED.
THE DOLLAR BEGINS A CONTINUOUS
SLIDE IN VALUE. GOLD BREAKS ABOVE
$400/OUNCE, AND SILVER GOES FROM
$4.50 TO $6.90/OUNCE. THE US DOLLAR
IS LOOSING ITS INTERNATIONAL
VALUE. A U.S. LED ALLIANCE INVADES
IRAQ. THE GENERAL STOCK MARKT
HAS A SLOW BUT CONTINUOUS RALLY
FROM SHORTLY AFTER THE INVASION
OF IRAQ. CHINA OPENS UP A GOLD
MARKET AND PERMITS IT CITIZENS TO
PURCHASE GOLD.

2004 A.D.

DURING JANUARY OVER 500,
INCLUDING TWO GENERALS, ARE
BAPTIZED IN CAMBODIA. A MEETING
AT KOH DACH HAS OVER 250 IN
ATTENDANCE AND 30 BAPTISMS.
MISSIONARIES INSIDE CHINA ASK
ABOUT THE SOURCE OF THE SI-A-
MEETREY INFORMATION AND IF IT HAS
BEEN TRANSLATED INTO CHINESE. BILL
SINGLETON TELLS THEM IT HAS NOT
BEEN TRANSLATED AND PUBLISHED IN
CHINESE, PROVIDES THEM WITH AN
ARTICLE ABOUT IT AND ASKS THEM
TO TRANSLATE. A BUDDHIST COLONY
INSIDE CHINA ASKS TO HEAR ABOUT
THE SI-A-MEETREY CONNECTION AND
THE GOSPEL. NAREN LOR, COUSIN-
IN-LAW TO THE KING OF CAMBODIA,
IS SPONSORING TWO CHURCHES OF
CHRIST AND WANTS TO SPONSOR
MORE. PAULEY, CHUNA SINGLETON'S

BROTHER, AN ELDER OF THE KOH DACH CHURCH OF CHRIST, AND HIS RELATIVES ESTABLISH TWO MORE CONGREGATIONS AT TONLEBET AND VIEL REIGN. A GROUP OF CHARLES SINGLETON'S FRIENDS IN AND AROUND PORTALES, N.M. BECOME THE CENTER OF THE FINANCIAL SUPPORT FOR THE PAULEY/SINGLETON CAMBODIAN OUTREACH. CHARLES IS THE FATHER OF BILL AND LEADS A JAIL MINISTRY IN PORTALES AND CLOVIS, N.M. IN 2004 HE HAS HIS 80TH BIRTHDAY. JAMES LORK CONTINUES THE WORK OF BOB BERARD AT THE PHNOM PENH CHURCH OF CHRIST, SUPPLYING A SOURCE OF BIBLE TRAINED TEACHERS. THE CENTRAL CHURCH OF CHRIST IN STOCKTON, CA. COMMITS TO SPONSORING JOHN SPROUL TO GO TO CAMBODIA IN 2005. AT THE CLOSE OF 2004 A.D. LIM SRENG ATTENDS A LEADERSHIP GATHERING OF CAMBODIAN MOSLEMS. HE HAS BEEN A LEADER IN THE MOSLEM MOVEMENT TO CHRIST AND IS NEPHEW OF THE MOSLEM CLERIC BAPTIZED IN 2003 THAT THEN BAPTIZED A 600 MEMBER MOSQUE. THAT CLERIC HAD BEEN OPPOSED BY A NUMBER OF MOSLEM LEADERS WITH EVEN A HANDGERNADE THROWN IN HIS FRONT YARD. DURING THAT MEETING THE LEADER OF THOSE OPPOSING THE SPREAD OF THE TEACHINGS OF CHRIST IN CAMBODIA COMES TO LIM SRENG AND ASKS TO HAVE HIS SON TAUGHT ABOUT JESUS. AFTER THIS

EVENT AL-QAIDA SEEMS TO QUIT
VISITING CAMBODIA. BEFORE THIS
WE WERE TOLD A NUMBER OF TIMES
TO AVOID CERTAIN AREAS BECAUSE
AL-QAIDA WOULD HAVE MEMBERS
IN OR AROUND THE LOCATION. AN
AREA WIDE POLITICAL GATHERING
AMONG SOUTHEAST ASIAN STATES
IS ALSO HELD AT THE END OF 2004.
AT THAT MEETING THE SUBJECT OF
U.S. MISSIONARIES IS BROUGHT UP.
A CAMBODIAN GENERAL STANDS UP
AND TELLS THE GROUP THEY HAVE
BEEN DEALING WITH THE AMERICAN
MISSIONARIES INCORRECTLY. HE SAYS
THE PROPER WAY TO WORK WITH
THEM IS TO LET THEM COME, PREACH,
CONVERT WHOEVER WANTS TO BE
CONVERTED. AS THEY WORK THEY
WILL LIFT UP THE WHOLE ECONOMY.
THE GENERAL FURTHER STATES
THAT HE HAS CHOSEN TO BECOME
CHRISTIAN HIMSELF. AS A RESULT OF
THIS LAOS REVERSES ITS OPPOSITION
TO AMERICAN MISSIONARIES. THE
SAM RAINSY PARTY WINS ABOUT 30%
OF THE SEATS IN THE CAMBODIAN
CONGRESS. THE RANARRIDH
PARTY LED BY RANARRIDH, SON OF
SIHANOUK AND HEIR APPARENT TO
THE THRONE OF CAMBODIA, WINS
ONLY ABOUT 15% OF THE SEATS IN THE
CAMBODIAN CONGRESS. HUN SEN AND
RANARRIDH AGREED TO DECLARE THE
SAM RANSY PARTY A TERRORIST GROUP
AND SEIZED THEIR SEATS GIVING
THEM TO RANARRIDH'S PARTY. HUN
SEN'S PARTY ALREADY HELD ABOUT

65% OF THE SEATS. THE HUN SEN
GOVERNMENT SEEMS TO CLEAR THEIR
MOVE AGAINST SAM RANSY WITH
CHINA. DURING THE TIME HUN SEN
WAS TALKING ON T.V. ABOUT HAVING A
SURPRISE FOR THE SAM RAINSY PARTY,
I VISITED IN BOUN LEANG'S HOME,
TAKING HIM A GIFT OF A COPY OF THE
SI-A-MEETREY INFORMATION AND
A CAMBODIAN BIBLE. BOUN LEANG
IS THE CAMBODIAN SECRETARY OF
INTERIOR AND BROTHER-IN-LAW TO
HUN SEN. BOUN LEANG AND HIS WIFE
WERE VERY POLITE AND RECEPTIVE.
THEY HAD A SON STUDYING IN A
UNIVERSITY ON THE WEST COAST OF
THE UNITED STATES AND PROVIDED
ME A PHONE NUMBER, ASKING ME
TO CONTACT HIM. NAREN LOR HAD
ARRANGED THE MEETING WITH BOUN
LEANG AND WENT WITH US. DURING
THE VISIT BOUN LEANG CONTINUALLY
REFERED TO HER AS "BOSS". THAT
SEEMED STRANGE AND HUMOROUS,
BUT COMPLETELY APPROPRIATE TO
ME. KNOWING NAREN'S PERSONALLITY
WOULD EXPLAIN THAT REACTION.
SHE IS AN OLD SCHOOL TEACHER/
PRINCIPAL WHO DOES LIKE TO BOSS.
HER COUSIN WAS THE THIRD WIFE OF
SIHANOUK. BOUN LEANG TOLD ME
SHE HAD SERVED CARRYING A RIFLE
IN THE JUNGLE WITH SIHANOUK
WHEN HE RAN FROM NOLL AND LATER
THE KHMER ROUGH. NAREN HAD
BEEN A REFUGEE IN STOCKTON, CA.
AND HAD ATTENDED THE CENTRAL
CHURCH OF CHRIST THERE IN THE

EARLY EIGHTIES. SHE BOASTED THAT
DURING THE KHMER ROUGH SHE
ATE RICE AT NORODOM SIHANOUK'S
TABLE. (THE GENERAL CAMBODIAN
POPULATION ATE RICE SOUP (MAINLY
WATER)). ABOUT TWO WEEKS AFTER
THE FIRST VISIT I HAD A FOLLOW-UP
VISIT WITH BOUN LEANG IN HIS
HOME IN PHENOM PENH. CHOUE
(JAMES) LORK WENT WITH ME. HUN
SEN HAD JUST DECLARED THE SAM
RAINSY GROUP A TERRORIST GROUP.
SAM RAINSY CONTINUALLY PREACHES
AN ANTI-CORRUPTION, PACIFIST
APPROACH. HE IS NOT A TERRORIST.
BOUN LEANG APPOLOGIZED FOR HIS
WIFE'S ABSENCE. HE SAID THEY HAD
JUST RETURNED FROM CHINA WHERE
HE HAD PARTICIPATED IN A POLITICAL
CONFERENCE WITH HIGH CHINESE
OFFICIALS. HIS WIFE WAS TIRED AND
SICK FROM THE TRAVEL. APPARENTLY
THERE WAS NO AIR CONDITIONING
AND THE WEATHER WAS MISERABLY
HOT. HE WAS VERY THANKFUL TO BE
BACK IN CAMBODIA WHERE LIVING
CONDITIONS WERE MUCH BETTER.

2005 A.D. BILL MCDONOUGH TAKES OVER
DIRECTING THE OPERATIONS OF
THE PHENOM PENH SCHOOL OF
PREACHING STARTED BY BOB BERARD
AND JAMES LORK BY INSERTING
HIMSELF IN THE FLOW OF AMERICAN
FUNDING SET-UP BY BOB BERARD.
JAMES LORK CONTINUES TO DO ALL
THE TEACHING. BILL MCDONOUGH
TELLS PAULEY AND BILL SINGLETON
THAT THEY MUST START PAYING $65/

MONTH FOR EACH RELATIVE THEY
HAVE IN THE SCHOOL. NORMALLY
ATTENDANCE IS FREE, SUPPORTED
BY CHURCHES IN AMERICA. THEY
HAVE A LOT OF RELATIVES THERE,
SO THEY TELL THEIR RELATIVES
TO LEAVE THE SCHOOL AND THEY
SET UP A SCHOOL OF PREACHING
IN KOH DACH (KAMPONG CHAM
PROVINCE). NORODOM SIHANOUK
PLACES HIS SON, SIHAMONI, ON
THE THRONE. RANARRIDH WAS
THE HEIR APPARENT, BUT THERE
SEEMS TO BE FAMILY CONFLICT
OVER HUN SEN AND RANARRIDH'S
MOVE AGAINST SAM RAINSY. THE
CONGREGATIONS SPONSORED IN
CAMBODIA THROUGH BILL SINGLETON
REACH TWELVE AS NOREA HOUT,
AT BILL SINGLETON'S REQUEST,
DURING A SCHOOL VACATION, GOES
TO BATDAMBANG TO ORGANIZE
CONGREGATIONS USING PREVIOUSLY
BAPTIZED GROUPS. NOREA IS AN
UPPER CLASSMAN AT THE PHENOM
SCHOOL. WHEN HE RETURNS TO THE
SCHOOL, MCDONOUGH REFUSES
TO CONTINUE HIS EDUCATION.
BILL SINGLETON AGREES TO HELP
IN HIS SUPPORT IF HE RETURNS TO
BATDAMBANG AND MINISTERS TO
THE THREE CONGREGATIONS HE
HAS JUST HELPED TO ESTABLISH.
BATDAMBANG IS WHERE HIS FAMILY
LIVES. TAWAN LORK, JAMES LORK'S
BROTHER, HAS JUST GRADUATED FROM
THE PHENOM PENH SCHOOL AND BILL
SINGLETON HELPS SET-UP SUPPORT

FOR HIM AS HE ENTERS HIS CHRISTIAN
MINISTRY CAREER. HE HAS OFTEN
SERVED AS TRAVELING TRANSLATOR
FOR BILL SINGLETON. TAWAN IS A
YOUNG, EXCEPTIONAL PREACHER OF
THE GOSPEL. DURING JUNE 257 ARE
BAPTIZED INTO CHRIST THROUGH THE
EFFORTS OF THE PAULEY/SINGLETON
GROUP. CHEN LEN LAM AND SOKOM
HUN ASKS TO BE CONSIDERED PART
OF THE PAULEY, BILL SINGLETON
OUT REACH TEAM IN CAMBODIA.
THE WOODARD PARK CAMBODIAN
CONGREGATION IN FRESNO, CA.
(CHEN LEN LAM'S SUPPORT GROUP)
BEGINS CARING FOR NOREA HOUT
AND THE CONGREGATIONS HE
ESTABLISHED IN THE BATDAMBANG
AREA. SOKHOM HUN AND HIS DALLAS,
TEXAS CAMBODIAN CHURCH OF
CHRIST BEGIN SUPPORTING THE
TANGKOK CHURCH GROUP THROUGH
PAULEY/BILL SINGLETON. THAT
CONGREGATION WAS ESTABLISHED
BY BOB BERARD ABOUT THREE WEEKS
BEFORE BOB'S DEATH. A SHORT TIME
LATER POEU SOKGEA, ITS PREACHER,
HAD APPROACHED PAULEY AND ASKED
TO BE HELPED BY THE KOH DACH
CHURCH THAT MET IN PAULEY'S
HOUSE. POEU SOKGEA HAS TAKEN INTO
HIS FAMILY ABOUT 10 ORPHANS. HIS
WIFE IS VERY POSSESSIVE AND QUICK
TO LET ALL KNOW THE ORPHANES ARE
NOT UP FOR ADOPTION. THEY ARE ALL
HER CHILDREN. HER LOVE FOR ALL OF
THEM IS VERY APPARENT.

Poe Sokgea and His Wife and Children

The Orphans that have been added to Poue Sokgea's Family

BILL SINGLETON TRAVELS AN
AMERICAN ENCAMPMENT CIRCUIT
SHARING INFORMATION ABOUT
THE CAMBODIAN OUTREACH AND
ASKING FOR HELP. THE HUGHSON,
CA. CHURCH OF CHRIST BEGINS
FUNCTIONING AS THE SPONSORING
CONGREGATION FOR THE PAULEY/
BILL SINGLETON CAMBODIAN
OUTREACH. ANH PAULEY BAPTIZES
THREE ARJAHS, THE TEACHING
LEADERSHIP OF TWO BUDDHIST
TEMPLES, INTO CHRIST. CHINA TALKS
ABOUT DE-LINKING ITS CURRENCY
FROM THE U.S. DOLLAR AND IRAN,
RUSSIA AND CHINA BEGIN TO
ATTEMPT TO UNDO THE DOLLAR-
PETRO SYSTEM SUPPORTING THE US
DOLLAR. CHINA BELIEVES BEFORE
YOU MAKE WAR ON A COUNTRY
YOU MUST FIRST DESTROY THEM
FINANCIALLY. JOHN SPROUL LOCATES
AT PHENOM PENH IN OCTOBER.
NORODOM AND SIHAMONI SPEND
NORODOM'S BIRTHDAY IN BEIJING.
NORODOM SIHANOUK IS REPORTED
TO HAVE CANCER. BOTH BEAR VALLEY
BIBLE INSTITUTE AND SUNSET BEGIN
EFFORTS TO ESTABLISH SCHOOLS OF
PREACHING IN CAMBODIA. TRUMAN
SCOTT AND CHRIS SWINSFORD LEAD
THIS EFFORT AT SUNSET. DENNY
PETRILLO, RALPH WILLIAMS, AND
DAVID HAMERICK LEAD IT FOR
BEAR VALLEY. LATE IN 2005 KASOL
PAYNE WAS KILLED IN A MOTOR
CYCLE/TRUCK ACCIDENT AS HE WAS
TRAVELING TO HELP NEW CHRISTIAN

VILLAGES HOLD MEANINGFUL
SUNDAY WORSHIPS. HE WAS THE
FIRST CAMBODIAN TO DIE CARRYING
THE GOSPEL FOR THE CHURCHES
OF CHRIST IN CAMBODIA. HIS
FATHER WAS INICIALLY VERY UPSET.
WE HONORED KASOL IN A PROPER
FASHION AND HIS FATHER, TWO
BROTHERS, AND THREE NEPHEWS
ENDED UP CARRYING THE GOSPEL.

2006-2010 A.D. PROJECTIONS OF THE EFFECTS OF THE
AIDS PLAGUE SUGGEST THAT BY THESE
DATES, IN ZIMBABWE, OVER 2/3RDS
OF THE WOMEN OF CHILDBEARING
AGE, AND THEIR CHILDREN WILL BE
DEAD. THE MELROSE CHURCH OF
CHRIST BECOMES THE SPONSORING
CONGREGATION FOR THE BILL
SINGLETON/PAULEY EFFORT, WHICH
CONTINUES TO BAPTIZE OVER ONE/
DAY. HUGHSON CHURCH OF CHRIST
HAS LOST ITS ELDERSHIP THROUGH
DEATH AND RESIGNATION, AND
IT IS DESIRED TO HAVE THE WORK
HELPED THROUGH THE ADVICE AND
LEADERSHIP OF A STRONG ELDERSHIP.
HUGHSON HAS BEEN A GREAT ASSET
AND FRIEND DURING ITS SERVICE AND
WILL ALWAYS BE APPRECIATED FOR
ITS SERVICE IN THE CAUSE OF CHRIST.
ABOUT THIRTY CONGREGATIONS HAVE
BEEN STARTED BY THE PAULEY/BILL
SINGLETON GROUP BY THE END OF
THIS TIME. PAULEY HAS PERSONALLY
BAPTIZED ALMOST 1700 PEOPLE INTO
CHRIST. A LEADERSHIP TRAINING
PROGRAM BEGINS IN 2006 WITH
OVER 30 LEADERS FROM VARIOUS

CONGREGATIONS ATTENDING TWO
DAY MEETINGS EVERY TWO OR THREE
MONTHS IN KAMPONG CHAM. BY
2010 THE ATTENDANCE IS REGULARLY
RUNNING

KASOL'S PARENTS WITH A MEMORIAL FOR KASOL

**KASOL'S HIGH SCHOOL HEARING THE
GOSPEL AND STORIES OF THEIR GRADUATES
WHO HAVE CARRIED THE GOSPEL**

OVER A HUNDRED. CHOEU LORK IS
CARING FOR FIVE CONGREGATIONS
AROUND PHNOM PENH LEFT BY
BOB BERARD AND HAS ADDED
TO THAT NUMBER FOUR MORE.
CHAN LORK, CHOEU'S YOUNGER
BROTHER, HAS JOINED THE BEAR
VALLEY EFFORT IN SIEM REAP AND
SEVERAL CONGREGATIONS HAVE BEEN
ESTABLISHED THERE. THE ORIGINAL
CONGREGATION IN THE SIEM REAP
AREA WAS STARTED BY PAULEY
FROM RELATIVES OF AN ADOPTED
DAUGHTER OF THE SINGLETON'S.
THAT CONGREGATION HAD PROVIDED
NEEDED POLITICAL SUPPORT FOR
BEAR VALLEY TO ESTABLISH THEIR
PRESENCE IN SIEM REAP PROVINCE.
TAWN LORK, ANOTHER LORK
BROTHER, IS WORKING WITH SUNSET
IN PHNOM PENH AND MAINTAINS A
CONGREGATION TO THE WEST OF
THE CAPITAL. BILL MCDONOUGH HAD
TURNED THE PHENOM SCHOOL OF
PREACHING OVER TO SUNSET, AND
CHOUE LORK HAD LEFT THE SCHOOL
TO CONCENTRATE ON BUILDING THE
PHENOM PENH CHURCH OF CHRIST
WITH THE HELP OF LYNN NELSON
AND THE RIVER ROAD CHURCH OF
CHRIST IN ALBANY, GEORGIA. THE
BILL SINGLETON/PAULEY GROUP IS
MAINTAINING A RADIO PROGRAM
WITH THE HELP OF "WORLD RADIO"
AND "KEY TO THE KINGDOM." IT
BROADCASTS THIRTY MINUTS/DAY
IN THE KAMPONG CHAM AREA AND
THIRTY MINUTES/DAY NATION WIDE.

THEY CENTER IN KAMPONG TOM AND KAMPONG CHAM PROVINCES. THEY ARE PRODUCING THREE OR FOUR NEW CONGREGATIONS PER YEAR. SOKHUM HUN IS FOCUSING ON DEVELOPING THE MOSLEM OUTREACH WITH LIM SRENG (AN EARLY MOSLEM CONVERT AND HIGH RANKING OFFICER WITH THE CAMBODIAN DEPARTMENT OF INTERIOR). CHEN LEN LAM IS DEVELOPING A GROUP AROUND BATDAMBANG AND SOUTHWEST OF PHNOM PENH. OTHERS ARE ALSO ACTIVE IN THE TEN YEAR OLD CAMBODIAN EVANGLISTIC EFFORT OF THE CHURCHES OF CHRIST.

2008 A.D.   DURING SEPTEMBER THE U.S. BANKING SYSTEM COMES VERY CLOSE TO FAILURE. EMERGENCY FUNDING IS APPROVED BY CONGRESS. THE HUGHSON CHURCH, THROUGH DEATH AND OLD AGE, HAS LOST ITS ELDERSHIP AND THE MELROSE CHURCH OF CHRIST BEGINS SPONSORING THE CAMBODIAN OUTREACH LEAD BY PAULEY AND BILL SINGLETON. SEVERAL MORE CONGREGATIONS ARE ADDED TO THE WORK.

CHAPTER FOURTEEN
A CHRISTIAN CHRONOLOGY OF HISTORY
(THE GREAT FRAUD – 2030 A.D.?)
A TIME LINE OF HUMAN HISTORY
FROM A CHRISTIAN PROSPECTIVE
Compiled by "God's Friend"

2008-2010 A.D.   BARRACK HUSAINE OBAMA, AN
APPARENT ILLEGAL ALIEN, IS ELECTED
PRESIDENT OF THE UNITED STATES.
DURING THE ELECTION CAMPAIGN
OBAMA HAS AN OVERWHELMING
FUNDING ADVANTAGE. AFTER THE
ELECTION THE PALESTINIANS AND
LIBYA'S MUAMMER GADDAFI CLAIM
THEY FINANCED OBAMA'S ELECTION,
"BUYING" THE ELECTION FOR HIM.
IF THIS IS TRUE IT WAS ILLEGAL.
OBAMA HIDES THE SOURCE OF
ABOUT $300,000,000.00 IN CAMPAIGN
DONATIONS. HE ADMITTED TO NOT
BEING A NATIVE BORN AMERICAN
IN A DEBATE WITH AMBASADOR
KEYES WHEN HE RAN FOR THE U.S.
SENATE. KEYES CHALLENGES HIS
ELIGIABILITY IN CALIFORNIA COURTS.
THE CONSTITUTION, THE HIGHEST
SECULAR LAW OF THE LAND, SAYS A
PRESIDENT MUST BE A NATIVE BORN
CITIZEN OF THE UNITED STATES.
THAT CASE IS DELAYED FOR MONTHS
AND THEN THE JUDGE REFUSES TO

HEAR IT AT THE REQUEST OF THE
U.S. JUSTICE DEPARTMENT. OBAMA
POSTS A HAWAIIAN BIRTH CERTIFICATE
(DECLARATION OF BIRTH) ON HIS
POLITICAL WEB SITE. THIS TYPE OF
CERTIFICATE CAN BE FILED BY ANYONE
AT ANYTIME AND IS NOT LEGAL FOR
MOST OFFICIAL PURPOSES. IT FAILS TO
IDENTIFY THE DOCTOR OR HOSPITAL.
REPORTEDLY A SOCIAL SECURITY
NUMBER USED BY OBAMA IS CHECKED
AND FOUND NEVER TO HAVE BEEN
USED IN ANY HAWAIIAN HOSPITAL.
IT ALSO APPEARS TO REPRESENT AN
IDENTITY THEFT. HIS MOTHER'S
SOCIAL SECURITY NUMBER IS ALSO
CHECKED WITH SIMILAR HOSPITAL
RESULTS. REPORTED ANALYSIS SAYS
THE BIRTH CERTIFICATE WAS PRINTED
ON A PRINTER FIRST MANUFACTURED
MANY YEARS AFTER OBAMA'S BIRTH.
OBAMA'S PATERNAL GRANDMOTHER
SAYS SHE WAS PRESENT AT HIS BIRTH
IN KENYA. THE AIRPORT IN NIAROBI,
KENYA PUTS UP A WELCOME SIGN
IDENTIFYING KENYA AS OBAMA'S BIRTH
PLACE. CONGRESSMEN IN THE KENYAN
LEGISLATURE EXCHANGE COMMENTS
ABOUT AMERICA CHOOSING KENYAN
BORN OBAMA AS THEIR PRESIDENT. AN
AMERICAN, LUCAS SMITH, TRAVELS TO
KENYA AND RETURNS WITH WHAT HE
CLAIMS IS A COPY OF OBAMA'S KENYAN
BIRTH CERTIFICATE. IT APPEARS MUCH
MORE LEGITIMATE THAN THE ONE
POSTED BY OBAMA ON HIS POLITICAL
WEB. (SEE THE ATTACHED LUCAS
SMITH'S LEGAL AFFIDAVIT ABOUT THE

SOURCE OF THE BIRTH CERTIFICATE.
PAGE # 199-200.) IF OBAMA WAS BORN
IN KENYA, IT IS UNCONSTITUTIONAL
FOR HIM TO HOLD THE OFFICE OF
PRESIDENT OF THE UNITED STATES. IT
IS CLAIMED OTHERS, UNDER COURT
ORDER, HAVE OBTAINED EVIDENCE
FROM OCCIDENTAL UNIVERSITY
INDICATING HE ATTENDED THAT
INSTITUTION AS A FOREIGN
NATIONAL. THIS HAPPENS WHILE HE
IS AN ADULT, IN HIS TWENTIES. THIS
IS BEFORE CITIZENS ARE ALLOWED
TO OBTAIN DUAL CITIZENSHIP. IF HE
DESERTED HIS AMERICAN CITIZENSHIP
TO BECOME A FOREIGN NATIONAL,
HE IS LEGALLY BARRED FROM EVER
REGAINING THAT CITIZENSHIP.
INDONESIAN SCHOOL RECORDS LIST
OBAMA AS AN INDONESIAN NATIONAL.

2008 A.D. IN NOVEMBER 2008, WHEN I
RETURNED TO CAMBODIA, KAMPONG
CHAM WAS FULL OF MOSLEMS FROM
MALAYSIA, INDONESIA, AND SOMALIA,
CLAIMING OBAMA HAD PROMISED
THEM THEY COULD MOVE TO THE
UNITED STATES. THEY WERE FILLING
OUT FORMS AND THEN DISAPPEARING
INTO THE COUNTRYSIDE WHILE
ANOTHER WAVE CAME IN TO FILL
OUT THE IMIGRATION FORMS.
KAMPONG CHAM IS NOT A CENTER
FOR FILLING OUT FORMS FOR
IMIGRATION, BUT THAT YEAR IT WAS.
THE MOSLEMS WERE REPORTING
THAT THEY EXPECTED TO LIVE IN THE
COUNTRYSIDE FOR A YEAR BEFORE
OBAMA WOULD GET THEM ENTRANCE

INTO THE UNITED STATES. THERE WAS
A NEW WAVE EVERY FOUR DAYS. THE
MOSLEMS SEEMED TO BE ALMOST ALL
MALES. THE YOUNGER ONES CLAIMED
TO BE RADIOLOGICAL EXPERTS,
BUT AN OLDER MAN SAID HE WAS A
COMMANDER OF A SOMALI MILITIA.
MY IMPRESSION WAS THE OLDER MAN
WAS THE ONLY ONE BEING TRUTHFUL.
THE YOUNGER ONES SEEMED TO
KNOW PRACTICALLY NO SCIENCE
AND WOULD QUICKLY CHANGE THE
SUBJECT OR LEAVE IF YOU TRIED
TO DISCUSS SCIENTIFIC SUBJECTS
RELATED TO THEIR CLAIMED FIELD
OF EXPERTISE. FOR TWO MONTHS
THIS MOSLEM POPULATION SEEMED
TO MAKE UP ABOUT A THIRD OF THE
KAMPONG CHAM POPULATION. THE
POPULATION OF KAMPONG CHAM IS
OVER A MILLION.

2009 A.D.   AN AMERICAN, LUCAS SMITH, TRAVELS
TO KENYA AND RETURNS WITH WHAT
HE CLAIMS IS A COPY OF OBAMA'S
KENYAN BIRTH CERTIFICATE. SOME
OBAMA SUPPORTERS CRITICISE THE
LUKAS CERTIFICATE BECAUSE THEY SAY
MOMBASA DID NOT BECOME PART OF
KENYA UNTIL DECEMBER 1963, WHEN
IT WAS CEDED BY ZANZIBAR. THIS
IGNORES HOSPITAL ADMINISTRATIVE
RECORDS. THE MOBASA HOSPITAL
WAS ESTABLISED IN 1891 WHEN THE
IMPERIAL BRITISH EAST AFRICA
COMPANY RECEIVED A DONATION
TO BUILD A HOSPITAL. ONLY THREE
YEARS EARLIER THEY HAD RECEIVED
THEIR OWN CHARTER FROM QUEEN

VICTORIA. THE RUNNING OF THE HOSPITAL WAS GIVEN TO THE HOLY GHOST FATHERS OF THE CATHOLIC CHURCH. GOVERNMENTAL OVERSITE OF THE HOSPITAL WAS UNDER THE EAST AFRICA BRITISH PROTECTORATE. AT THAT TIME THE HEADQUARTERS OF THE PROTECTORATE WAS IN MOMBASA, BUT LATER MOVED TO NAIROBI IN 1907. IN 1920 THE EAST AFRICA BRITISH PROTECTORATE BECAME THE KENYA COLONY AND PROTECTORATE. THE BRITISH APPOINTED GOVERNOR OF THE KENYA PROTECTORATE EVEN HAD THE MOBASA HOSPITAL NURSES LIVING IN HIS GOVERNMENT HOME FACILITY FROM 1944 TO 1952. THE HOSPITAL WAS ADMINISTERED AND STAFFED BY CATHOLIC NUNS AND PRIESTS. IT WAS INITIALLY ONLY FOR THE EUROPEAN POPULATION, THOUGH LATER ITS SERVICE WAS EXTENDED TO AFRICANS. IT WAS NEVER UNDER THE GOVERNMENT OF THE MOSLEM SULTAN OF ZANZIBAR, WHOSE RELIGIOUS STANDARD, THE QURAN, ENDORSES AND APPROVES OF THE ABUSE AND MURDER OF CHRISTIAN WOMEN. CALL IT COLONIAL ARROGANCE OR PERSONNAL SURVIVAL, THE NUNS AND CATHOLIC PRIESTS, WHO SUPERVISED AND STAFFED THE MOBASA HOSPITAL, WERE ALWAYS UNDER THE GOVERNMENTAL PROTECTION OF THE BRITISH CROWN, UNTIL THE DAY THEY WERE PLACED UNDER THE REPUBLIC OF KENYA.

THE IDENTIFIED GOVERNMENT
AUTHORITY ON THE BIRTH
CERTIFICATE OFFERED BY LUCAS
SMITH IS THE CORRECT GOVERNMENT
AUTHORITY FOR THE MOBASSA COAST
PROVINCE GENERAL HOSPITAL AT
THE DATE OF THE BIRTH OF OBAMA.
IT IS REPORTED THAT AT THE TIME
OF OBAMA'S BIRTH, THIS HOSPITAL
HAD THE BEST MATERNITY WARD
IN THE REGION. THAT SHOULD BE A
REASON FOR ACCEPTANCE AND NOT
THE FALLACIOUS CHALLENGE BEING
VOICED BY OFFICIAL DEMOCRATES.

2009 A.D.   OTHO ROGERS AND BUTCH CROZIER,
OF THE MELROSE CHURCH, VISITED
CAMBODIA. WITH PAULEY'S HELP
THEY HELD A TWO DAY TEACHING
SESSION FOR TEN DENOMINATIONAL
CONGREGATIONS WITH OVER 50
LEADER IN ATTENDANCE. THEY THEN
TRAINED OVER EIGHTY CHURCH
OF CHRIST LEADERS IN A TWO DAY
MEETING. MORE CONGREGATIONS
ARE BEING STARTED BY THE GROUP
THE MELROSE CHURCH HELPS
FINANCE.

Denominational Preachers Trained
By Otho Rogers

Otho Rogers is the one with the mustache.

The Church of Christ Leaders Trained
By Otho Rogers

Dr. Orly Taitz, Attorney-at-Law
(California SBN 223433)
Orly Taitz Law Offices
26302 La Paz, Suite 211
Mission Viejo, California 92691
Telephone: (949) 683-5411
E-Mail: dr_taitz@yahoo.com

UNITED STATES DISTRICT COURT
FOR THE CENTRAL DISTRICT OF CALIFORNIA
SANTA ANA (SOUTHERN) DIVISION

Captain Pamela Barnett, et al.,
        Plaintiffs,

      v.

Barack Hussein Obama,
Michelle L.R. Obama,
Hillary Rodham Clinton, Secretary of State,
Robert M. Gates, Secretary of Defense,
Joseph R. Biden, Vice-President and
President of the Senate,
        Defendants.

Civil Action:

SACV09-00082-DOC (Anx)

28 U.S.C. §1746 Declaration of Lucas Daniel Smith

1. My name is Lucas Daniel Smith. I am over 18 years old, am of sound mind and free of any mental disease or psychological impairment of any kind or condition.

2. I am a citizen of the United States of America, I am 29 years old and I was born in the state of Iowa.

3. I have personal knowledge of all the facts and circumstances described herein below in this declaration and will testify in open court to all of the same.

4. On February 19, 2009 I visited the Coast General hospital in Mombasa, Kenya.

5. I visited the hospital accompanied by one more person, a natural born citizen of the Democratic Republic of Congo (formerly known as

DR. ORLEY TAITZ
FOR THE PLAINTIFFS
26302 LA PAZ SUITE 211
MISSION VIEJO, CALIFORNIA 92691
(949) 683-5411

"Zaire" and before independence as the "Belgian Congo").

6. I traveled to Kenya and Mombasa in particular with the intent to obtain the original birth certificate of Barack Hussein Obama, as I was told previously that it was on file in the hospital and under seal, due to the fact that the prime minister of Kenya Raela Odinga is Barack Hussein Obama's cousin.

7. I had to pay a cash "consideration" to a Kenyan military officer on duty to look the other way, while I obtained the copy of the birth certificate of Barack Hussein Obama.

8. The copy was signed by the hospital administrator.

9. The copy contain the embossed seal.

10. The true and correct photocopy of the Birth certificate obtained, is attached to this affidavit as Exhibit A.

11. I declare, certify, verify, state, and affirm under penalty of perjury under the laws of the United States of America that the foregoing statements of fact and descriptions of circumstances and events are true and correct.

12. I have not received any compensation for making this affidavit.

Further, Declarant saith naught.

Signed and executed in on this 3rd day of September, 2009.

By: _____
Lucas Daniel Smith

DR. ORLEY TAITZ
FOR THE PLAINTIFFS
26302 LA PAZ SUITE 211
MISSION VIEJO, CALIFORNIA 92691

2010 A.D.   THE ONE WHO WON THE HAWAIAN GOVERNORSHIP PLEDGED DURING HIS CAMPAIGN HE WOULD MAKE OBAMA'S LONG FORM BIRTH CERTIFICATE PUBLIC. WHEN HE TRIES TO FULFILL THE PLEDGE, HE FINDS HE CAN NOT FIND AN OBAMA BIRTH CERTIFICATE IN THE STATE RECORDS. OBAMA DOES NOT HOLD THE VISA REQUIRED TO LEGALIZING THE PRESENCE OF A FOREIGN NATIONAL IN THE UNITED STATES. THEREFORE, IT APPEARS MOST LIKELY HE IS AN ILLEGAL ALIEN. IT ALSO SEEMS PROBABLE THAT HE HOLDS THE OFFICE OF PRESIDENT THROUGH FRAUD AND DECEPTION. OBAMA FURTHER HAS COURT MARSHALLED AN OUTSTANDING MILITARY OFFICIER, LTC TERRY LAKIN, DENYING HIM DISCOVERY RIGHTS DURING HIS TRIAL. LTC LAKIN RESPONSIBLY SOUGHT PROOF THAT OBAMA WAS A CONSTITUTIONAL PRESIDENT. INSTEAD OF DISCOVERY RIGHTS, LTC LAKIN WAS IMPRISONED. HIS COURT MARTIAL MAKES AN OXYMORON OUT OF THE TERM, "MILITARY JUSTICE." THE GUILTY IS GOING FREE AND THE COURAGEOUS PATRIOT STANDING UP FOR THE CONSTITUTION IS INCARCERATED. THERE WAS A TIME WHEN RESPONSIBLE MILITARY AUTHORITIES UNDERSTOOD SOLDIERS HAD A DUTY AND RIGHT TO ASSURE THEMSELVES THAT THEIR ORDERS CAME FROM A VALID SOURCE. THEY UNDERSTOOD OFFICERS HAD THE DUTY TO CONFIRM

THIS WHEN THERE WAS REASONABLE
DOUBT. THERE IS CERTAINLY
REASONABLE DOUBT THAT OBAMA IS A
CONSTITUTIONAL PRESIDENT.
OBAMA VERBALLY CLAIMS TO BE
A CHRISTIAN WHEN SPEAKING TO
THE AMERICAN VOTERS, BUT HIS
ACTIONS SPEAK MUCH LOUDER
THAN HIS WORDS. HE ALSO TALKS
ABOUT HIS "MOSLEM FAITH", WHEN
AWAY FROM THE STATES, ORDERED
BIBLES BURNED IN AFGHANISTAN,
OBJECTED TO THE BURNING OF A
QURAN IN FLORIDA, ORDERED NAVY
CROSSES REMOVED FROM ARLINGTON
CEMETARY AND THE PUBLIC INTERNET
HISTORIC RECORD OF THOSE CROSSES
ERASED, USES TAX DOLLARS TO BUILD
MOSQUES, AND FINANCED THE
TRAVEL OF A MOSLEM CLERIC TO
RECRUIT SUPPORT FOR THE BUILDING
OF A MOSQUE AT GROUND ZERO IN
NEW YORK. HE ALSO HELPS TO IMPORT
MOSLEMS FROM INDONESIA, SOMALIA
AND PALESTINE INTO THE UNITED
STATES. HE REFUSES TO PROTECT THE
U.S. BORDER AND IS ATTEMPTING TO
GIVE THOSE RECENTLY BROUGHT
INTO THE UNITED STATES U.S.
CITIZENSHIP AND VOTING RIGHTS.
HE IS ALSO ATTEMPTING TO REMOVE
THE RIGHT TO HAVE FIRE ARMS
AND HAS INCLUDED IN THE HEALTH
CARE BILL A MEASURE TO LET HIM
FORM, ARM, TRAIN, AND EQUIP A
SEVERAL THOUSAND MAN ARMY
FOR HIS PERSONAL USE INSIDE THE
CONTINENTAL UNITED STATES. HE

HAS OPENLY TRIED TO INTIMIDATE
THE JUSTICES OF THE SUPREME
COURT WITH EMPEACHMENT (WITH
THE HELP OF REID AND PELOSI),
CONSTANTLY RIDICULES THE USE
OF CHRISTIAN INFLUENCE IN THE
CREATION OF LAWS, AND INDICATES
THE U.S. CONSTITUTION SHOULD BE
IGNORED. HIS ADMINISTRATION TOLD
CHRISTIAN SOLDERS THEY COULD
NOT PROSELYTE, ORDERING THEM
TO BREAK A COMMAND OF JESUS OR
FACE COURT-MARTIAL. HE OFTEN
REFUSES TO ENFORCE OR DEFEND
ENACTED LAWS AND HAS DEMANDED
THE LEGISLATION OF POWERS DENIED
HIM BY THE CONSTITUTION THAT
ENDANGERS AMERICAN CITIZENS,
INCLUDING THE ARREST AND
INDEFINATE DETENTION OF CITIZENS
WITHOUT CHARGES.
MOSLEMS HAVE GATHERED IN
THAILAND. A MOSLEM GENERAL JOINS
WITH THE KING OF THAILAND TO
REMOVE THE ELECTED BUDDHIST
GOVERNMENT. THE PEOPLE OF
THAILAND ARE ILL PREPARED TO
RESIST THIS. THEY HAVE GIVEN UP
THEIR WEAPONS UNDER A U.N.
INICIATIVE. THE BUDDHIST ARE TOLD
TO MOVE FROM THE DEVELOPED PART
OF THEIR COUNTRY OR THEY WILL BE
KILLED WHEN THEY COME OUT FOR
FOOD. THE MOSLEMS THEN SHELL
CAMBODIA. CAMBODIA ASKS THE U.S.
FOR HELP. INSTEAD OF HELPING THEM,
OBAMA SENDS THE MOSLEM FORCES

2011- 2014 A.D.

F-16s. THE LEADERSHIP OF CAMBODIA IS PUSHED INTO THE ARMS OF CHINA. ON APRIL 27, 2011 PRESIDENT OBAMA POSTS A LONG FORM HAWAIIAN BIRTH CERTIFICATE ON THE INTERNET. EXAMINATION OF THE CERTIFICATE INDICATES THAT IT IS A POOR FORGERY. CONSTITUANTS OF MARICOPA COUNTY SHERIFF JOE ARPAIO ASK THE SHERIFF TO INVESTIGATE THE LEGAL IMPLICATIONS OF THE NEWLY POSTED OBAMA BIRTH CERTIFICATE. HE AGREES TO APPOINT A GRAND JURY TO LOOK INTO THE MATTER, BUT APPEARED TO EXPECT NO IRREGULARITIES. MIKE ZULLO, AN EXPERIENCED, FORMER LAW ENFORCEMENT OFFICIER, IS CHOSSEN TO LEAD THE GRAND JURY. SHERIFF ARPAIO, HIMSELF SPENT 25 YEARS AS A FEDERAL INVESTIGATOR WITH THE FEDERAL DRUG ENFORCEMENT ADMINISTRATION. I SPENT FIVE YEARS AS A YOUNG MAN SERVING AS A FEDERAL FOOD AND DRUG INVESTIGATOR. THE DRUG ENFORCEMENT ADMINISTRATION WAS A SPIN-OFF FROM THE FOOD AND DRUG ADMINISTRATION. MY EARLY EXPERIENCE TELLS ME JOE ARPAIO RECEIVED SOME OF THE BEST INVESTIGATIVE TRAINING MONEY COULD BUY. JOE WAS BORN ON JUNE 14, 1932 AND IS IN HIS EARLY 80's. HE HAS BEEN ELECTED BY HIS MARICOPA CONSTITUANTS AS COUNTY SHERIFF AT LEAST SIX TIMES WITH

SIGNIFICANT VOTER MARGINS. AS
THE INVESTIGATION DEVELOPED IT
BECAME EVIDENT THAT THE LONG
FORM BIRTH CERTIFICATE WAS
FRAUDULANT. OTHER FRAUDULANT
IDENTIFICATION INCLUDES OBAMA'S
SOCIAL SECURITY CARD NUMBER 042-
68-4425. IT WAS ORIGINALLY ISSUED
TO JEAN PAUL LUDWIG, BORN IN 1890
IN FRANCE. HE IMMIGRATED TO THE
U.S. IN 1924. HE DIED IN HAWAII IN
EARLY 1977 WHERE IT WAS POSSIBLE
FOR OBAMA'S GRAND MOTHER TO
IDENTIFY THE SOCIAL SECURITY
NUMBER AS A POSSIBLY SAFE NUMBER
TO USE FOR HER GRAND SON. OBAMA'S
SELECTIVE SERVICE CARD HAS ALSO
BEEN RECOGNIZED AS FRAUDULANT.
ITS DATE DOES NOT APPEAR TO BE
OF 1980 ORIGIN, BUT TO BE DATED
BY A 2008 STAMP, WITH THE FIRST 2
AND 0 REMOVED FROM THE DATE
STAMP, AND THEN THE STAMP TURNED
UPSIDE DOWN TO PRODUCE THE
IMPRINT OF "80" INSTEAD OF "1980".
RECENTLY OBAMA HAS IDENTIFIED
LORETTA FUNDY AS THE PERSON WHO
OBTAINED THE LONG FORM BIRTH
CERTIFICATE FOR HIM. LORETTA DIED
IN A PLANE CRASH IN LATE 2013 AND
CAN NOT BE QUESTIONED ABOUT
HER SOURCE. THERE WERE A NUMBER
IN THE PLANE WHEN IT CRASHED,
BUT SHE WAS THE ONLY FATALITY.
AFTER ARPAIO HELD HIS FIRST PUBLIC
INFORMATION MEETING ABOUT THE
GRAND JURY'S FINDINGS, OBAMA
AND HIS ADMINISTRATION HAVE

INVESTIGATED HIM AND TRIED TO
BRING HIM GRIEF IN MANY WAYS. SO
FAR HIS CONSTITUANTS HAVE ALWAYS
HAD HIS BACK.

DURING THIS TIME CHEN LEN LAM
AND TAWAN BOTH PASS AWAY. CHEN
HAD HAD A WEAK HEART FOR A LONG
TIME AND DIED OF HEART FAILURE.
TAWAN WAS KILLED IN A MOTOR CYCLE
/TRUCK ACCIDENT AND MEDICAL
AFTER-MATH. BOTH WERE GREATLY
APPRECIATED DURING THEIR LIVES,
WHICH SERVED THE PEOPLE OF
CAMBODIA WELL. BY THIS TIME PAULEY
HAS PERSONALLY BAPTIZED OVER 2000.

AFTER TAWAN IS TRANSFERRED TO
HEAVEN, HIS WIFE CONTINUED
SERVING THE CONGREGATION HER
AND HER HUSBAND HAD WORKED
HARD TO CREATE AND BUILD.

IN PORTALES IN THE ROOSEVELT
COUNTY DETENTION CENTER
ROBERT MATA, ADRIAN FIERRA AND
OTHERS ARE BAPTIZED INTO CHRIST.
ACCORDING TO INMATES ROBERT IS A
SHOT CALLER FOR SPANISH GANGS IN
SOUTHERN NEW MEXICO. MATA SENDS
ADRIAN BACK TO ARTISIA TO HELP
MEDIATE A FAMILY DISPUTE. ADRIAN
IS GUNNED DOWN ON THE STREETS
OF ARTESIA. MATA SEEMS EXCITED
OVER BECOMING EVANGELISTIC FOR
CHRIST, BUT IS SHIPPED OUT OF THE
PORTALES FACILITY. THE INMATES
FROM THE CARLSBAD AND ARTESIA

AREA SEEM TO HAVE A NEW ATTITUDE AND BEGIN STUDYING THE BIBLE AND HELPING BRING OTHERS TO CHRIST. IN 2013 FIFTY ARE BAPTIZED INTO CHRIST IN THE ROOSEVELT COUNTY DETENTION CENTER. THE CURRY COUNTY DETENTION CENTER IS HAVING SIMILAR RESULTS. THE WORK IN CLOVIS IS LED BY BOB NORRIS AND GARVIN CHANDLER. BOTH WORKS WERE SERVED AT THEIR BEGINNINGS BY CHARLES SINGLETON, THE FATHER OF BILL. GOD TRANSFERS GARVIN TO HEAVEN IN EARLY 2014. JERRY STOKES HELPS BOTH MINISTRIES. JERRY TRIED TO SAVE A FARM AND MARRIAGE BY COOKING METH. BECAUSE OF THAT HE LOST BOTH THE MARRIAGE AND FARM AND ENDED UP SERVING THIRTEEN YEARS AS A GUEST OF THE FEDS. HE RELATES WITH THE INMATES IN MANY OF THEIR PROBLEMS. WHEN BILL IS NOT IN CAMBODIA HE HELPS IN THE PORTALES WORK. CHARLES AND JEAN SINGLETON (FATHER AND MOTHER OF BILL) ARE IN THEIR LATE EIGHTIES AND EARLY NINETIES AND CARE FOR THE BAPTISTRY THAT SERVES THE PORTALES JAIL MINISTRY.

(SEE MORE IN THE NEXT EDITION, LORD WILLING.) (PRAY FOR AMERICA AND ITS CITIZENS' INALIENABLE RIGHTS. MAY THESE BE MAINTAINED WITHOUT INTERNAL MILITARY CONFLICT.)

IF YOU WOULD LIKE TO HELP THE CAMBODIAN
MISSION MENTIONED IN THESE PAGES FOLLOWING
2000 A.D., PLEASE CONTACT OR SEND HELP TO:

**CAMBODIAN MISSIONS
MELROSE CHURCH OF CHRIST
340 NORTH 8ᵀᴴ ST.
MELROSE, N.M. 88124**

BECAUSE OF FEAR AND INTIMIDATION THE CHRISTIANS
HAVE TENDED TO FAIL TO EVANGELIZE THE MOSLEMS.
NOW GOD IS PERMITTING THEM TO ENTER OUR
INCUBATOR. IF WE WISH TO LIVE LIVES WITHOUT HEAVY,
LIFE THREATENING PERSECUTION, WE MUST EVANGELIZE.
THIS IS SOMETHING WE SHOULD HAVE BEEN DOING ALL
ALONG. THE QURAN TELLS THEM THAT JESUS IS GREATLY
HONORED IN THIS WORLD AND AMONG THOSE NEAREST
TO GOD. HE CAME WITH A SIGN FROM GOD SO THEY
SHOULD FEAR GOD AND OBEY HIM (Sura Al-Imran 3:42-57).
THEY ARE VERY RELIGIOUS, BUT IMPROPERLY ZEALOUS,
LIKE FIRST CENTURY JEWS WHO PERSECUTED CHRISTIANS.
JESUS IS THE ONLY ONE WHO CAN SOLVE THEIR SIN
PROBLEM. THEY NEED TO KNOW ABOUT **JESUS** !

The only way to heaven is through JESUS.

ABOUT THE AUTHOR

God's Friend was education at many of our nation's very best colleges and universities. He did undergraduate work at Lubbock Christian University, the University of New Mexico and Abilene Christian University. He received his B.S.E. from A.C.U. in Biology and Chemistry, placing in the top one percentile on the National Teachers' Examination, among graduates specializing in Biology and Science. After a tour in Vietnam and five military medals, he returned to do graduate work in Biology at New Mexico Highlands University. During five years as a Food and Drug Investigator he received further science oriented training at Temple Buell College, The University of Wisconsin, The University of Rhode Island, Denver Metro State College, The University of Idaho, and Cornell University. He then attended the Preston Road School of Preaching, graduating and doing graduate work in Bible related studies at Pepperdine University. Education and science related graduate work was also completed at California State at Stanislaus.

He has been responsible for all F.D.A. operations in Montana and a third of all operations in a six state region.

He has filled the pulpits of many of the churches of Christ. He has been a full time pulpit minister for the Singing Oaks church of Christ in Denton, Texas and the Livermore Church of Christ in Livermore, California. He preached for over eight years for the Lathrop Church of Christ. He was a volunteer Chaplain for the California Department of Corrections for fifteen years prior to becoming a missionary to Cambodia. He has worked in that country longer than any other missionary in the churches of Christ and he and his converts have baptized over one/day among the Buddhist, to include the baptism of three arjahwats (teacher leaders of Buddhist temples). His work among the Moslem population has helped establish 10 congregations there with the baptism of a leading Moslem cleric.

He has been the Science Chair person for two different Science Departments in the Stockton Unified School District. He served many years on the Executive Board of Directors for the Stockton Teachers' Association. His students received more honors in county and state competition of the Science Fairs' than students of any other teacher in the county. As a school teacher he has taught Biology, General Science, Introductory Physical Science, Physical Science, Earth Science, Life Science, History, Math, and Algebra.

He has served on the Board of Directors for five corporations.

His literature efforts have resulted in his work being included in "The Best Poems and Poets of 2003," "2004," and "2005." He has published on three continents in two languages. In recognition of outstanding achievement his biographic sketch has been listed in "Who's Who among America's Teachers," "Who's Who in American Education," "Who's Who in the West," and other similar listings.